THE SPIRITUAL EXERCISES
OF SAINT IGNATIUS

THE SPIRITUAL EXERCISES
OF SAINT IGNATIUS

A Translation and Commentary by
GEORGE E. GANSS, S.J.

THE INSTITUTE OF JESUIT SOURCES

St. Louis

This edition is for sale only in
North and South America, Europe,
Australia, and New Zealand

There is another edition,
for sale only in Asia and Africa, by
Gujarat Sahitya Prakash,
P. Box 70
Anand 388 001, India

© 1992 The Institute of Jesuit Sources
3700 West Pine Blvd.
St. Louis, Missouri 63108-3386
TEL 314 652 5737
FAX 314 652 0810

Library of Congress Catalog Card Number: 91-77119
ISBN 0-912422-84-X clothbound
ISBN 0-912422-86-6 paperbound

CONTENTS

Preface vii

INTRODUCTION 1

THE TEXT OF THE *SPIRITUAL EXERICISES* 15
Contents of the *Spiritual Exercises* 17

List of Abbreviations Used in the Notes 140
ENDNOTES ON THE *EXERCISES* 143

Appendix I. Scripture Texts: God's Plan of Salvation
            and Spiritual Growth 201
Appendix II. Toward the Deeper Study of the
            Foundation 208

Selected Bibliography 215
Editorial Note on the Term "Spiritual Exercises" 221
Index 223

PREFACE

This new edition of St. Ignatius' *Spiritual Exercises*, with its accompanying introduction and commentary, is intended for use as a manual by those making, directing, or studying the *Exercises*.

In the case of retreatants, their chief aim is to foster the experience of prayer, prayerful deliberation, and cooperation with God's graces which St. Ignatius intended his Exercises to induce in those who are making them. A retreat, therefore, is a time predominantly of prayer rather than of study. Although judicious use of explanatory notes is sometimes useful during a retreat, the retreat experience should be kept in mind as the norm for using them. Notes should be employed to the extent that they foster this experience and omitted when they distract from it. Because of this norm we thought it better to print our explanations in the form of endnotes rather than footnotes.

After the Exercises have been made, however, the experience and spiritual benefits they bring can be immensely deepened by study of the book itself, Ignatius' *Spiritual Exercises*. His book is a practical application of God's great plan of creation, Redemption, and spiritual growth; and growing insight into that design is simultaneously insight into the deposit of faith itself. Such study often becomes prayerful and brings heart-warming motivation along with closeness to God. It clinches the benefits of the retreat and often lasts for the rest of one's life. It puts an intellectual foundation under one's spiritual practices and grows into an activity in which the knowledge in the intellect leads to love in the will and increasing union with God through wonder and awe. In this case the distinction between study and prayer fades into insignificance. Along this line some centers of spirituality have developed unusually beneficial programs.

They have their retreatants make Ignatius' Exercises for a month and then spend another month or more in study and discussion of his book. This manual aims to open the way both to the prayerful experience and such subsequent deepening.

Directors, too, often find it useful to have at hand both the text of the *Exercises* and some commentary on their more important features. Perhaps, too, with the aid of a book such as this they will be able to induct many retreatants into the beneficial and prayerful study sketched above.

Our chief editorial conventions are explained in the Editorial Note on pages 221-222 One item, however, seems to require mention here. According to modern editorial conventions superior numbers are not used with display type in titles. Ignatius, however, wrote his titles or other words which modern editors in varying ways convert into titles or sub-headings before these conventions arose. Especially in the case of the *Exercises*, his titles often contain words which have his own highly technical meanings or nuances and do not reoccur in the text below. If these words are not explained immediately, uninitiated readers will misunderstand his thought. Hence for the purposes of this book we make an exception to the modern conventions and use superior numbers in the titles.

The New Verse Numbers for Computerized Studies

The present edition of the *Exercises* is the first translation in English to employ the recently devised verse enumerations for use with computers and the many concordances, word-processor programs, and studies in Ignatius' use of words which are certain to emerge from them. Some explanation of this seems desirable here.

To make references easier, Arturo Codina in 1928 divided the *Exercises* into 370 numbered sections, with the numbers enclosed in square brackets to indicate that they were an addition not found in Ignatius' manuscript. In this system, for example, the Foundation is in *Exercises*, [23], and the Incarnation in [101-109]. By now these section numbers have become standard and universally used. Sometimes the section numbers are placed in margins, with or without the brackets. Similar divisions into sections have become standard in most of the other writings of Ignatius, except his Letters.

The advent of the computer age has brought further developments in the same direction. Ignatius often uses words with highly personalized meanings of his own, and these meanings or at least their nuances differ from context to context. To further linguistic and lexicographical studies of his meanings, one project in the celebration of the Ignatian Year of 1990-1991 has been the preparation of a complete electronic edition of all his extant writings. By now the texts of all his works and letters in their original languages have been typed or scanned into computers and will become available on disks. By use of the search key and query programs now standard on most all computers, it will soon be possible to bring up on a computer screen a list of all occurrences of some word (such as "glory") in the *Exercises*, or *Constitutions*, or *Spiritual Diary*, or Letters, along with enough context to study its nuances in each instance.

Under the leadership of Fathers Roberto Busa in Gallarate, Italy (who prepared the *Index Thomisticus* published by IBM in 1974-1975) and Edouard Gueydan in Chantilly, France, an international team of Jesuit Ignatian experts has been at work since 1983 on this project of producing a computerized electronic edition or data base. The team is working in collaboration with Doctor Manfred Thaller at the prestigious Max Planck Institut für Geschichte in Göttingen, Germany.

In his *Vocabulario de Ejercicios Espirituales: Ensayo de hermenéutica Ignaciana* (Rome: CIS, 1972), the expert Ignacio Iparraguirre chose fifteen words particularly important in Ignatius' spiritual doctrine and treated their meanings in his various writings. For example, on pages 11-27 he studies the founder's nuances of "love" (*amor*) as God's love of us and our response of love to him in (1) the *Exercises*; (2) the *Constitutions*; (3) Ignatius' general teachings; (4) its resonances from the Bible; and (5) from the documents of Vatican Council II. Beyond doubt this electronic edition along with its computer programs will stimulate many similarly profitable linguistic and lexicographical studies of Ignatius' words and teachings. When these programs are fully ready the Institute of Jesuit Sources will be one of the centers of distribution to the public. Readers of this new edition of the *Spiritual Exercises* will be able to use it in connection with these expected studies.

In this computerization of Ignatius' texts, the earlier and now standard section numbers have been retained; for instance, *Exercises* 23; *Constitutions*, 101; *Autobiography*, 87. But sometimes a word such as glory will occur two or more times within one section. Consequently further divisions into thought units (often called verses) have been found necessary to specify individual instances of occurrence; for example, *Exercises*, 23:2; *Constitutions*, 101:4,5,9; *Autobiography*, 87:3. We have here similarities with the verses which Robert Estienne introduced into the chapters of the Bible in 1551.

These new verse numbers have been inserted in *Ignace de Loyola: Ecrits, traduits et présentés sous la direction de Maurice Giuliani, S.J.* (Paris, 1991), published in 1,110 pages. They will also be used in the edition of Ignatius' complete major works which is being prepared in the Institute of Jesuit Sources. They are certain to become equally as standard and universal as the section numbers already are. Hence we employ them in this new translation of the *Exercises*. This will enable our readers to use this book in connection with the references which will be found in the many studies which will employ them in the years ahead.

In the vast majority of instances in the present book, the reference to the section number alone suffices, just as it did in the past. To add the new verse numbers in all cases would be unnecessarily cumbersome. But on occasions when it is necessary or useful, we do add the new verse number to the section number. Our usage in this and other editorial problems pertaining to the *Spiritual Exercises* is shown by exemplification in the Editorial Note on the Term "Spiritual Exercises" at the end of this book, pages 221-222.

Acknowledgments

The present translation was first published as a part of this writer's earlier volume, *St. Ignatius of Loyola: The Spiritual Exercises and Selected Works*, number 72 in the series The Classics of Western Spirituality published by the Paulist Press. I am grateful to Dr. John Farina of Paulist Press for inviting me to produce that book, and for arranging the agreement by which I might, with appropriate revisions and additions, reuse its contents later for other purposes; also to Dr. Bernard McGinn, editor of the series, for his constructive and welcomed criticisms which I gratefully received. In this new present manual the translation and endnotes have been slightly revised as well as augmented by two appendices.

To name all the others from whom this writer has received highly valued help is impossible. But he desires to show his deep gratitude explicitly to at least some of them: to Father John W. Padberg for continual encouragement toward carrying this work steadily forward; to Father Martin E. Palmer for constant help of many kinds; to Fathers Vincent J. O'Flaherty and Joseph A. Tetlow for scrutinizing my translation of and notes on the *Exercises* and making valued suggestions which reflect their long experience as directors; to Fathers Philip C. Fischer and John L. McCarthy for their competent editorial help; and to Sisters Elizabeth A. Johnson, C.S.J., and Frances Krumpelman, S.C.N., both of whom carefully read the translation and gave me helpful suggestions, particularly in regard to gender-inclusive language.

George E. Ganss, S.J.
Feast of St. Ignatius, in the
500th year of his birth
July 31, 1991

INTRODUCTION

1. St. Ignatius' Worldview 1
2. Nature and Gradual Composition of the *Exercises* 2
3. The Exercitants 4
4. Structure of the Book 5
5. Its Influence 8
6. The Manuscript Texts 8
7. The Aims and Style of This Translation 10
8. Directories 12
9. Varying Interpretations of the *Exercises* 13

INTRODUCTION

1. St. Ignatius' Worldview

St. Ignatius of Loyola (1491-1556) had an outlook on God, the created universe, and the role of human beings within it that led him to inspire many others to be seriously concerned with their spiritual growth and apostolic zeal. This worldview was firmly based on five chief truths of God's revelation: God's purpose in creating human beings; their fall from grace through original sin; the Incarnation of his Son; the Redemption by which Christ restored humankind to God's grace through his life, Passion, and Resurrection; and the destiny of humankind to eternal salvation, that full satisfaction of each person's capacities and desires in the joy of the beatific vision. In other words, Ignatius' outlook was based on God's plan of creation and spiritual development for human beings who use their free wills wisely as this divine design evolves in the history of salvation.[1] This plan is what St. Paul enthusiastically called "the mystery of Christ" (Eph. 1:7-8; 3:3-21). It had long remained hidden but was fully revealed through Christ.

As a result of that expansive outlook, Ignatius habitually viewed all things as proceeding from God, and then becom-

---

1. For a brief collection of texts from Scripture which give a bird's-eye view of the stages by which this divine plan evolves in the history of salvation, see Appendix I, pp. 201-207 below. This list can well be used for "prayerful reading" (*lectio divina*). Ignatius did not have or use this modern terminology, "history of salvation." But his worldview clearly contained the reality designated by the modern term.

For a LIST OF THE ABBREVIATIONS used throughout this book, see pp. 140-141 below at the beginning of the ENDNOTES on the *Exercises*.

For our EDITORIAL USAGES, e.g., *Exercises* (in italic type) and Exercises (in roman), see the Editorial Note, pp. 221-222.

ing a means by which human beings could make their way toward happiness by praising or glorifying God here and hereafter.

This worldview took its first vague shape during Ignatius' own experience of conversion to spiritual living at Loyola in 1521, particularly from his readings in the *Life of Christ* by Ludolph of Saxony. It was further formed by the extraordinary divine illuminations which Ignatius received at Manresa in 1522. Already in that city he felt an urge to share his spiritual experiences with others; and this led him to write notes which became the core of his worldview which he gradually wrote into his *Spiritual Exercises*.[2] This core was matured and revised through some twenty-five years until his book was published in 1548. It is a practical manual aiming to guide others to a somewhat similar yet fully personalized spiritual experience.

2. The Nature and Gradual Composition of the Book

The *Spiritual Exercises* is beyond doubt the best-known among Ignatius' books. Through it most of those who have become followers of his spirituality have made their first acquaintance with its chief principles and inspirational force. Among all his works, this small book contains the marrow of his spiritual outlook and most quickly mirrors to us the synthesis of his principles.

In its final published form this book is not a treatise on

---

2. For a detailed account of Ignatius' intellectual and spiritual formation through which he matured that worldview, see G. E. Ganss, *St. Ignatius of Loyola: the Spiritual Exercises and Selected Works*, no. 72 in "The Classics of Western Spirituality" (Mahwah, N.J.: Paulist, 1991), pp. 12-44 hereafter referred to as *IgnCLWS*. This treatment will also be included in the edition of St. Ignatius' complete major works which is being prepared in the Institute of Jesuit Sources.

For further background on Ignatius' assimilation of God's plan of salvation and spiritual growth as evolving in the history of salvation, see G. Cusson, *BibThSpEx*, pp. 3-43; On the divine plan itself, see J. A. Fitzmyer, "God and His Plan of Salvation History," nos. 37-47 in "Pauline Theology," *The New Jerome Biblical Commentary* (Englewood Cliffs, N.J., 1989), pp. 1390-1393.

the spiritual life, nor was it composed to communicate its message through reading by a retreatant. Instead, it is a manual to guide exercises which were to be carried out by an exercitant, ordinarily with counsel from a director. Thus it is comparable to a book on "How to Play Tennis." Some profit comes to anyone who reads it, but the far more substantial benefit accrues to the one who carries out the practices suggested.

Ignatius began the composition of the *Exercises* shortly after his outstanding mystical illumination at Manresa in August or September of 1521. With a view to helping others, he was recording what he had experienced in his own soul during his conversion to spiritual living at Loyola, Montserrat, and his previous months at Manresa. Hence it can be truly said that he made the Exercises before he wrote them. With a view to helping others, he started by writing notes intended as aids for himself in his spiritual conversations with others there and at Barcelona (*Autobiog*, 21, 32, 34, 37). He was enticing them to perform exercises of prayer, confession, and other activities of a more intensive spiritual life. From Laínez we know that the book was written at Manresa "at least in its substance."[3] Documentary evidence establishes probability that in that "substance" were contained the meditations on the Kingdom and Two Standards; the division into four Weeks and their fundamental meditations aptly combined to attain the end of the Exercises, to order one's life to God without coming to a decision through inordinate attachments; some instructions for making an election; and some of the rules for discernment more suitable for the First Week. The Principle and Foundation too was probably present in some sketchy form, although no document mentions it.[4] Such no doubt were the notes which he used in 1527 at Alcalá where "he was engaged in giving spiritual exercises," and at Salamanca when he gave to Bachelor Frías

---

3. *FN*, 1:82 and *DalmIgn*, pp. 64-65.
4. Leturia, *Estudios Ignacianos*, 2:21; *DalmIgn*, pp. 65-86; *SpExMHSJ69*, pp. 30-32.

"all his papers, which were the Exercises, to be examined" (57, 60, 67). He continued his revisions and additions until the text was complete in 1541.[5] His further corrections until 1556 were few and chiefly verbal. After the Vulgate Latin translation was published in 1548 Ignatius' book became a guide also for other directors in their conversational presentations of the Exercises (such as those whom he trained to give them in Paris near to 1533). Early directors sometimes left some points in writing with the retreatant.

3. The Exercitants

While composing his book Ignatius was aiming to furnish a director with the helps which would be needed for an ideal type of exercitant: a person who sincerely desires to discover how he or she can please and serve God best, and who for about thirty days can withdraw from ordinary occupations (whence arose the name "retreat"), in order to make four or five contemplations a day, alone with God in complete solitude (*SpEx* 20). Since the printing of the book in 1548 it has been used profitably by both directors and retreatants.

However, Ignatius himself and his contemporary Jesuits continually used the book to direct persons who in varying ways did not exemplify all the features of this ideal case. He clearly intended it to be a flexible guide from which a director would select and adapt what was likely to be most helpful to each particular retreatant in his or her circumstances (18-20). He and others whom he trained gave these Exercises to many kinds of persons and in many different ways; for example, for two or three days, or one week, or three, or four; to some persons who were deliberating about the choice of a state of life, and to others who had no such election to make. The topics and directions were presented in conversations between the director and the retreatant. Retreats to groups, however, began already during Ignatius' lifetime.[6] For example, in 1551 Jay gave the Exercises to

---

5. *SpEx*MHSJ69, p. 33.
6. See *DeGuiJes*, p. 303-304, and esp. note 71 on p. 304.

Cardinal Truchsess "and others." The practice of preaching the topics to a group of retreatants had some precedents before 1556, but its greatest development probably came through the founding of retreat houses about 1660.[7] Such retreats certainly brought great spiritual fruit. The preached retreat still continues. Each type of retreat, that individually directed and that preached to a group, has its own advantages and disadvantages which are absent from the other.

4. The Structure of the Book

The book opens with twenty introductory explanations, some chiefly for the director and others for the exercitant. Then it states the purpose of the Exercises: to help one (1) to discard disordered attachments and (2) through this means to order one's life toward God, without coming to a decision from some disordered attachment pleasing more to self than to God —even if this requires the conquering of self necessary when selfish urges would impede this goal. Then comes the Principle and Foundation, which presents the principles for the logical reasoning which functions through the rest of the book. This Foundation presents (1) an inspiring goal, eternal self-fulfillment as the purpose of life on earth; (2) the means to the goal, creatures rightly used; (3) a preliminary attitude for their wise use: making oneself "indifferent" or undecided until the sound reasons for choice appear; (4) a criterion of choice: Which option is likely to be more conducive to the end, greater praise or glory to God? The Exercises are indeed far more than an application of logical reasoning. But there is a logical sequence of ideas which runs through them all and links them together.

The remaining exercises are divided into four groups, called "Weeks." The First Week consists of exercises characteristic of the purgative way, the purification of the soul which frees it to advance toward God. It also makes the retreatant aware of how small he or she is in the sight of

---

7. *DeGuiJes*, pp. 303-305.

God. Still further, it views the whole history of sin and its consequences, the attempted wrecking of God's plan for human beings endowed with the freedom to give or refuse cooperation. It includes the exercitant's own role in this history, and God's loving mercy. The Exercises bring into play any or all the abilities any exercitant has, such as the intellect, will, imagination, and emotions. All these are stimulated, with a stress on each one at its own proper time.

The Second Week presents exercises proper to the illuminative way, the acquiring of virtues in imitation of Christ. The spirit of the Week is set by means of an opening contemplation on Christ's call to participate with him in spreading his Kingdom. Then follow about three days devoted respectively to contemplations on the Incarnation, Nativity, and Hidden Life of Christ (101-134). They prepare the way for about six more days (135-189) when two series of exercises run concurrently: (1) contemplations on selected mysteries of the public life of Christ; and (2) principles (especially those on indifference and the norm of choice drawn from the Principle and Foundation), applied now to "Three Times Suitable for Making a Sound Election" and the "Two Methods" of making it about some important matter, such as choice of a state of life. In series 1, during all the contemplations on the events in the life of Christ, the exercitant prayerfully strives to gain "an interior knowledge of our Lord, who has become man for me, that I may love him more and follow him more closely" (104). In series 2, the fourth day of this Week is devoted to two meditations aimed at confirming the necessary attitude for a rightly ordered decision: that of "indifference" (attained by suspending one's decision in order to avoid acting from mere impulse of likes or dislikes, or from some other disordered motive). The first meditation is on the Two "Standards" (banners, flags), respectively of Christ and of Satan, to point out the opposite tactics of these two leaders. The second, on Three Classes of Persons (postponers, half-hearted, and wholeheartedly decisive), fosters an adherence of the heart to total commitment to God, even if sacrifice is involved. A third exercise, called a consideration, begins on day six (or even earlier: 164). It is about the Three Ways of Being Humble. They reach a climax in the third way, which aims to evoke a desire to be as like to Christ as possible in an attitude of loving humility, no matter what the cost. This attitude is especially useful in an option where the pros and cons seem equal. These principles form a background which should function in all the contemplations on the public life for the rest of the Second Week.

Another important point about the principles for a good election should be noticed. Ignatius' text itself is focused concretely on one typical case, that of someone deliberating about the choice of a state of life. But the principles and methods he gives are equally applicable to other cases and any options which occur in life. Further, not all retreatants are concerned with an election about something new. The Exercises should be adjusted to their condition, and for them Ignatius gives some suggestions about renewal of life. This, however, can be regarded as a species of election.

The Third and Fourth Weeks bring contemplations characteristic of the unitive or perfective way: activities to establish habitual and intimate union with God, through Christ. The exercitant associates himself or herself closely with Christ in his sufferings during the Third Week, and in his joys in the Fourth. By this sympathetic association the retreatant is confirmed in his or her choice, if this has been a retreat of election; or if not, in whatever resolutions one has reached. The Exercises conclude with a contemplation to increase one's love of God. By now the exercitant has reviewed God's entire plan of creation and redemption evolving in the history of salvation, from creation, through the fall of the angels and Adam, as well as the Incarnation and Redemption which lead one all the way to the destiny of the beatific vision. The exercitant, too, has been striving to fit himself or herself cooperatively into this divine plan. For many an exercitant this whole sequence of exercises has produced a powerful psychological impact and given a new orientation of life.

Finally, as appendages at the end of his book Ignatius places sets of suggestions on a variety of topics: Three

Methods of Praying; a list of Mysteries of Christ's life especially suitable for a time of retreat; Rules for the Discernment of Spirits; the Distribution of Alms; Notes on Scruples; and Rules for Thinking, Judging, and Feeling Rightly within the Church.

5. Its Influence

It is through the *Exercises* that Ignatius has exerted his most effective and widespread influence directly upon individual persons. During his own lifetime from Manresa onward he gave these Exercises continually to innumerable men and women with whom he dealt. By means of the Exercises, too, he won and trained the first followers with whom he founded the Society of Jesus. Thereupon they too directed innumerable others in making them. From Ignatius' day until now all Jesuit novices have been obliged to make them for the full thirty days. For almost all of them probably no other element in their training was more effective in forming their outlook on life and their spiritual practices. Since 1616 all Jesuit priests have repeated the Exercises through thirty days during their final year of spiritual training called the "tertianship." From Ignatius' day until now virtually all Jesuit priests have carried on the apostolate of the Exercises in various forms and adaptations. The book has been published unusually often. According to one plausible estimate worked out in 1948, by then the *Exercises* had been published, either alone or with commentaries, some 4,500 times—an average of once a month for four centuries—and the number of copies printed was around 4,500,000.[8] Throughout the world today the Exercises are being made by greater numbers than ever before.

6. The Manuscript Texts

Ignatius completed his last substantial revisions of the *Spiritual Exercises* in Rome between 1539 and 1541. The texts

---

8. *Obrascompl*, p. 225.

of the three chief editions, critically edited by the expert Cándido de Dalmases, are printed in parallel columns on pages 140-415 in the 850 pages of Volume 100 (1969) in the series Historical Sources of the Society of Jesus.[9] Their designations and names are:

A, the Autograph text in Spanish, Ignatius' own copy left at his death in 1556. This was a copy, made probably in 1544, of his earlier text. He used it during his remaining fourteen years and on it wrote 32 verbal corrections, because of which it received its name of "Autograph."

P^1, the *Versio Prima* or first translation into scholastic Latin, made in Paris, probably about 1534 and by Ignatius himself. This text exists in a manuscript copied in 1541, and in a later copy, P^2, made in 1547 and containing a few additions.

V, the *Versio Vulgata,* made from the Spanish Autograph into stylistic classical Latin to present it, along with the *Versio Prima* in text P^2,[10] to Pope Paul III for the approval which was granted in 1548. Ignatius used it from 1548 to 1556. It was named *Vulgata* because it was spread in a printed edition of 500 copies. It was the text in greatest use until Jan Roothaan's new Latin version of the Autograph in 1835.

Most modern scholars think that the Autograph, text *A,* best reproduces Ignatius' thought and its nuances. However, since the First Latin Version and the Vulgate (*V*) were used by Ignatius, they have approval by him and are substantial helps for interpreting *A* in passages where obscurities occur. The present translation of the *Exercises* is based chiefly on this critical text *A* published by Dalmases in 1969, with aid from the Latin versions printed in his parallel columns.

Recently Dalmases himself updated and adjusted his

---

9. S. Ignatii de Loyola, *Exercitia Spiritualia: Textuum antiquissimorum nova editio*, Monumenta Historica Societatis Iesu (Rome, 1969).

10. *DalMan*, p. 27; *SpExMHSJ69*, p. 135.

previous critical text for practical use as a manual by directors, retreatants, and students of the *Exercises*, for whom the earlier volume of 850 pages was too unwieldy. He left this small book virtually complete when he died in 1986, and it was posthumously published by his colleague, Father Manuel Ruiz Jurado, with the title: Ignacio de Loyola, *Ejercicios Espirituales: Introducción, texto, notas y vocabulario* por Cándido de Dalmases, S.J. (Santander: Sal Terrae, 1987), to which we refer hereafter as *DalmMan*. His introductions, brief interpretative footnotes, and dictionary (*vocabulario*) of selected Ignatian terms were a great help both for the translation and the explanatory footnotes. Similar help was also obtained from José Calveras, *Ejercicios espirituales, Directorio, y Documentos de S. Ignacio: Glosa y Vocabulario* (henceforth referred to as *Vocabulario*, and from the recent French translation: Ignace de Loyola, *Exercices Spirituels: Traduction du texte Autographe* par Edouard Gueydan, S.J. (Paris, 1986). This version is the result of teamwork by an editorial committee and its consultation with experts, among whom was Father Dalmases. We also acknowledge extensive help obtained from the *Vocabulario de Ejercicios Espirituales: Ensayo de hermenéutica Ignaciana* (Rome: CIS, 1972) by Ignacio Iparraguirre, and from the well-known *Obras completas de San Ignacio* in the series Biblioteca de autores cristianos.

7. The Aims and Style of This Translation

Like Dalmases' manual edition, the present translation is intended for practical use, especially by retreatants, directors, and those who are undertaking a deeper study of the *Exercises*. Attention has also been paid to the needs of those reading them for the first time. For these users this translator thought it best to aim, not at a literal translation strictly so called, but rather at one of "functional equivalence." That is, the ideal and aim of the present version is to express Ignatius' ideas altogether accurately, with no concept added to or subtracted from his own thought in the Autograph Spanish text of his *Exercises*. However, it does not seek to do this by "formal equivalence," namely, word for word, clause for clause, and participle by participle, pretty much in the sentence structure of the original language. Instead it is an endeavor to reproduce the thought of the original more as a modern English-speaking writer would be likely to express it. It aims to adjust Ignatius' Spanish text to the thought patterns and habits of English-speaking persons in such a way that a reader today can grasp the thought accurately and with reasonable ease, usually on the first reading.

Each of these two types of translation has, for its respective purposes, advantages and disadvantages which are absent from the other; and whichever is chosen, the translator must sacrifice something if he or she is to achieve the particular goals which are being sought. Usually the version of functional equivalence is better for quick intelligibility in practical use or for popular audiences, but the strictly literal version is better and even indispensable for scholarly investigation of technicalities and nuances. What our translation loses are some traits of Ignatius' style. It may make him appear to be more concerned with form and more literary than he really was.

Several excellent literal translations of the *Exercises* exist, such as those by Elder Mullan (1909), John Morris (1913), W. H. Longridge (1919), and others. We by no means seek to replace or disparage the more literal versions. Rather, if in some instances a reader wonders whether our translation has missed a nuance of Ignatius' thought, we invite him or her to investigate the matter with the help of a more literal version.

While the ideals mentioned above were being pursued in practice, many difficulties were met which required arbitrary decisions. The use of gender-inclusive language has been sincerely sought but at times found difficult in practice. Ignatius himself sometimes changes his pronoun within one paragraph, for example, from we (*nosotros*) to him or her (*le*) in 157, or from third person singular (*el hombre*) to first person plural (*nosotros*) in 23. Hence we too sometimes follow his example and make similar changes of person or from singular to plural in cases where this does not risk inaccurate rendition of his thought.

In some difficult instances, however, as is natural in the present state of English, whatever was tried in efforts to avoid gender-specific language pleased some and displeased others. To solve these and related problems, we decided to follow as far as possible the principles and precedents set by the committee which produced the most recent translation of the Bible, the *New Revised Standard Version* (1989).[11] In regard, too, to the use of masculine pronouns referring to God we have followed that committee's precedents, by reducing the number of such pronouns when it seemed possible without infidelity to Ignatius' text.

8. Directories

The *Exercises* were printed in 1548, more as a set of directives intended to be carried out in practice than as a book to be read. Its appearance in this form immediately provoked many questions. Just how was it to be used and interpreted? Requests for further directions came from many Jesuits. Successive sets of such directives arose, each called a "Directory." Ignatius himself started to work on this problem, especially because of questions raised by Polanco. But by 1556 he completed only a few fragments and gave some instructions orally which others wrote down.[12] After 1556 the First

---

11. This committee has stated its principles in *The Holy Bible: New Revised Standard Version* (Nashville: Nelson, 1989), on an unnumbered page which is page 3 of the Preface to the Readers at the beginning of the book. Much similar help is gratefully acknowledged from the committees which have produced two other gender-inclusive versions only a little less recent. They have stated their principles as follows: in the revised *Jerusalem Bible* (New York: Doubleday, 1985), on page 3, in the Preface; in *The New American Bible* (New York: The Catholic Book Publishing Company, 1986), on pp. [5], [6], and [7] of the Preface to the Revised Edition of the New Testament, placed immediately before the text of the New Testament. How these three committees respectively applied their principles in practice can be observed, for example, in the following sample texts: Genesis 1:31, 2:3; Luke 1:47-55, 68-79; John 1:2-3, 8:54, 14:16-17. See also the texts cited in Appendix I on pp. 201-207 below.

12. These are now referred to as the Autograph Directory (found in *Obrascompl*, pp. 295-298), and as Dictated Directories (of which examples can be seen ibid., pp. 299-303).

General Congregation, the early generals, and various committees or prominent persons such as Miró and Polanco produced Directories. During the generalate of Claudio Aquaviva (1581-1615) this work was brought to a synthesis. In 1599 he sent to all the provinces an official *Directory of the Spiritual Exercises* (Florence, 1599), intended to be a guide useful to all directors of the Exercises.[13] It contains forty short chapters. All these Directories enshrine the early traditions and are great helps for the interpretation and use of the *Exercises*.

9. Varying Interpretations of the Exercises

Since Ignatius' style was so terse and his book intended for flexible use, differing opinions about its meanings and proper use have been abundant from its first appearance in 1548. In these controversies, usually neither protagonist fully convinced his or her opponent, but both parties felt their efforts well repaid by all they had learned during their discussions. A fortunate result has been an ever-growing insight into the inexhaustible spiritual treasures hidden in Ignatius' little book. Only a few of these varying opinions, worthy though they are, can be mentioned in our limited space, and we apologize to those whose favorite theories must be left in silence.

In our endnotes in Part III below our foremost hope is to help toward the accurate understanding and interpretation of Ignatius' text. In the cases of differing opinions we aimed to give always a position which is solidly based and gets to the heart of the matter, to indicate on occasions at least some of the differing views, and to give some bibliographical aids for those who wish to explore them further.

---

13. This Directory is contained in *Directoria Exercitiorum Spiritualium (1540-1599)* (Rome, 1955), pp. 569-751. Two English translations exist: *Directory of the Spiritual Exercises of Our Holy Father Ignatius: Authorized Translation* (London: Manresa Press, 1925), and another in *The Spiritual Exercises of Saint Ignatius of Loyola*, trans. by W. H. Longridge (London, 1919), pp. 271-358. For the history of the Directories see *DeGuiJes*, pp. 243-247.

In judging such opinions and in studying the *Exercises*, we should distinguish carefully between two questions: (1) In any given passage, precisely what did Ignatius mean? and (2) what are the uses which we today can legitimately make of his thought? Since he intended his brief remarks to set exercitants on the way to thinking things out for themselves,[14] there is wide room for directors, exercitants, and students to enrich his texts by the knowledge they bring to it, for example, from updated writings in systematic, spiritual, or biblical theology. In general, the more such knowledge one brings to his text the more one gets from it.[15] Many exercitants have found treasures in Ignatius' book of which he himself was unaware; and precisely that was his hope. In many a case, the discoveries made in prayer during the Exercises have led to enriching study through the rest of the retreatant's life. Since the *Exercises* present a comprehensive view of God's whole plan for the salvation of human beings, growing insight into the *Exercises* brings deepening understanding of the deposit of faith itself. Although Ignatius never intended the *Exercises* to be a well-rounded treatise on the spiritual life, no other work of his introduces us better into the chief principles of his spirituality. His book of *Exercises* was perfected simultaneously with the maturing of his spirituality, and virtually all the rest of his achievements and writings can be considered to be commentaries on them or applications of them to particular situations.

---

14. *SpEx*, 2.

15. See *BibThSpEx*, pp. 39-43, 219-233, particularly 220 and 224, 278-279, 296-301; also *DeGuiJes*, pp. 539-543, 564.

THE TEXT OF THE

SPIRITUAL EXERCISES

CONTENTS
OF THE *SPIRITUAL EXERCISES*

Section numbers

Introductory Explanations   *1–20*

THE FIRST WEEK

The Purpose	*21*
Presupposition	*22*
Principle and Foundation	*23*
Daily Particular Examination of Conscience	*24–31*
General Examination of Conscience	*32–43*
General Confession, with Holy Communion	*44*
The Exercises of the First Week:	
1st: Meditation on the First, Second, and Third Sins	*45–54*
2nd: Meditation on Our Own Sins	*55–61*
3rd: Repetition of the First and Second Exercises	*62–63*
4th: Résumé by Making Three Colloquies	*64*
5th: Meditation on Hell	*65–71*
Additional Directives	*73–90*

THE SECOND WEEK

The Contemplation of the Kingdom of Christ	*91–99*
The Exercises of the First Day:	
1st Contemplation: on the Incarnation	*101–109*
2nd Contemplation: on the Nativity	*110–117*
3rd Contemplation: Repetition of Contemplations	
1 and 2	*118–119*
4th Contemplation: Repetition of Contemplations	
1 and 2	*120*
5th Contemplation: Application of the Five Senses	
to Contemplations 1 and 2	*121–126*
Second Day: The Presentation in the Temple and	
The Flight into Egypt	*132*

Third Day: The Hidden Life and the Finding in
                            the Temple   134
Fourth Day:
  Preamble to the Consideration of the States of Life   135
  Meditation on Two Standards: of Christ and
        of Lucifer   136–147
  Meditation on the Three Classes of Persons   149–156
  Note on Overcoming Repugnances to Poverty   157
Fifth Day: Contemplation on Christ's Departure
                            from Nazareth and on His Baptism   158
Sixth Day: The Temptations of Christ in the Desert   161
Seventh Day: Christ Calls the Apostles   161
Eighth Day: The Sermon on the Mount: the Beatitudes   161
Ninth Day: Christ Calms the Storm on the Lake   161
Tenth Day: Christ Preaches in the Temple   161
Eleventh Day: The Raising of Lazarus   161
Twelfth Day: Palm Sunday   161
Three Ways of Being Humble   165–168

The Election

Introduction to the Making of an Election   169
The Matters about Which an Election Should
        Be Made   170–174
Three Times Suitable for Making a Good Election   175–178
  1. When God Strongly Attracts One's Will   175
  2. When Clarifying Consolations and Desolations
        Are Experienced   176
  3. By Reasoning in a Time of Mental Calm   177
        The First Method   178–183
        The Second Method   184–188
Toward Amending and Reforming One's Own Life
        and State   188

THE THIRD WEEK

First Day: Contemplation, from Bethany through
                            the Last Supper   190–199
                    From the Last Supper to the Garden,
                            inclusively   200–203
Notes on Procedures   204–207

Second Day: From the Garden to the House of Annas   *208*

               From the House of Annas to That
                   of Caiaphas   *208*
               Third Day: From Caiaphas to Pilate   *208*
               From Pilate to Herod   *208*
Fourth Day: From Herod to Pilate   *208*
Fifth Day: From Pilate to the Crucifixion   *208*
               Christ on the Cross   *208*
Sixth Day: From the Cross to the Sepulcher   *208*
               From the Sepulcher to Our Lady's House   *208*
Seventh Day: Contemplation of the Passion as a Whole   *208*
Note   *209*
Rules to Order Oneself in the Taking of Food   *210–217*

THE FOURTH WEEK

First Contemplation: Christ Appears to Our Lady   *218–225*
Notes on the Contemplations of the Fourth Week   *226–229*
Contemplation to Attain Love   *230–237*

SUPPLEMENTARY MATTER

Three Methods of Praying   *228–260*
    The First: On the Commandments, Capital Sins,
        Faculties of the Soul, and Five Senses
        of the Body   *238–247*
    The Second: Contemplating Each Word of a Prayer   *249–257*
    The Third: Praying according to a Rhythmic
        Measure   *258–260*
The Mysteries of the Life of Christ   *261–312*
Rules to Perceive and Somewhat Understand the Mo-
        tions Caused in the Soul by the Diverse Spirits *313–327*
Rules for a More Probing Discernment of Spirits   *328–336*
Rules for the Ministry of Distributing Alms   *337–344*
Notes toward Perceiving and Understanding Scruples   *345–351*
Rules for Thinking, Judging, and Feeling with
        the Church   *352–370*

THE PRAYER "SOUL OF CHRIST"
(ANIMA CHRISTI)

Soul of Christ, sanctify me.
Body of Christ, save me.
Blood of Christ, inebriate me.
Water from the side of Christ, wash me.
Passion of Christ, strengthen me.
O good Jesus, hear me.
Within your wounds hide me.
Do not allow me to be separated from you.
From the malevolent enemy defend me.
In the hour of my death call me,
and bid me come to you,
that with your saints I may praise you
forever and ever. Amen.*

---

*This prayer, the *Anima Christi*, was not in Ignatius' text of the *Exercises*. However, because it is less widely known today than in the sixteenth century, most modern editions print it here. See endnote 46 on p. 157 below.

SPIRITUAL EXERCISES

IHS

1 *1* INTRODUCTORY EXPLANATIONS,[1]
TO GAIN SOME UNDERSTANDING
OF THE SPIRITUAL EXERCISES WHICH FOLLOW,
AND TO AID BOTH THE ONE WHO GIVES THEM
AND THE ONE WHO IS TO RECEIVE THEM.

2 The First Explanation. By the term Spiritual Exercises we mean every method of examination of conscience, meditation, contemplation, vocal or mental prayer, and other spiritual activities, such as will be mentioned later.
3 For, just as taking a walk, traveling on foot, and running are physical exercises, so is the name of spiritual exercises given to any means of preparing and disposing our
4 soul to rid itself of all its disordered affections[2] | and then, after their removal, of seeking and finding God's will in the ordering of our life for the salvation of our soul.

2 *1 The Second.* The person who gives to another the method and procedure for meditating or contemplating should accurately narrate the history[3] contained in the contemplation or meditation, going over the points with only a
2 brief or summary explanation. For in this way the person who is contemplating, by taking this history as the authentic foundation, and by reflecting on it and reasoning about it for oneself, can thus discover something that will bring better understanding or a more personalized
3 concept of the history—either through one's own reasoning or insofar as the understanding is enlightened
4 by God's grace. This brings more spiritual relish and spiritual fruit than if the one giving the Exercises had

lengthily explained and amplified the meaning of the
5 history. For what fills and satisfies the soul consists, not
in knowing much, but in our understanding the realities
profoundly and in savoring them interiorly.

3 1 *The Third*. In all the following Spiritual Exercises we use
the acts of the intellect in reasoning and of the will in
2 eliciting acts of the affections. In regard to the affective
acts which spring from the will we should note that
when we are conversing with God our Lord or his saints
3 vocally or mentally, greater reverence is demanded of us
than when we are using the intellect to understand.

4 1 *The Fourth*. Four Weeks are taken for the following
Exercises, corresponding to the four parts into which
2 they are divided. That is, the First Week is devoted to the
consideration and contemplation of sins; the Second, to
the life of Christ our Lord up to and including Palm
3 Sunday; | the Third, to the Passion of Christ our Lord;
and the Fourth, to the Resurrection and Ascension. To
this Week are appended the Three Methods of Praying.
4 However, this does not mean that each Week must
5 necessarily consist of seven or eight days. For during the
First Week some persons happen to be slower in finding
what they are seeking, that is, contrition, sorrow, and
6 tears for their sins. Similarly, some persons work more
diligently than others, and are more pushed back and
7 forth and tested by different spirits.[4] In some cases,
therefore, the Week needs to be shortened, and in others
lengthened. This holds as well for all the following
Weeks, while the retreatant is seeking what corresponds
8 to their subject matter. But the Exercises ought to be
completed in thirty days, more or less.

5 1 *The Fifth*. The persons who make the Exercises will
benefit greatly by entering upon them with great spirit
and generosity toward their Creator and Lord, and by
2 offering all their desires and freedom to him | so that His

Divine Majesty[5] can make use of their persons and of all they possess in whatsoever way is in accord with his most holy will.

6 1 *The Sixth.* When the one giving the Exercises notices that the exercitant is not experiencing any spiritual motions[6] in his or her[7] soul, such as consolations or desolations, or is not being moved one way or another
2 by different spirits, the director should question the retreatant much about the Exercises: Whether he or she is making them at the appointed times, how they are
3 being made, and whether the Additional Directives are being diligently observed. The director should ask about
4 each of these items in particular. Consolation and desolation are treated in [316-324], the Additional Directives in [73-90].

7 1 *The Seventh.* If the giver of the Exercises sees that the one making them is experiencing desolation and temptation, he or she should not treat the retreatant severely or
2 harshly, but gently and kindly. The director should encourage and strengthen the exercitant for the future, unmask the deceptive tactics of the enemy of our human nature, and help the retreatant to prepare and dispose himself or herself for the consolation which will come.

8 1 *The Eighth.* According to the need perceived in the exercitant with respect to the desolations and deceptive
2 tactics of the enemy, and also the consolations, | the giver of the Exercises may explain to the retreatant the rules of the First and Second Weeks for recognizing the different kinds of spirits, in [313-327 and 328-336].

9 1 *The Ninth.* This point should be noticed. When an exercitant spiritually inexperienced is going through the First Week of the Exercises, he or she may be tempted
2 grossly and openly, for example, by being shown obstacles to going forward in the service of God our Lord, in

the form of hardships, shame, fear about worldly honor,
3 and the like. In such a case the one giving the Exercises should not explain to this retreatant the rules on differ-
4 ent kinds of spirits for the Second Week. For to the same extent that the rules of the First Week will help him or her, those of the Second Week will be harmful. They are too subtle and advanced for such a one to understand.

10 1 *The Tenth.* When the one giving the Exercises perceives that the retreatant is being assailed and tempted under the appearance of good, the proper time has come to explain to the retreatant the rules of the Second Week
2 mentioned just above. For ordinarily the enemy of human nature tempts under the appearance of good more often when a person is performing the Exercises in the illuminative life,[8] which corresponds to the Exercises
3 of the Second Week, | than in the purgative life, which corresponds to those of the First Week.

11 1 *The Eleventh.* It is helpful for a person receiving the Exercises of the First Week to know nothing about what
2 is to be done in the Second, but to work diligently during the First Week at obtaining what he or she is seeking, just as if there were no anticipation of finding anything good in the Second.

12 1 *The Twelfth.* The one giving the Exercises should insist strongly with the person making them that he or she should remain for a full hour in each of the five Exer-
2 cises or contemplations which will be made each day; and further, that the recipient should make sure always to have the satisfaction of knowing that a full hour was spent on the exercise—indeed, more rather than less. For
3 the enemy usually exerts special efforts to get a person to shorten the hour of contemplation, meditation, or prayer.

13 1 *The Thirteenth.* This too should be noted. In time of consolation it is easy and scarcely taxing to remain in contemplation for a full hour, but during desolation it is
2 very hard to fill out the time. Hence, to act against the desolation and overcome the temptations, the exercitant ought to remain always a little longer than the full hour, and in this way become accustomed not merely to resist the enemy but even to defeat him.

14 1 *The Fourteenth.* If the one giving the Exercises sees that the exercitant is proceeding with consolation and great fervor, he or she should warn the person not to make some promise or vow which is unconsidered or hasty.
2 The more unstable the director sees the exercitant to be, the more earnest should be the forewarning and caution.
3 For although it is altogether right for someone to advise another to enter religious life, which entails the taking
4 of vows of obedience, poverty, and chastity; and although a good work done under a vow is more meritori-
5 ous than one done without it, still one ought to bestow much thought on the strength and suitability of each person, and on the helps or hindrances one is likely to meet with in carrying out what one wishes to promise.

15 1 *The Fifteenth.* The one giving the Exercises should not urge the one receiving them toward poverty or any other promise more than toward their opposites, or to one state
2 or manner of living more than to another. Outside the Exercises it is lawful and meritorious for us to counsel those who are probably suitable for it to choose conti-nence, virginity, religious life, and all forms of evangeli-
3 cal perfection. But during these Spiritual Exercises when a person is seeking God's will, it is more appropriate and far better that the Creator and Lord himself should
4 communicate himself to the devout soul, embracing it in love and praise, and disposing it for the way which will
5 enable the soul to serve him better in the future. Accord-ingly, the one giving the Exercises ought not to lean or

incline in either direction but rather, while standing by
6 like the pointer of a scale in equilibrium, | to allow the
Creator to deal immediately with the creature and the
creature with its Creator and Lord.

16 1 *The Sixteenth.* For this purpose—namely, that the
Creator and Lord may with greater certainty be the one
2 working in his creature—if by chance the exercitant
feels an affection or inclination to something in a
disordered way, it is profitable for that person to strive
with all possible effort to come over to the opposite of
3 that to which he or she is wrongly attached. Thus, if
someone is inclined to pursue and hold on to an office
or benefice,[9] not for the honor and glory of God our
Lord or for the spiritual welfare of souls, but rather for
4 one's own temporal advantages and interests, | one
should try to bring oneself to desire the opposite. One
should make earnest prayers and other spiritual exercises
5 and ask God our Lord for the contrary; that is, to have
no desire for this office or benefice or anything else
unless the Divine Majesty has put proper order into
those desires, and has by this means so changed one's
6 earlier attachment that | one's motive in desiring or
holding on to one thing rather than another will now be
only the service, honor, and glory of the Divine Majesty.

17 1 *The Seventeenth.* It is very advantageous that the one
who is giving the Exercises, without wishing to ask
about or know the exercitant's personal thoughts or sins,
2 should be faithfully informed about the various agitations and thoughts which the different spirits stir up in
3 the retreatant. For then, in accordance with the person's
greater or lesser progress, the director will be able to
communicate spiritual exercises adapted to the needs of
the person who is agitated in this way.

18 1 *The Eighteenth.* The Spiritual Exercises should be adapted to the disposition of the persons who desire to make

2 them, that is, to their age, education, and ability.[10] In this way someone who is uneducated or has a weak constitution will not be given things he or she cannot well bear or profit from without fatigue.

3   Similarly exercitants should be given, each one, as much as they are willing to dispose themselves to receive, for their greater help and progress.

4   Consequently, a person who wants help to get some instruction and reach a certain level of peace of soul can be given the Particular Examen [24-31], and then the

5 General Examen [32-43], | and further, the Method of Praying, for a half hour in the morning, on the Commandments [238-243], the Capital Sins[11] [244-245], and

6 other such procedures [238; 246-260]. Such a person can also be encouraged to weekly confession of sins and, if possible, to reception of the Eucharist every two weeks

7 or, if better disposed, weekly. This procedure is more appropriate for persons who are rather simple or illiterate. They should be given an explanation of each of the commandments, the seven capital sins, the precepts of the Church, the five senses, and the works of mercy.

8   Likewise, if the one giving the Exercises sees that the one making them is a person poorly qualified or of little natural ability from whom much fruit is not to be

9 expected, it is preferable to give to such a one some of

10 these light exercises until he or she has confessed, and then to give ways of examining one's conscience and a program for confession more frequently than before, that

11 the person may preserve what has been acquired. But this should be done without going on to matters pertaining to the Election or to other Exercises beyond the First

12 Week. This is especially the case when there are others with whom greater results can be achieved. There is not sufficient time to do everything.

19 1 *The Nineteenth.* A person who is involved in public
   2 affairs or pressing occupations | but educated or intelligent may take an hour and a half each day to perform

the Exercises.[12] To such a one the director can explain
3 the end for which human beings are created. Then he or
she can explain for half an hour the particular examen,
then the general examen, and the method of confessing
4 and receiving the Eucharist. For three days this exercitant should make a meditation for an hour each
5 morning on the first, second, and third sins [45-53]; then
for another three days at the same hour the meditation
6 on the court-record of one's own sins [55-61]; then for a
further three days at the same hour the meditation on
7 the punishment corresponding to sins [65-72]. During
these three meditations the ten Additional Directives [73-
8 90] should be given the exercitant. For the mysteries of
Christ our Lord this exercitant should follow the same
procedure as is explained below and at length throughout the Exercises themselves.

20 1 *The Twentieth.* A person who is more disengaged, and
who desires to make all the progress possible, should be
given all the Spiritual Exercises in the same sequence in
2 which they proceed below. Ordinarily, in making them
an exercitant will achieve more progress the more he or
she withdraws from all friends and acquaintances, and
3 from all earthly concerns; for example, by moving out of
one's place of residence and taking a different house or
room where one can live in the greatest possible soli-
4 tude, and thus be free to attend Mass and Vespers daily
5 without fear of hindrance from acquaintances. Three
principal advantages flow from this seclusion, among
many others.

6   First, by withdrawing from friends and acquaintances
and likewise from various activities that are not well
ordered, in order to serve and praise God our Lord, we
gain much merit in the eyes of the Divine Majesty.

7   Second, by being secluded in this way and not
having our mind divided among many matters, but by
concentrating instead all our attention on one alone,
namely, the service of our Creator and our own spiritual

8 progress, we enjoy a freer use of our natural faculties for seeking diligently what we so ardently desire.

9   Third, the more we keep ourselves alone and secluded, the more fit do we make ourselves to approach and

10 attain to our Creator and Lord; and the more we unite ourselves to him in this way, the more do we dispose ourselves to receive graces and gifts from his divine and supreme goodness.

THE FIRST WEEK[13]

SPIRITUAL EXERCISES
TO OVERCOME ONESELF,
AND
TO ORDER ONE'S LIFE,[14]
WITHOUT REACHING A DECISION
THROUGH SOME DISORDERED AFFECTION.[15]

PRESUPPOSITION

1 That both the giver and the maker of the Spiritual Exercises may be of greater help and benefit to each *2* other, it should be presupposed that every good Christian ought to be more eager to put a good interpretation *3* on a neighbor's statement than to condemn it. Further, if one cannot interpret it favorably, one should ask how the other means it. If that meaning is wrong, one should *4* correct the person with love; and if this is not enough, one should search out every appropriate means through which, by understanding the statement in a good way, it may be saved.[16]

23   *1*   PRINCIPLE AND FOUNDATION[17]

2 Human beings are created to praise, reverence, and serve
     God our Lord,[18] and by means of doing this to save their
     souls.[19]

3   The other things on the face of the earth are created
     for the human beings, to help them in the pursuit of the
     end for which they are created.

4   From this it follows that we ought to use these things
     to the extent that they help us toward our end, and free
     ourselves from them to the extent that they hinder us
     from it.

5   To attain this it is necessary to make ourselves indif-
     ferent[20] to all created things, in regard to everything
6 which is left to our free will and is not forbidden.[21] Con-
     sequently, on our own part we ought not to seek health
     rather than sickness, wealth rather than poverty, honor
     rather than dishonor, a long life rather than a short one,
     and so on in all other matters.

7   Rather, we ought to desire and choose only that
     which is more conducive to the end for which we are
     created.[22]

24 1 ## DAILY PARTICULAR EXAMINATION
OF CONSCIENCE.[23]
It comprises three times in the day
and two examinations of conscience.

2 *The First Time* is in the morning. Upon arising the retreatant should resolve to guard carefully against the particular sin or fault he or she wants to correct or amend.

25 1 *The Second Time* is after the noon meal.[24] The exercitant should ask God our Lord for what she or he desires, namely, grace to recall how often one has fallen into the particular sin or fault, in order to correct it in the future.

2 Then the retreatant should make the first examination, exacting an account of self with regard to the particular matter decided upon for correction and improvement. He

3 or she should run through the time, hour by hour or period by period, from the moment of rising until the

4 present examination. On the upper line of the g====[25] one should enter a dot for each time one fell into the

5 particular sin or fault. Then one should renew one's resolution to do better during the time until the second examination which will be made later.

26 1 *The Third Time* is after supper. The exercitant should make the second examination, likewise hour by hour starting from the previous examination down to the

2 present one. For each time he or she fell into the particular sin or fault, a dot should be entered on the lower line of the g====.

27 1   **FOUR ADDITIONAL DIRECTIVES**
to help toward quicker riddance
of the particular sin or fault.

2 *The First Directive*. Each time one falls into the particular sin or fault, one should touch one's hand to one's
3 breast in sorrow for having fallen. This can be done even in public without its being noticed by others.

28 1 *The Second*. Since the upper line of the g═══ s represents the first examination and the lower line the second, the retreatant should look at night to see if there was any improvement from the first line to the second, that is, from the first examination to the second.

29 1 *The Third*. The exercitant should compare the second day with the first, that is, the two examinations of each day with those of the previous day, to see whether any improvement has been made from one day to the next.

30 1 *The Fourth*: He or she should compare this week with the previous one, to see if any improvement has been made during the present week in comparison with the one before.

31 1 It should be noted that the first large G on the top line indicates Sunday, the second and smaller g Monday, the third Tuesday, and so on.

2   G ══════════════════════════════
   g ──────────────────────────────
   g ──────────────────────────────
   g ──────────────────────────────
   g ──────────────────────────────
   g ──────────────────────────────
   g ──────────────────────────────

32 *1*   **GENERAL EXAMINATION OF CONSCIENCE**
to purify oneself, and
to make a better confession.[26]

2 I assume that there are three kinds of thoughts in myself. That is, one kind is my own, which arises strictly from *3* my own freedom and desire; and the other two come from outside myself, the one from the good spirit and the other from the evil.[27]

33 *1*   **Thoughts**

2 There are two ways in which I can merit from an evil thought that comes from outside myself.

3   The first occurs when a thought of committing a mortal sin comes to me, and I resist it immediately, and it remains conquered.

34 *1*   The second way to merit occurs when this same bad thought comes to me, and I resist it, but it keeps coming back and I resist it continually, until it is overcome and *2* goes away. This second way gains more merit than the first.

35 *1* I sin venially when this same thought of committing a mortal sin comes to me and I give some heed to it, by *2* dwelling on it slightly | or admitting some pleasure in the senses, or when I am somewhat slack in repulsing the thought.

36 *1* There are two ways of sinning mortally. The first occurs when I consent to the bad thought, intending at that time to carry out what I have assented to, or to do so if it becomes possible.

37 *1* The second way of sinning mortally occurs when one actually carries out the sin. This is graver, for three *2* reasons: | first, the longer time involved; second, the greater intensity; and third, through greater harm to other persons.

38 *1* **Words**

2 It is not permissible to swear, either by God or by a creature, unless it is done with truth, necessity, and *3* reverence. With necessity, that is, to affirm with an oath, not just any truth at all, but only one of some importance for the good of the soul, or the body, or temporal *4* interests. With reverence, that is, when in pronouncing the name of our Creator and Lord one acts with consideration and manifests that honor and reverence which are due to him.

39 *1* In an unnecessary oath, it is a more serious sin to swear by the Creator than by a creature. However, we should *2* note, it is harder to swear by a creature with the proper truth, necessity, and reverence than to swear by the Creator, for the following reasons.

3   *The First.* When we desire to swear by a creature, our very desire to name a creature makes us less careful and cautious about speaking the truth or affirming it with necessity than is the case when our urge is to name the Lord and Creator of all things.

4   *The Second.* When we swear by a creature, it is not as easy to maintain reverence and respect for the Creator as it is when we swear by the name of the Creator and Lord himself. For our very desire to name God our Lord carries with it greater respect and reverence than desire *5* to name a creature. Consequently, to swear by a creature is more permissible for persons spiritually far advanced *6* than for those less advanced. The perfect, through constant contemplation and enlightenment of their understanding, more readily consider, meditate, and contemplate God our Lord as being present in every *7* creature by his essence, presence, and power. Thus when they swear by a creature, they are more able and better disposed than the imperfect to render respect and reverence to their Creator and Lord.

8   *The Third.* To swear continually by a creature brings a risk of idolatry that is greater in the imperfect than in the perfect.

40 1 It is not permissible to speak idle words. I take this to mean words that are of no benefit to myself or anyone else, and are not ordered toward such benefit.

2 Consequently, words that benefit or are intended to benefit my own or another's soul, body, or temporal

3 goods are never idle. Nor are they idle merely because they are about matters outside one's state of life; for example, if a religious talks about wars or commerce.

4 However, in all that has been mentioned, there is merit if the words are ordered to a good end, and sin if they are directed to a bad end, or by one's talking uselessly.

41 1 We may not say anything to harm the reputation of others or to disparage them. If I reveal another person's mortal sin that is not publicly known,[28] I sin mortally; if a venial sin, venially; if a defect, I expose my own defect.

2   When one has a right intention, there are two cases where it is permissible to speak about someone else's sin or fault.

3   *The First.* When the sin is public, for example, in the case of a known prostitute, a judicial sentence, or a public error infecting the minds of those with whom we live.

4   *The Second.* When a hidden sin is revealed to another person so that he or she can help the sinner arise from this state. But in that case there must be conjectures or probable reasons to think that this person will be able to help the sinner.[29]

42 1   **Deeds**

  2 Here the subject matter takes in the ten commandments,
     the precepts of the Church, and the official recommen-
     dations of our superiors. Any action performed against
     these three headings is a sin, more serious or less in
  3 accordance with its nature. By official recommendations
     of our superiors I mean, for example, the bulls about
     crusades and other indulgences, such as those for
     peaceful reconciliations on condition of confession and
  4 reception of the Eucharist. For it is no small sin to act or
     cause others to act against these pious exhortations and
     recommendations of our superiors.

43 1   **A METHOD FOR MAKING**
         THE GENERAL EXAMINATION OF CONSCIENCE. [30]
                      It contains five points.

  2 *The First Point* is to give thanks to God our Lord for the
     benefits I have received.
  3   *The Second* is to ask grace to know my sins and rid
     myself of them.
  4   *The Third* is to ask an account of my soul from the
     hour of rising to the present examen, hour by hour or
  5 period by period; first as to thoughts, then words, then
     deeds, in the same order as was given for the particular
     examination [25].
  6   *The Fourth* is to ask pardon of God our Lord for my
     faults.
  7   *The Fifth* is to resolve, with his grace, to amend them.
     Close with an Our Father.

44 1

GENERAL CONFESSION,
WITH HOLY COMMUNION

2 For a person who voluntarily desires to make a general confession, to make it here in the time of retreat will bring three benefits, among others.

3   *The First.* It is granted that a person who confesses annually is not obliged to make a general confession.

4 Nevertheless, to make it brings greater profit and merit, because of the greater sorrow experienced at present for all the sins and evil deeds of one's entire life.

5   *The Second.* During these Spiritual Exercises one reaches a deeper interior understanding of the reality and malice of one's sins than when one is not so con-

6 centrated on interior concerns. In this way, by coming to know and grieve for the sins more deeply during this time, one will profit and merit more than was the case on earlier occasions.

7   *The Third.* As a result of having made a better confession and come to a better disposition, one is worthier and better prepared to receive the Holy Sacra-

8 ment. Furthermore, the reception of it helps, not only to avoid falling into sin, but also to preserve the increase of grace.

9   The general confession is best made immediately after the Exercises of the First Week.

45 *1* ### THE FIRST EXERCISE

IS A MEDITATION[31]
BY USING THE THREE POWERS OF THE SOUL
ABOUT THE FIRST, SECOND, AND THIRD SINS.

2 **It contains,**
after a preparatory prayer and two preludes,
three main points and a colloquy.

46 *1* *The Preparatory Prayer*[32] is to ask God our Lord for the
grace that all my intentions, actions, and operations[33]
may be ordered purely to the service and praise of the
Divine Majesty.

47 *1* *The First Prelude* is a composition[34] made by imagining
2 the place. Here we should take notice of the following.
When a contemplation or meditation is about something
that can be gazed on, for example, a contemplation of
3 Christ our Lord, who is visible, ⌐the composition will be
to see in imagination the physical place where that
4 which I want to contemplate is taking place. By physical
place I mean, for instance, a temple or a mountain where
Jesus Christ or our Lady happens to be, in accordance
with the topic I desire to contemplate.
5   When a contemplation or meditation is about something abstract and invisible, as in the present case about
the sins, the composition will be to see in imagination
and to consider my soul as imprisoned in this corruptible
6 body, and my whole compound self as an exile in this
valley [of tears] among brute animals. I mean, my whole
self as composed of soul and body.[35]

48 *1* *The Second Prelude* is to ask God our Lord for what I
2 want and desire.[36] What I ask for should be in accordance with the subject matter. For example, in a contemplation on the Resurrection, I will ask for joy with Christ

3 in joy; | in a contemplation on the Passion, I will ask for pain, tears, and suffering with Christ suffering.

4   In the present meditation it will be to ask for shame and confusion about myself, when I see how many people have been damned for committing a single mortal

5 sin, and how many times I have deserved eternal damnation for my many sins.

49 1 *Note.* All the contemplations or meditations ought to be preceded by this same preparatory prayer, which is never changed, and also by the two preludes, which are sometimes changed in accordance with the subject matter.

50 1 *The First Point* will be to use my memory, by going over the first sin, that of the angels; next, to use my under-

2 standing, by reasoning about it; | and then my will.³⁷ My aim in remembering and reasoning about all these matters is to bring myself to greater shame and confu-

3 sion, by comparing the one sin of the angels with all my own many sins. For one sin they went to hell; then how often have I deserved hell for my many sins!

4   In other words, I will call to memory the sin of the angels: How they were created in grace and then, not wanting to better themselves by using their freedom to

5 reverence and obey their Creator and Lord, they fell into pride, were changed from grace to malice, and were

6 hurled from heaven into hell. Next I will use my intellect to ruminate about this in greater detail, and then move myself to deeper emotions by means of my will.

51 1 *The Second Point* will be meditated in the same way. That is, I will apply the three faculties to the sin of Adam

2 and Eve. I will recall to memory how they did long penance for their sin, and the enormous corruption it brought to the human race, with so many people going

3 to hell. Again in other words, I will call to memory the second sin, that of our first parents: How Adam was

created in the plain of Damascus[38] and placed in the earthly paradise; and how Eve was created from his rib;

4 how they were forbidden to eat of the tree of knowl-

5 edge, but did eat, and thus sinned; and then, clothed in garments of skin and expelled from paradise, they lived out their whole lives in great hardship and penance,

6 deprived of the original justice which they had lost. Next I will use my intellect to reason about this in greater detail, and then use the will, as is described just above.

52 1 *The Third Point* will likewise be to use the same method on the third sin, the particular sin of anyone who has gone to hell because of one mortal sin; and further, of innumerable other persons who went there for fewer sins than I have committed.

2   That is, about this third particular sin too I will follow the same procedure as above. I will call to memory the gravity and malice of the sin against my Creator

3 and Lord; then I will use my intellect to reason about it —how by sinning and acting against the Infinite Goodness the person has been justly condemned forever. Then I will finish by using the will, as was described above.

53 1 *Colloquy.*[39] Imagine Christ our Lord[40] suspended on the cross before you, and converse with him in a colloquy: How is it that he, although he is the Creator, has come to make himself a human being? How is it that he has passed from eternal life to death here in time, and to die in this way for my sins?

2   In a similar way, reflect on yourself and ask: What have I done for Christ? What am I doing for Christ? What ought I to do for Christ?

3   In this way, too, gazing on him in so pitiful a state as he hangs on the cross, speak out whatever comes to your mind.

54 1 A colloquy is made, properly speaking, in the way one

friend speaks to another, or a servant to one in authority
2 —now begging a favor, now accusing oneself of some misdeed, now telling one's concerns and asking counsel about them. Close with an Our Father.

55 *1*

THE SECOND EXERCISE
IS A MEDITATION ON OUR OWN[41] SINS.
It comprises, after the preparatory prayer and preludes, five points and a colloquy.

2 *The Preparatory Prayer* will be the same.
3   *The First Prelude* will be the same composition of place.
4   *The Second Prelude* will be to ask for what I desire. Here it will be to ask for growing and intense sorrow and tears for my sins.

56 *1* *The First Point* is the court-record[42] of my sins. I will call to memory all the sins of my life, looking at them year
2 by year or period by period. ¹ For this three things will be helpful: first, the locality or house where I lived; second, the associations which I had with others; third, the occupation I was pursuing.

57 *1* *The Second Point* is to ponder these sins, looking at the foulness and evil which every mortal sin would contain in itself, even if it were not forbidden.

58 *1* *The Third Point.* I will reflect upon myself, by using examples which humble me:
      First, what am I when compared with all other human beings?
2   Second, what are they when compared with all the angels and saints in paradise?
3   Third, what is all of creation when compared with God? and then, I alone—what can I be?
4   Fourth, I will look at all the corruption and foulness

of my body.

5   Fifth, I will look upon myself as a sore and abscess from which have issued such great sins and iniquities and such foul poison.

59 1 *The Fourth Point.* I will consider who God is against whom I have sinned, by going through his attributes and comparing them with their opposites in myself: God's
    2 wisdom with my ignorance; God's omnipotence with my weakness; God's justice with my iniquity; God's goodness with my malice.

60 1 *The Fifth Point.* This is an exclamation of wonder and surging emotion, uttered as I reflect on all creatures and wonder how they have allowed me to live and have
    2 preserved me in life. The angels: How is it that, although they are the swords of God's justice, they have borne
    3 with me, protected me, and prayed for me? The saints: How is it that they have interceded and prayed for me? Likewise, the heavens, the sun, the moon, the stars, and
    4 the elements; the fruits, birds, fishes, and animals. ¹ And the earth: How is it that it has not opened up and swallowed me, creating new hells for me to suffer in forever?

61 1 *I will conclude with a colloquy* of mercy—conversing with God our Lord and thanking him for granting me life until now, and proposing, with his grace, amendment for the future. Our Father.

62 *1* THE THIRD EXERCISE
IS A REPETITION OF
THE FIRST AND SECOND EXERCISES,
BY MAKING THREE COLLOQUIES.

2 After the preparatory prayer and two preludes, this exercise will be a repetition[43] of the first and the second exercises. I should notice and dwell on those points where I felt greater consolation or desolation, or had a *3* greater spiritual experience. Then I will make three colloquies in the manner which follows.

63 *1* *The First Colloquy* will be with our Lady, that she may obtain for me from her Son and Lord grace for three things:

2 First, that I may feel an interior knowledge of my sins and also an abhorrence of them;

3 Second, that I may perceive the disorder in my actions, in order to detest them, amend myself, and put myself in order;

4 Third, that I may have a knowledge of the world,[44] in order to detest it and rid myself of all that is worldly and vain. Then I will say a Hail Mary.[45]

5 *The Second Colloquy.* I will make the same requests to the Son, asking him to obtain these graces for me from the Father. Then I will say the prayer Soul of Christ.[46]

6 *The Third Colloquy.* I will address these same requests to the Father, asking that he himself, the eternal Lord, may grant me these graces. Then I will say an Our Father.

64 1   **THE FOURTH EXERCISE**
IS TO MAKE A REPETITION OF THE THIRD.

2 I have used the word repetition because the intellect, aided by the memory, will without digressing reflect on the matters contemplated in the previous exercises. It concludes with the same three colloquies.

65 1   **THE FIFTH EXERCISE**
IS A MEDITATION ON HELL.
It contains,
after the preparatory prayer and two preludes,
five points and a colloquy.

2 *The Preparatory Prayer* will be the same as usual.

3   *The First Prelude*, the composition of place. Here it will be to see in imagination the length, breadth, and depth of hell.

4   *The Second Prelude*, to ask for what I desire. Here it will be to ask for an interior sense of the pain suffered

5 by the damned, so that if through my faults I should forget the love of the Eternal Lord, at least the fear of those pains will serve to keep me from falling into sin.

66 1 *The First Point* will be to see with the eyes of the imagination the huge fires and, so to speak, the souls within the bodies full of fire.

67 1 *The Second Point.* In my imagination I will hear the wailing, the shrieking, the cries, and the blasphemies against our Lord and all his saints.

68 1 *The Third Point.* By my sense of smell I will perceive the smoke, the sulphur, the filth, and the rotting things.

69 1 *The Fourth Point.* By my sense of taste I will experience the bitter flavors of hell: tears, sadness, and the worm of conscience.

70 1 *The Fifth Point.* By my sense of touch, I will feel how the flames touch the souls and burn them.

71 1 *The Colloquy.* I will carry on a colloquy with Christ our Lord. I will call to mind the souls who are in hell: Some are there because they did not believe in Christ's coming; and others who, although they believed, did not act
  2 according to his commandments. I will group these persons into three classes.
>
> First, those lost before Christ came.
> Second, those condemned during his lifetime.
> Third, those lost after his life in this world.

  3   Thereupon I will thank Christ because he has not, by
  4 ending my life, let me fall into any of these classes. I will also thank him because he has shown me, all through my life up to the present moment, so much pity and mercy. I will close with an Our Father.[47]

72 1 *Note.* The first exercise will be made at midnight; the second, soon after arising in the morning; the third, before or after Mass, but always before the noon meal; the fourth, at the time of Vespers; and the fifth, an hour
  2 before the evening meal. This distribution of the hours is intended to be followed, more or less, throughout the four Weeks. The norm is the help found by the exercitant in making the five exercises or fewer, in accordance with his or her age, physical or mental disposition, and temperament.

73 1 ### ADDITIONAL DIRECTIVES[48]
FOR MAKING THE EXERCISES BETTER
AND
FINDING MORE READILY WHAT ONE DESIRES.

2 *The First Directive.* Upon going to bed at night, just before I fall asleep, I will think for the length of a Hail Mary about the hour when I should arise, and for what purpose; and I will briefly sum up the exercise I am to make.

74 1 *The Second.* Upon awakening, while keeping out any other thoughts, I will immediately turn my attention to what I will contemplate in the first exercise, at midnight. I will strive to feel shame for my many sins, by using 2 examples, such as that of a knight who stands before his king and his whole court, shamed and humiliated because he has grievously offended him from whom he has received numerous gifts and favors.

3 Similarly, in the second exercise I will imagine myself as a great sinner in chains; that is, as if I were being brought in chains to appear before the supreme and 4 eternal Judge; taking as an example how chained prisoners, already deserving death, appear before their 5 earthly judge. As I dress I will keep thoughts like these in mind, or others proper to the subject matter.

75 1 *The Third.* A step or two away from the place where I will make my contemplation or meditation, I will stand 2 for the length of an Our Father. I will raise my mind and think how God our Lord is looking at me, and other such thoughts. Then I will make an act of reverence or humility.

76 1 *The Fourth.* I will enter upon the contemplation, now kneeling, now prostrate on the floor, or lying face

upward, or seated, or standing—but always intent on
2 seeking what I desire. | Two things should be noted.
First, if I find what I desire while kneeling, I will not
change to another posture; so too, if I find it while
3 prostrate, and so on. Second, if in any point I find what
I am seeking, there I will repose until I am fully satisfied,
without any anxiety to go on.[49]

77 1 *The Fifth*. After finishing the exercise, for a quarter of an
hour, either seated or walking about, I will examine how
2 well I did in the contemplation or meditation. If poorly,
I will seek the reasons; and if I find them, I will express
3 sorrow in order to do better in the future. If I did well,
I will thank God our Lord and use the same procedure
next time.

78 1 *The Sixth*. I should not think about pleasant or joyful
things, such as heavenly glory, the Resurrection, and so
forth. For if we desire to experience pain, sorrow, and
tears for our sins, any thought of happiness or joy will
2 be an impediment. Instead, I should keep myself intent
on experiencing sorrow and pain; and for this it is better
to think about death and judgment.

79 1 *The Seventh*. For the same purpose I will deprive myself
of all light, by closing the shutters and doors while I am
in my room, except for times when I want to read the
office or other matters, or eat.

80 1 *The Eighth*. I should not laugh, or say anything that
would arouse laughter.

81 1 *The Ninth*. I should restrain my sight, except to receive
or say goodbye to someone with whom I speak.

82 1 *The Tenth*. This pertains to penance, which is divided
2 into interior and exterior. Interior penance is grieving for
one's sins with a firm intention not to commit those or

3 any other sins again. Exterior penance, a fruit of the former, is self-punishment for the sins one has committed. This is done in three principal ways.

83 1 The first way pertains to eating. That is, when we abstain from what is superfluous we are practicing, not
2 penance, but temperance. We practice penance when we abstain from what is ordinarily suitable. And the more we subtract the better is the penance, provided that we do not weaken our constitution or bring on noteworthy illness.

84 1 The second way pertains to our manner of sleeping. Again, when we abstain from the superfluous in things
2 delicate and soft, this is not penance. But we do practice penance when we deprive ourselves of what is ordinarily suitable; and the more we so deprive ourselves, the better is the penance, provided we do not harm our-
3 selves or weaken our constitution. However, we should not deprive ourselves of the amount of sleep ordinarily good for us, except perhaps in an effort to find the right mean when one has a bad habit of sleeping too much.

85 1 The third way is to chastise the body, that is, to inflict pain on it, by wearing hairshirts, cords, or iron chains; by scourging or wounding oneself; and by similar austerities.

86 1 *Note.* The most suitable and safest form of penance seems to be that which produces physical pain but does not penetrate to the bones, so that it brings pain but not
2 illness. Therefore the most suitable form of penance is to hurt oneself with light cords that inflict the pain on the surface, rather than some other manner which might cause noteworthy illness inside.

87 1 *A First Observation.* Exterior penances are performed chiefly for three purposes:

First, to satisfy for one's past sins.

2 Second, to overcome ourselves; that is, to keep our bodily nature obedient to reason and all our bodily faculties[50] subject to the higher.

3 Third, to seek and obtain some grace or gift which one wishes and desires, such as interior contrition for

4 one's sins, or abundant tears because of them or of the pains and sufferings which Christ our Lord underwent in his Passion; or to obtain a solution to some doubt in which one finds oneself.

88 1 *A Second Observation.* The first and second additional directives should be used for the exercises at midnight and early morning, but not for those which will be made

2 at other times. The fourth additional directive will never be practiced in church in the presence of others, but only privately, for example, in one's house, and so forth.

89 1 *A Third Observation.* When someone making the Exercises fails to find what he or she desires, such as tears, consolation, and the like, it is often useful to make some change in eating, sleeping, and other forms of penance,

2 so that we do penance for two or three days, and then omit it for two or three days. Furthermore, for some persons more penance is suitable, and for others less.

2 Further still, on many occasions we give up penance because of love of our bodies and judge erroneously that a human being cannot endure such penance without

4 notable illness. On the other hand, we sometimes do excessive penance, thinking that the body can bear it.

5 Now since God our Lord knows our nature infinitely better than we do, through changes of this sort he often enables each of us to know what is right for ourselves.

90 1 *A Fourth Observation.* The particular examination should be made to get rid of faults and negligences pertaining to the exercises and Additional Directives. This holds true also during the Second, Third, and Fourth Weeks.

THE SECOND WEEK

[THE CONTEMPLATION
OF THE KINGDOM OF JESUS CHRIST][51]

91 *1*   THE CALL OF THE TEMPORAL KING,
AS AN AID TOWARD CONTEMPLATING
THE LIFE OF THE ETERNAL KING.[52]

2   *The Preparatory Prayer* will be as usual [46].

3   *The First Prelude.* A composition by imagining the place. Here it will be to see with the eyes of the imagination the synagogues, villages, and castles[53] through which Christ our Lord passed as he preached.

4   *The Second Prelude* is to ask for the grace which I desire. Here it will be to ask grace from our Lord that I may not be deaf to his call, but ready and diligent to accomplish his most holy will.

92 *1*   *The First Point.* I will place before my mind a human king, chosen by God our Lord himself, whom all Christian princes and all Christian persons reverence and obey.[54]

93 *1*   *The Second Point.* I will observe how this king speaks to
2   all his people, saying, "My will is to conquer the whole land of the infidels. Hence, whoever wishes to come with me has to be content with the same food I eat, and the
3   drink, and the clothing which I wear, and so forth. So too each one must labor with me during the day, and
4   keep watch in the night, and so on, ⌐ so that later each may have a part with me in the victory, just as each has

shared in the toil."[55]

94 1 *The Third Point.* I will consider what good subjects
2 ought to respond to a king so generous and kind; and
how, consequently, if someone did not answer his call,
he would be scorned and upbraided by everyone and
accounted as an unworthy knight.

95 1 **THE SECOND PART OF THIS EXERCISE**
consists in applying
the above parable of a temporal king
to Christ our Lord,
according to the three points just mentioned.[56]

2 *The First Point.* If we give consideration to such a call
3 from the temporal king to his subjects, how much more
worthy of our consideration it is to gaze upon Christ our
Lord, the eternal King, and all the world assembled
before him. He calls to them all, and to each person in
4 particular he says: "My will is to conquer the whole
world and all my enemies, and thus to enter into the
5 glory of my Father. Therefore, whoever wishes to come
with me must labor with me, so that through following
me in the pain he or she may follow me also in the glory."[57]

96 1 *The Second Point.* This will be to reflect that all those
who have judgment and reason will offer themselves
wholeheartedly for this labor.

97 1 *The Third Point.* Those who desire to show greater
devotion and to distinguish themselves in total service to
their eternal King and universal Lord, will not only offer
2 their persons for the labor, | but go further still. They
will work against[58] their human sensitivities[59] and
against their carnal and worldly love, and they will make
offerings of greater worth and moment, and say:

98 1 "Eternal Lord of all things, I make my offering, with your favor and help. I make it in the presence of your infinite Goodness, and of your glorious Mother, and of 2 all the holy men and women in your heavenly court. I wish and desire, and it is my deliberate decision, provid- 3 ed only that it is for your greater service and praise, | to imitate you in bearing all injuries and affronts, and any 4 poverty, actual[60] as well as spiritual, | if your Most Holy Majesty desires to choose and receive me into such a life and state."

99 1 *First Note.* This exercise will be made twice during the day, that is, on rising in the morning and an hour before the noonday or the evening meal.

100 1 *Second Note.* During the Second Week, and also the following Weeks, it is profitable to spend occasional periods in reading from *The Imitation of Christ*, the Gospels, or lives of the saints.

101 *1*

THE FIRST DAY.

ON IT THE FIRST CONTEMPLATION[61] IS DEVOTED TO THE INCARNATION.[62]
It contains, after the preparatory prayer, three preludes, three points, and a colloquy.

2 The usual Preparatory Prayer.

102 *1 The First Prelude* is to survey the history[63] of the matter I am to contemplate. Here it is how the three Divine Persons gazed on the whole surface or circuit of the *2* world, full of people; and how, seeing that they were all going down into hell, they decide in their eternity that the Second Person should become a human being,[64] in *3* order to save the human race. And thus, when the fullness of time had come, they sent the angel St. Gabriel to Our Lady [see 262 below].

103 *1 The Second Prelude* is a composition, by imagining the place. Here it will be to see the great extent of the circuit *2* of the world, with peoples so many and so diverse; ¹ and then to see in particular the house and rooms of Our Lady, in the city of Nazareth in the province of Galilee.

104 *1 The Third Prelude* will be to ask for what I desire. Here it will be to ask for an interior knowledge[65] of Our Lord, who became human for me, that I may love him more intensely and follow him more closely.

105 *1 Note.* It should be noted here that this same preparatory prayer, without any change, should be made throughout this and the following Weeks, as was stated at the *2* beginning. Similarly the same three preludes are to be made throughout this and the following Weeks; but their procedure is changed in accordance with the subject

matter.

106 1 *The First Point.* I will see the various persons, some here, some there.

2 First, those on the face of the earth, so diverse in dress and behavior: | some white and others black, some in peace and others at war, some weeping and others laughing, some healthy and others sick, some being born and others dying, and so forth.

3 Second, I will see and consider the three Divine Persons, seated, so to speak, on the royal canopied throne of Their Divine Majesty. They are gazing on the whole face and circuit of the earth; and they see all the peoples in such great blindness, and how they are dying and going down to hell.

4 Third, I will see Our Lady and the angel greeting her. Then I will reflect on this to draw some profit from what I see.

107 1 *The Second Point.* I will listen to what the persons on the face of the earth are saying; that is, how they speak with

2 one another, swear and blaspheme, and so on. Likewise, I will hear what the Divine Persons are saying, that is, "Let us work the redemption of the human race," and so

3 forth. Then I will listen to what the angel and Our Lady are saying. Afterwards I will reflect on this, to draw profit from their words.

108 1 *The Third Point.* Here I will consider what the people on the face of the earth are doing: How they wound, kill, go

2 to hell, and so on. Similarly, what the Divine Persons are doing, that is, bringing about the most holy Incarnation,

3 and other such activities. Likewise, what the angel and Our Lady are doing, with the angel carrying out his office of ambassador and Our Lady humbling herself

4 and giving thanks to the Divine Majesty. Then I will reflect on these matters, to draw some profit from each of them.

109 1 *Colloquy.* At the end a colloquy should be made. I will
think over what I ought to say to the Three Divine
Persons, or to the eternal Word made flesh, or to our
2 Mother and Lady. I will beg favors according to what I
perceive in my heart, that I may better follow and imitate
Our Lord, who in this way has recently become a human
being. Our Father.

110 1 ## THE SECOND CONTEMPLATION
IS ON THE NATIVITY.

2 *The Preparatory Prayer* as usual.

111 1 *The First Prelude* is the history. Here it will be to recall
how Our Lady, pregnant almost nine months and, as we
2 may piously meditate, seated on an ass, | together with
Joseph and a servant girl leading an ox, set forth from
Nazareth to go to Bethlehem and pay the tribute which
Caesar had imposed on all those lands [264].

112 1 *The Second Prelude.* The composition, by imagining the
place. Here it will be to see in imagination the road from
Nazareth to Bethlehem. Consider its length and breadth,
whether it is level or winds through valleys and hills.
2 Similarly, look at the place or cave of the Nativity: How
big is it, or small? How low or high? And how is it
furnished?

113 1 *The Third Prelude.* This will be the same as in the
preceding contemplation, and made with the same
procedure [104].

114 1 *The First Point.* This is to see the persons; that is, to see
Our Lady, Joseph, the maidservant, and the infant Jesus
2 after his birth. I will make myself a poor, little, and
unworthy slave, gazing at them, contemplating them,
and serving them in their needs, just as if I were there,

3 with all possible respect and reverence. Then I will
reflect upon myself to draw some profit.

115 1 *The Second Point.* I will observe, consider, and contemplate what they are saying. Then, reflecting upon myself,
I will draw some profit.

116 1 *The Third Point.* This is to behold and consider what
they are doing; for example, journeying and toiling, in
2 order that the Lord may be born in greatest poverty; and
that after so many hardships of hunger, thirst, heat, cold,
injuries, and insults, he may die on the cross! And all
3 this for me! Then I will reflect and draw some spiritual
profit.

117 1 *Colloquy.* Conclude with a colloquy, as in the preceding
contemplation, and with an Our Father.

118 1 ### THE THIRD CONTEMPLATION
WILL BE A REPETITION
OF THE FIRST AND SECOND EXERCISES.

2 After the preparatory prayer and the three preludes, the
exercitant should make a repetition of the first and
3 second exercises. Always he or she will note some more
important points where some insight, consolation, or
desolation was experienced. Also, at the end a colloquy
should be made, and an Our Father recited.

119 1 *Note.* In this repetition, and in all those which follow,
the order of procedure will be the same as what was
used in the repetitions of the First Week [62-64]. The
subject matter is changed but the same procedure is kept.

120 1
THE FOURTH CONTEMPLATION
WILL BE A REPETITION
OF THE FIRST AND SECOND CONTEMPLATIONS,
just as was done in the preceding repetition.

121 1
THE FIFTH CONTEMPLATION
WILL BE AN APPLICATION OF THE FIVE SENSES[66]
to the subject matter
of the first and second contemplations.

2 After the preparatory prayer and the three preludes, it is profitable to use the imagination and to apply the five senses to the first and second contemplations, in the following manner.

122 1 *The First Point*. By the sight of my imagination I will see the persons, by meditating and contemplating in detail all the circumstances around them, and by drawing some profit from the sight.

123 1 *The Second Point*. By my hearing I will listen to what they are saying or might be saying; and then, reflecting on myself, I will draw some profit from this.

124 1 *The Third Point*. I will smell the fragrance and taste the infinite sweetness and charm of the Divinity, of the soul, of its virtues, and of everything there, appropriately for
2 each of the persons who is being contemplated. Then I will reflect upon myself and draw profit from this.

125 1 *The Fourth Point*. Using the sense of touch, I will, so to speak, embrace and kiss the places where the persons walk or sit. I shall always endeavor to draw some profit from this.

126 1 *Colloquy*. Conclude with a colloquy, as in the first and

second contemplations [101, 110], and with an Our Father.

127   **[NOTES FOR THE SECOND WEEK]**

1 *The First Note.* For this and the following Weeks this should be observed. I should read only about the mys-
2 tery which I shall immediately contemplate. In this way I will avoid reading about a mystery foreign to my contemplation for that day or that hour. The purpose is to keep the consideration of one mystery from interfering with that about another.

128 1 *Second Note.* The first exercise, that on the Incarnation, will be at midnight; the second exercise, on awakening in the morning; the third, near the hour of Mass; the fourth, at the hour of Vespers; and the fifth, before the
2 evening meal. The exercitant should remain for an hour in each of these five exercises. This same order of the day should be followed on all the remaining days.

129 1 *Third Note.* This too should be noted. If the one making the Exercises is aged or weak, or even if he or she is strong but has been left somewhat weakened by the First
2 Week, during the Second Week it is better for this person not to arise at midnight, at least sometimes. Instead one contemplation should be made in the morning, a second
3 at the hour of Mass, a third before the noon meal, ¹ the repetition near the hour of Vespers, and the application of the senses before the evening meal.

130 1 *Fourth Note.* In the observance of the ten Additional Directives given in the First Week, during the Second Week modifications should be made in the second, sixth, seventh, and part of the tenth.
2   The second Additional Directive [74] will be that when I awaken I should call to mind the contemplation I am about to make in my desire to know better the

eternal Word made flesh, so that I may better serve him and follow him.

3   The sixth [78] will be frequently to call to mind the life and mysteries of Christ our Lord, from his Incarnation up to the place or mystery I am presently contemplating.

4   The seventh [79] will become this: I should make use of darkness or light, good weather or its opposite, to the extent that I find them profitable for myself and helpful toward finding what I desire.

5   In regard to the tenth Additional Directive [82], the exercitant ought to adjust his or her practice of penance in accordance with the mysteries being contemplated. For some of them call for penance, and others do not.

6   In this way all ten Additional Directives should be carried out with great care.

131 1 *Fifth Note.* In all the exercises, except those at midnight and in the morning, the equivalent of the second Additional Directive [74] should be observed in the following way.

2   As soon as I recall that the time to make the exercise has come, before I begin it I will call to mind where I am going and before whom I shall appear, and I will briefly
3 survey its subject matter. Then I will carry out the third Additional Directive [75] and begin the exercise.

132 1   **THE SECOND DAY**

On the second day, for the first and second contemplations the exercitant should take the Presentation in the
2 Temple [268] and the Flight into exile in Egypt [269]. The two repetitions will be made about this pair of contemplations, and then an application of the senses to them. This is done in the same way as on the preceding day [101-126].

133 1 *Note.* On this second day and through the fourth day, it is sometimes profitable, even when an exercitant is strong and well-disposed, to make changes in procedure, 2 to help him or her in finding what is desired. One contemplation might be taken at dawn, another near the hour of Mass, and the repetition at the hour of Vespers, and the application of the senses before the evening meal.

134 1   **THE THIRD DAY**

On the third day the exercitant will contemplate how the child Jesus was obedient to his parents at Nazareth [271], and next how they found him in the temple [272]. After this will come the two repetitions and the application of the senses.

[THE ELECTION]

135 *1*

INTRODUCTION TO
THE CONSIDERATION OF THE STATES OF LIFE[67]

2 We have already considered the example which Christ our Lord gave us for the first state of life, which consists in the observance of the commandments. He gave this example when he lived in obedience to his parents.

3 We have also considered the example he gave us for the second state, that of evangelical perfection,[68] when he remained in the temple, separating himself from his adoptive father and human mother in order to devote himself solely to the service of his eternal Father.

4 While continuing our contemplations of his life, we now begin simultaneously to explore and inquire: In which state or way of life does the Divine Majesty wish us to serve him?

5 Therefore to gain some introduction to this matter, we shall in our next exercise observe the intention of Christ our Lord and, in contrast, that of the enemy of

6 human nature. We shall also think about how we ought to dispose ourselves in order to come to perfection in whatsoever state or way of life God our Lord may grant us to elect.

136 *1*   THE FOURTH DAY
A MEDITATION ON TWO STANDARDS,[69]
THE ONE OF CHRIST,
OUR SUPREME COMMANDER AND LORD,
THE OTHER OF LUCIFER,
THE MORTAL ENEMY OF OUR HUMAN NATURE.

   2 The Preparatory Prayer will be as usual.

137 *1* *The First Prelude.* This is the history. Here it will be to consider how Christ calls and desires all persons to come under his standard, and how Lucifer in opposition calls them under his.

138 *1* *The Second Prelude.* A composition, by imagining the place. Here it will be to imagine a great plain in the region of Jerusalem, where the supreme commander of
   2 the good people is Christ our Lord; then another plain in the region of Babylon, where the leader of the enemy is Lucifer.

139 *1* *The Third Prelude.* It is to ask for what I desire. Here it will be to ask for insight into the deceits of the evil
   2 leader, and for help to guard myself against them; | and further, for insight into the genuine life which the supreme and truthful commander sets forth, and grace to imitate him.[70]

[PART I. THE STANDARD OF SATAN]

140 *1* *The First Point.* Imagine the leader of all the enemy in that great plain of Babylon. He is seated on a throne of fire and smoke, in aspect horrible and terrifying.

141 *1* *The Second Point.* Consider how he summons uncountable devils, disperses some to one city and others to

2 another, ¹ and thus throughout the whole world, without missing any provinces, places, states, or individual persons.

142 1 *The Third Point.* Consider the address he makes to them: How he admonishes them to set up snares and chains;

2 how first they should tempt people to covet riches (as he usually does, at least in most cases), so that they may more easily come to vain honor from the world, and

3 finally to surging pride. In this way, the first step is riches, the second is honor, and the third is pride; ⁷¹ and from these three steps the enemy entices them to all the other vices.

[PART II. THE STANDARD OF CHRIST]

143 1 Similarly, in contrast, gaze in imagination on the supreme and true leader, who is Christ our Lord.

144 1 *The First Point.* Consider how Christ our Lord takes his place in that great plain near Jerusalem, in an area which is lowly, beautiful, and attractive.

145 1 *The Second Point.* Consider how the Lord of all the world chooses so many persons, apostles, disciples, and the like. He sends them throughout the whole world, to spread his doctrine among people of every state and condition.

146 1 *The Third Point.* Consider the address which Christ our Lord makes to all his servants and friends whom he is

2 sending on this expedition. He recommends that they endeavor to aid all persons, by attracting them, first, to

3 the most perfect spiritual poverty ¹ and also, if the Divine Majesty should be served and should wish to choose them for it, even to no less a degree of actual poverty; ⁷²

4 and second, by attracting them to a desire of reproaches and contempt, since from these results humility.

5   In this way there will be three steps: the first, poverty
in opposition to riches; the second, reproaches or contempt in opposition to honor from the world; and the
6   third, humility in opposition to pride. Then from these
three steps they should induce people to all the other
virtues. [73]

147 1 *A Colloquy* should be made with Our Lady. I beg her to
obtain for me grace from her Son and Lord that I may be
2   received under his standard; and first, in the most
perfect spiritual poverty; and also, if his Divine Majesty
should be served and if he should wish to choose me for
3   it, to no less a degree of actual poverty; and second, in
bearing reproaches and injuries, that through them I
may imitate him more, if only I can do this without sin
on anyone's part and without displeasure to the Divine
Majesty. Then I will say a Hail Mary.
4   *A Second Colloquy.* It will be to ask the same grace
from the Son, that he may obtain it for me from the
Father. Then I will say the Soul of Christ.
5   *A Third Colloquy* will be to ask the same grace from
the Father, that he may grant it to me. Then I will say an
Our Father.

148 1 *Note.* This exercise will be made at midnight and again
after arising. There will also be two repetitions of it, one
near the hour of Mass and one near that of Vespers.
2   Each of these exercises will close with the three colloquies: one with Our Lady, one with the Son, and one
3   with the Father. Then the following exercise on the
typical persons will take place before the evening meal.

149 *1* ON THIS SAME FOURTH DAY,
A MEDITATION[74] IS MADE
ON THE THREE CLASSES OF PERSONS,[75]
to aid one toward embracing what is better.

2 *The Preparatory Prayer* will be as usual.

150 *1* *The First Prelude.* It is the history,[76] that of three persons, each typical of a class. Each of them has acquired
ten thousand ducats, but not purely or properly for the
2 love of God. Each desires to save his or her soul and to
find God our Lord in peace, by discarding the burden
and obstacle to this purpose which this attachment to the
acquired money is found to be.[77]

151 *1* *The Second Prelude* is a composition, by seeing the place.
Here it will be to imagine myself as standing before God
and all his saints, that I may desire and know what will
be more pleasing to the Divine Goodness.

152 *1* *The Third Prelude* will be to ask for what I desire. Here
I will ask for the grace to choose that which is more to
the glory of the Divine Majesty and the salvation of my
soul.[78]

153 *1* *The Person Typical of the First Class* would like to get
rid of this attachment[79] to the acquired money, in order
to find God in peace and be able to attain salvation. But
this person does not take the means, even to the hour of
death.

154 *1* *The Person Typical of the Second Class* also desires to get
rid of the attachment, but in such a way that she or he
will keep the acquired money; and that thus God will
2 come to where this person desires. No decision is made
to dispose of the money in order to go to where God is,

even though that would be the better state for this individual.

155 1 *The Person Typical of the Third Class* desires to get rid of the attachment, but in such a way that there remains no inclination either to keep the acquired money or to
2 dispose of it. Instead such a one desires to keep it or reject it solely according to what God our Lord will move[80] one's will to choose, and also according to what the person himself or herself will judge to be better for the service and praise of the Divine Majesty.
3   In the meantime this person endeavors to take an attitude by which, as far as the affections are concerned, he or she is giving up everything.[81] [In other words], one strives earnestly not to desire that money or anything else, except when one is motivated solely by the service
4 of God our Lord; in such a way that the desire to be able to serve God our Lord better is what moves one to take or reject any object whatsoever.[82]

156 1 *Colloquy.* The same three colloquies should be made as in the preceding contemplation on the Two Standards [147].

157 1 *Note.* When we feel an inclination or repugnance against actual poverty, or when we are not indifferent to poverty
2 or riches, a great help toward overcoming this disordered attachment is to beg the Lord in the colloquies to choose oneself to serve him in actual poverty (even though it is
3 contrary to our lower nature); and further that one desires it, begs for it, and pleads for it, provided only that it would be for the service and praise of the Divine Majesty.

158 1   **THE FIFTH DAY**

The contemplation will be on the departure of Christ our

Lord from Nazareth for the river Jordan, and how he was baptized [273].[83]

159 1 *First Note.* This contemplation will be made once at midnight, and a second time in the early morning. Then there will be two repetitions of it, one near the hour of Mass and one near that of Vespers, and an application of
2 the five senses before the evening meal. In each of these five exercises the usual preparatory prayer and three preludes will be used, in the manner explained for the contemplation on the Incarnation [102] and the Nativity
3 [111]. Moreover, the triple colloquy should be that of the Three Classes of Persons [147], or according to the note which follows that meditation [157].[84]

160 1 *Second Note.* The particular examination of conscience after the noonday and evening meals will be about one's faults and negligences during the day in regard to the exercises and the Additional Directives. This same procedure should be used also for the following days.

161 1   THE SIXTH DAY

The contemplation will be on how Christ our Lord went from the river Jordan to the desert inclusively, and on his temptations there [274]. The same manner of proceeding should be followed as on the fifth day.

2   THE SEVENTH DAY

How St. Andrew and others followed Christ our Lord [275].

3   THE EIGHTH DAY

The Sermon on the Mount, which is on the eight beatitudes [278].

4

THE NINTH DAY

How Christ our Lord appeared to his disciples on the waves of the sea [280].

5

THE TENTH DAY

How Christ our Lord preached in the temple [288].

6

THE ELEVENTH DAY

On the raising of Lazarus [285].

7

THE TWELFTH DAY

On Palm Sunday [287].

162 1 *First Note.* In this Second Week the number of the contemplations can be increased or lessened, according to the number of days each exercitant wants to spend in 2 this Week or finds profitable. If the Week is to be prolonged, one can take the mysteries of Our Lady's visitation to Elizabeth, the Shepherds, the Circumcision of the Infant Jesus, the Three Kings, and others similar. 3 If the Week is to be shortened, even some of those which were assigned can be omitted. For the purpose of these meditations is to furnish an introduction and a method for meditating and contemplating, that one may do this better and more completely later on.

163 1 *Second Note.* The exposition of the material pertaining to an election will be begun on the Fifth Day, the day

devoted to the contemplation of Christ's departure from Nazareth for the Jordan, in accordance with the explanations given below [169-189].

164 1 *Third Note*. Before entering into the deliberations about an election, an exercitant who desires to become lovingly
2 attached to the genuine teaching of Christ our Lord I will profit much from considering and pondering the three ways of being humble which are described immediately below. One should mull them over from time to time
3 throughout the whole day,[85] and make colloquies, as will be explained [168].

[THREE WAYS OF BEING HUMBLE][86]

165 1 *The First Way of Being Humble* is necessary for eternal salvation, and consists in this. I so lower and humble myself, as far as is in my power, that in all things I may be obedient to the law of God our Lord.
2   Consequently, even though others would make me lord of all the creatures in this world, or even to save my temporal life, never would I reach a decision to violate a commandment either human or divine which binds me under mortal sin.

166 1 *The Second Way of Being Humble* is more perfect than the first. It is what I have when I find myself in this
2 disposition: If my options are equally effective[87] for the
1 service of God our Lord and the salvation of my soul, I I do not desire or feel myself strongly attached to having wealth rather than poverty, or honor rather than dishonor, or a long life rather than a short one.[88]
2   Furthermore, neither for all creation nor to save my life would I ever reach a decision to commit a venial sin.

167 1 *The Third Way of Being Humble* is the most perfect, and consists in this. When I possess the first and second

ways, and when the options equally further the praise
2 and glory of God, in order to imitate Christ our Lord
3 better and to be more like him here and now, I desire
and choose poverty with Christ poor rather than wealth;
contempt with Christ laden with it rather than honors.
4 Even further, I desire to be regarded as a useless fool for
Christ, who before me was regarded as such, rather than
as a wise or prudent person in this world.[89]

168 1 *Note.* One who desires to obtain this third way of being
humble will profit much by making the colloquies of the
meditation on the Three Classes of Persons, as presented
2 above [147, 156]. In order to imitate and serve our Lord
better, he or she should beg him to be chosen for this
third, a greater and better way of being humble, if the
service and praise to the Divine Majesty would be equal
or greater.

169 1

INTRODUCTION
TO THE MAKING OF AN ELECTION[90]

2 In every good election, insofar as it depends on us, the eye of our intention ought to be single. I ought to focus only on the purpose for which I am created, to praise
3 God our Lord and to save my soul. Accordingly, anything whatsoever that I elect ought to be chosen as an aid toward that end.

I ought not to order or drag the end into subjection
4 to the means, but to order the means to the end. In this way it happens, for example, that many choose firstly to marry, which is the means, and secondly to serve God our Lord in marriage, although[91] the service of God is
5 the end. Similarly, there are others who first seek to possess benefices, and afterwards to serve God in them.
6 Thus these persons do not go directly to God, but desire God to come directly to their disordered attachments. As a result they transform the end into a means and the means into the end; and consequently what they should fasten on in the first place they take up in the last.
7 For I ought to aim first at desiring to serve God, which is the end, and secondarily at accepting the benefice or marrying if that is more suitable for me, which is the means to the end.
8 Finally, nothing whatever ought to move me to choose such means or deprive myself of them except one alone, the service and praise of God our Lord and the eternal salvation of my soul.[92]

170   **[A CONSIDERATION]**[93]

1   **TO ACQUIRE KNOWLEDGE OF THE MATTERS
ABOUT WHICH AN ELECTION SHOULD BE MADE.
It contains four points and one note.**

2 *The First Point.* It is necessary that all the matters about
which we wish to make an election should in themselves
be either indifferent or good, so that they function
constructively within our Holy Mother the hierarchical
Church, and are not bad or opposed to her.[94]

171 *1* *The Second.* Some matters fall under the heading of an
unchangeable election, such as priesthood, marriage, and
2 the like. Others fall under the heading of a changeable
election; for example, we may take or leave benefices; we
may take or reject temporal goods.

172 *1* *The Third.* In the case of an unchangeable election, once
it has been made there is nothing further to elect, since
the first one cannot be undone. Examples are marriage,
2 priesthood, and the like. But if this election was not
made properly and in a rightly ordered way, free from
disordered affections, the only thing that can be considered is to repent and then explore how to lead a good
3 life within the decision made. An election of this kind
does not seem to be a divine vocation, since it is some-
4 thing improperly ordered and indirect. This is a way in
which many are in error; for they take up a predisposed
or bad choice and then regard it as a divine vocation.
5 For every vocation from God is something pure, stain-
less, and without mingling of the flesh or any other
poorly ordered affection.

173 *1* *The Fourth.* In regard to matters under the heading of a
changeable election, if someone has made one in a

proper and well-ordered way, and with no admixture of
2 the flesh or the world, there is no reason to make a new
election. Instead one should perfect oneself as much as
possible in accordance with the former choice.

174 1 *Note.* This too should be noticed. If such a changeable
election was made but not in a sincerely and rightly
2 ordered way, | then, if one desires fruits to spring from
it which are noteworthy and very pleasing to God our
Lord, it is profitable to make it anew in a properly
ordered way.

175 1   **THREE TIMES,**
          EACH OF THEM SUITABLE
   FOR MAKING A SOUND AND GOOD ELECTION.

2 *The First Time* is an occasion when God our Lord moves
and attracts the will in such a way that a devout person,
without doubting or being able to doubt, carries out
3 what was proposed. This is what St. Paul and St. Matthew did when they followed Christ our Lord.[95]

176 1 *The Second Time* is present when sufficient clarity and
knowledge are received from the experience of consolations and desolations, and from experience in the
discernment of various spirits.[96]

177 1 *The Third Time* is one of tranquility. I consider first the
end for which human beings are born, namely, to praise
2 God our Lord and to save their souls; then, desiring this,
as the means I elect a life or state of life within the limits
of the Church, in order to be helped in the service of my
Lord and the salvation of my soul.[97]
3   By a time of tranquility I mean one when the soul is
not being moved one way and the other by various
spirits and uses its natural faculties in freedom and
peace.

178 *1*   If an election is not made in the first or second time, two methods are given below for making it in this third time.

2   ## THE FIRST METHOD
OF MAKING A SOUND AND GOOD ELECTION.
It contains six points.

3 *The First Point* is to put before myself the matter about which I wish to make an election, for example, an office or a benefice to be taken or relinquished, or any other thing which falls under the heading of a changeable election.

179 *1* *The Second Point*. It is necessary to keep as my objective the end for which I am created, to praise God our Lord
2 and save my soul. Furthermore, I ought to find myself indifferent,[98] that is, without any disordered affection, to such an extent that I am not more inclined or emotionally disposed toward taking the matter proposed rather than relinquishing it, nor more toward relinquishing it rather than taking it.
3   Instead, I should find myself in the middle, like the pointer of a balance, in order to be ready to follow that which I shall perceive to be more to the glory and praise of God our Lord and the salvation of my soul.

180 *1* *The Third Point*. I should beg God our Lord to be pleased to move my will and to put into my mind what I ought to do in regard to the matter proposed, so that it
2 will be more to his praise and glory. I should beg to accomplish this by reasoning well and faithfully with my intellect, and by choosing in conformity with his most holy will and good pleasure.

181 *1* *The Fourth Point*. I should consider and reason out how many advantages or benefits accrue to myself from

having the office or benefice proposed, all of them solely
for the praise of God our Lord and the salvation of my
2 soul; and on the contrary I should similarly consider the
3 disadvantages and dangers in having it. Then, acting in
the same manner in the second part, I should consider
the advantages and benefits in not having it, and
contrarily the disadvantages and dangers in not having
it.[99]

182 1 *The Fifth Point.* After I have thus considered and rea-
soned out all the aspects of the proposed matter, I should
2 see to which side reason more inclines. It is in this way,
namely, according to the greater motion arising from
reason,[100] and not according to some motion arising from
sensitive human nature, that I ought to come to my decision[101] about the matter proposed.

183 1 *The Sixth Point.* When that election or decision has been
made, the person who has made it ought with great
2 diligence to go to prayer before God our Lord | and to
offer him that election, that the Divine Majesty may be
pleased to receive and confirm it, if it is conducive to his
greater service and praise.

184 1 ## THE SECOND METHOD
OF MAKING A SOUND AND GOOD ELECTION.[102]
It contains four rules and a note.

2 *The First Rule.* That love which moves me and brings me
to choose the matter in question should descend from
3 above, from the love of God; in such a way that the
person making the election should perceive beforehand
that the love, whether greater or less, which he or she
has for the matter being chosen is solely for the sake of
our Creator and Lord.

185 1 *The Second Rule.* I will imagine a person whom I have

never seen or known. Desiring all perfection for him or her, I will consider what I would say in order to bring such a one to act and elect for the greater glory of God our Lord and the greater perfection of his or her soul.

2 Then, doing the same for myself, I will keep the rule which I set up for another.

186 1 *The Third Rule.* I will consider, as if I were at the point of death, what procedure and norm[103] I will at that time wish I had used in the manner of making the present election. Then, guiding myself by that norm, I should make my decision on the whole matter.

187 1 *The Fourth Rule.* Imagining and considering how I will find myself on judgment day, I will think how at that time I will wish I had decided in regard to the present

2 matter. And the rule which I will then wish I had followed is what I shall apply now, in order that then I may be in complete contentment and joy.

188 1 *Note.* After I have observed the rules presented above for my salvation and eternal contentment, I shall make my election and offer it to God our Lord, in the manner described in point 6 of the First Method of Making an Election [183].

189 1   TOWARD AMENDING AND REFORMING
          ONE'S OWN LIFE AND STATE[104]

2 In regard to those persons who are established in an
ecclesiastical office or in the state of matrimony (whether
they possess an abundance of temporal goods or not),
3 there is either no possibility of a change, or else no ready
will to make an election about matters subject to a
changeable election.

4   For them it is very profitable to present, in place of
an election, a procedure and method for each one of
5 them to improve and reform his or her life and state, by
setting before them the purpose of each one's creation,
life, and state of life: the glory and praise of God our
Lord and the salvation of their own soul.

6   To make progress toward this end and attain to it,
one ought to consider and work out in detail, during the
Exercises and by means of the Methods of Making an
7 Election as explained above [175-188], how large a house
and how many persons in it one ought to maintain, how
one ought to direct and govern its members, and how to
8 teach them by word and example. So too persons such as
these should examine their resources, how much they
ought to assign for the house and household, and how
9 much for the poor and other good works. In all this and
by it, each one should desire and seek nothing except
the greater praise and glory of God our Lord.

10   For everyone ought to reflect that in all spiritual
matters, the more one divests oneself of self-love, self-
will, and self-interests, the more progress one will
make.[105]

THE THIRD WEEK[106]

THE FIRST DAY

1
THE FIRST CONTEMPLATION,
at Midnight.
HOW CHRIST OUR LORD WENT FROM BETHANY
TO JERUSALEM FOR THE LAST SUPPER [289].
It contains the preparatory prayer, three
preludes, six points, and a colloquy.

2 *The Preparatory Prayer* is as usual.

191 1 *The First Prelude* is to survey the history. Here it is to recall how Christ our Lord sent two disciples from Bethany to Jerusalem to prepare the supper, and later 2 went there himself with his other disciples; and how, after eating the Paschal Lamb and finishing the meal, he washed their feet and gave his Most Holy Body and 3 Precious Blood to his disciples; and further, how he addressed his farewell discourse to them, after Judas had left to sell his Lord.

192 1 *The Second Prelude.* A composition, by imagining the place. Here it will be to see in imagination the road from Bethany to Jerusalem, whether it is broad, or narrow, or 2 level, and so on. In similar manner, imagine the room of the supper, whether it is large, or small, or arranged in one way or another.

193 1 *The Third Prelude* is to ask for what I desire. Here it will be to ask for sorrow, regret, and confusion, because the Lord is going to his Passion for my sins.

194 1 *The First Point* is to see the persons at the supper; and then, by reflecting on myself, to endeavor to draw some profit from them.

2 *The Second Point* is to listen to what they are saying, and similarly to draw profit from that.

3 *The Third Point* is to see what they are doing, and to draw profit from it.

195 1 *The Fourth Point.* Consider what Christ our Lord suffers in his human nature, or desires to suffer, according to

2 the passage being contemplated. Then one should begin here with much effort to bring oneself to grief, sorrow, and tears, and in this same manner to work through the points which follow.

196 1 *The Fifth Point.* Consider how his divinity hides itself; that is, how he could destroy his enemies but does not, and how he allows his most holy humanity to suffer so cruelly.

197 1 *The Sixth Point.* Consider how he suffers all this for my sins, and so on; and also ask: What ought I to do and suffer for him? [107]

198 1 *The Colloquy.* Finish with a colloquy to Christ our Lord, and at its end recite an Our Father.

199 1 *Note.* Attention should be called to a matter which was partially explained before [54]. In the colloquies we ought to converse and beg according to the subject mat-

2 ter [108]; that is, in accordance with whether I find myself tempted or consoled, desire to possess one virtue or another, or to dispose myself in one way or another, or to experience sorrow or joy over the matter I am contem-

3 plating. And finally I ought to ask for what I more earnestly desire in regard to some particular matters.

4 In carrying out this procedure, we may make one colloquy to Christ our Lord or, if the topic or devotion

moves us, make three colloquies, one to the Mother, one
5 to the Son, and one to the Father—using the same
procedure that was explained in the Second Week in the
Meditation on the Three[109] Classes [156] and the note
after it [157].

200 1

THE SECOND CONTEMPLATION,
in the Morning.
FROM THE SUPPER TO THE GARDEN,
INCLUSIVELY [290].

2 *The Preparatory Prayer* will be as usual.

201 1 *The First Prelude* is the history. Here it will be how
Christ our Lord descended with his eleven disciples from
2 Mt. Sion, where the supper had been eaten, | into the
3 Valley of Jehoshaphat. He left eight of them in one part
4 of the valley and three in an area of the garden. He
began to pray, and his sweat became like drops of blood.
After he had prayed three times to his Father and
awakened his disciples, his enemies fell back at his
5 words. Then Judas gave him the kiss of peace | and St.
Peter cut off the ear of Malchus, but Christ put it back in
6 place. He was arrested as a malefactor, and his captors
led him down the valley and up its other side to the
house of Annas.

202 1 *The Second Prelude* is to imagine the place. Here it will
be to consider the road from Mt. Sion down into the
Valley of Jehoshaphat, and the Garden, whether it is
small or large, whether of one appearance or another.

203 1 *The Third Prelude* is to ask for what I desire. Here it is
what is proper for the Passion: sorrow with Christ in
sorrow; a broken spirit with Christ so broken; tears; and
interior suffering because of the great suffering which
Christ endured for me.

204 1 *First Note.* In this second contemplation, after the preparatory prayer and the three preludes already mentioned, the exercitant will follow the same manner of proceeding through the points and colloquy as in the 2 first contemplation on the supper. At the hour of Mass and of Vespers two repetitions will be made, and after that, but before the evening meal, an application of the 3 senses to both the contemplations mentioned above. The preparatory prayer and the three preludes will always be used, adjusted to the subject matter, in the same manner of proceeding indicated and explained above in the Second Week [119, 152; see also 72].

205 1 *Second.* According to what is most helpful in view of the exercitant's age, condition, and temperament, there will be five exercises each day or fewer.

206 1 *Third.* During this Third Week the second and sixth Additional Directives will be changed in part.
  2   The second will be that as soon as I awaken I will think of where I am going and for what purpose. In my mind I will briefly run over the coming contemplation I intend to make, in accordance with the mystery at hand.
  3 While I am arising and dressing, | I will endeavor to make myself sad and sorrowful over the great sorrow and suffering of Christ our Lord.
  4   The sixth will be adjusted thus. I will not admit joyful thoughts, even though they are good and holy, such as those about the Resurrection and heavenly glory. Instead, I will try to foster an attitude of sorrow, suffer-
  5 ing, and heartbreak, | by calling often to memory the labors, fatigue, and sufferings which Christ our Lord suffered, from his birth up to whatever mystery of his Passion I am contemplating at the time.

207 1 *Fourth.* The Particular Examination of Conscience will be made about the exercises and Directives for the present Week, just as was done during the past Week [160].

208 *1* <h2 style="text-align:center">THE SECOND DAY</h2>

At midnight, the contemplation will be about the events from the Garden to the house of Annas, inclusively [291]; and in the morning, on those from the house of Annas *2* to that of Caiaphas, inclusively [292]. The two repetitions and the application of the senses will follow, according to what has been already stated [204].

3 <h2 style="text-align:center">THE THIRD DAY</h2>

At midnight, from the house of Caiaphas to that of Pilate, inclusively [293]; and in the morning, from Pilate *4* to Herod [294]; and later the two repetitions and application of the senses, by using the same procedure already described [204].

5 <h2 style="text-align:center">THE FOURTH DAY</h2>

From Herod to Pilate [295]. The contemplation at midnight will take in half the mysteries in the house of *6* Pilate, [|] and the later one, in the morning, the remaining events which took place in the same house. The repetitions and the application of the senses will be done as was described above [204].

7 <h2 style="text-align:center">THE FIFTH DAY</h2>

At midnight, what happened from the house of Pilate up to the crucifixion [296], and in the morning, from the raising of the cross until Christ expired [297]. Then the two repetitions and the application of the senses.

8   **THE SIXTH DAY**

At midnight, from the taking down from the cross to the
burial in the sepulcher, exclusively; and in the morning,
from the placing in the tomb [298] to the house where
Our Lady went after the burial of her Son.

9   **THE SEVENTH DAY**
        A CONTEMPLATION OF ALL THE PASSION
                TAKEN AS A WHOLE,
   during the exercise at midnight and in the morning.

10 In place of the repetitions and the application of the
senses, the exercitant should consider, throughout that
whole day and as frequently as possible, how the most
holy body of Christ our Lord was separated from his
soul and remained apart from it, and where and how it
11 was buried. Consider, too, Our Lady's loneliness along
with her deep grief and fatigue; then, on the other hand,
the fatigue of the disciples.

209   *Note.* If someone wishes to extend the time spent on the
  1 Passion, in each contemplation he or she should take
fewer mysteries. That is, in the first contemplation [289]
only the supper [point 1]; in the second, the washing of
  2 the feet [ibid., point 2]; in the third, Christ's institution
of the Holy Eucharist [ibid., point 3]; in the fourth, his
farewell discourse to his apostles; and so on through the
other contemplations and mysteries. Similarly, after
  3 finishing the Passion such a one should devote one full
day to half of it, another day to the other half, and a
third day to a review of the whole.

    On the contrary, one who wants to abbreviate the
  4 time spent on the Passion will take: at midnight, the
supper; in the morning, the Garden; at the hour of Mass,
the house of Annas; at the hour of Vespers, the house of
Caiaphas; and during the hour before the evening meal,

5 the house of Pilate. In this way the exercitant, omitting the repetitions and the application of the senses, will make five distinct exercises; and in each exercise, a distinct mystery of Christ our Lord will be taken.

6 When the whole Passion has been completed, he or she can take another day to review it as a whole, either in one exercise or in several, according to what will seem to be more fruitful.

210 *1*   **RULES**[110] **TO ORDER ONESELF HENCEFORTH
IN THE TAKING OF FOOD.**[111]

2 The First Rule. In regard to bread there is less need to abstain, because it is not a food to which the appetite ordinarily urges us in a disordered way, or to which we are tempted as strongly as we are to other foods.

211 *1 The Second.* In regard to drink there seems to be more
2 need of abstinence than about eating bread. Therefore, we ought to consider much more carefully what is better for us, in order to accept it, and what is harmful to us, to reject it.

212 *1 The Third.* In regard to foods greater and more complete abstinence ought to be practiced. For in this area just as the appetite is more prone to become disordered, so is
2 temptation more likely to assail us. Hence, toward avoiding what is disordered in the taking of food, abstinence can be practiced in two ways. One is to accustom oneself to eating ordinary foods, and the other, if the foods are dainties, to take them in small quantity.

213 *1 The Fourth.* Provided care is taken not to fall into sickness, the more one abstains from what is ordinarily sufficient, the sooner will one find the right mean to keep for oneself in eating and drinking, for two reasons.
2 First, by making this progress and disposing oneself through it, on many occasions one will more clearly perceive interior lights, consolations, and divine inspirations which guide one to the mean suitable to oneself.
3 Second, if in abstinence of this sort one finds oneself lacking in the physical energy and disposition to carry on the present spiritual exercises, one will soon be able to judge what is more suitable to one's own bodily sustenance.

214 1 *The Fifth.* While one is eating, it is good to imagine Christ our Lord eating in company with his apostles, and to observe how he eats, how he drinks, how he looks about, and how he converses, and then to try to imitate

2 him. In this way one's mind will be occupied chiefly with the consideration of our Lord and less with the

3 sustenance of the body. Thus one gains a better method and order in regard to how one ought to conduct and govern oneself.

215 1 *The Sixth.* At another time, while one is eating one can use a different consideration, drawn from a life of the saints, or some pious contemplation, or some spiritual

2 project at hand. When the attention is thus directed to some good object, a person will be less concerned with the sensible pleasure from the bodily food.

216 1 *The Seventh.* Above all, one should be on guard against being totally absorbed in what one is eating or letting

2 oneself be completely dominated by the appetite. Rather, one should be master of oneself, both in the manner of eating and the amount one takes.

217 1 *The Eighth.* To rid oneself of disordered excess it is very profitable, after dinner or supper or at some other hour

2 when the appetite to eat or drink is not strong, to settle with oneself how much food is to be taken at the next

3 dinner or supper, and further, to do this every day. Then one should not exceed this amount either because of appetite or of temptation, but overcome every occurrence of disordered appetite and of temptation from the enemy, whether his temptation is to take more food or less. [112]

THE FOURTH WEEK

218 *1* ### THE FIRST CONTEMPLATION.
HOW CHRIST OUR LORD
APPEARED TO OUR LADY [299].[113]

2 *The usual Preparatory Prayer.*

219 *1* The *First Prelude* is the history. Here it is how, after
Christ died on the cross, his body remained separated
from his soul but always united with his divinity. His
blessed soul, also united with his divinity, descended to
2 hell.[114] Then, releasing the souls of the just from there,
returning to the sepulcher, and rising again, he appeared
in body and soul to his Blessed Mother.[115]

220 *1* *The Second Prelude.* A composition, by imagining the
place. Here it will be to see the arrangement of the holy
sepulcher; also, the place or house where Our Lady was,
including its various parts, such as a room, an oratory,
and the like.

221 *1* *The Third Prelude.* It is to ask for what I desire. Here it
will be to ask for the grace to be glad and to rejoice
intensely because of the great glory and joy of Christ our
Lord.[116]

222 *1* *The First, Second, and Third Points* will be respectively
the usual ones which were used about the last supper of
Christ our Lord [194].

223 *1* *The Fourth Point.* Consider how the divinity, which
seemed hidden during the Passion, now appears and
manifests itself so miraculously in this holy Resurrection,
through its true and most holy effects.

224 1 *The Fifth Point.* Consider the office of consoler which Christ our Lord carries out, and compare it with the way friends console one another.

225 1 *Colloquy.* Finish with a colloquy, according to the subject matter, and recite the Our Father.

226 1 *First Note.* In the following contemplations, the exercitant should proceed through all the mysteries of the Resurrection up to and including the Ascension in the 2 manner indicated immediately below [227]. The procedure and method throughout the Week on the Resurrection should be the same as they were in the whole Week 3 on the Passion [204]. Therefore, the first contemplation on the Resurrection should be taken as the guiding model in regard to the preludes, which are varied 4 according to the subject matter. The five points should remain the same as immediately above [222-224], as do also the Additional Directives which are given below 5 [229]. In everything else the exercitant can be guided by the procedure used in the Week on the Passion; for example, in regard to the repetitions, applications of the five senses, the shortening or lengthening of the time devoted to the mysteries, and the like [204, 205].

227 1 *Second Note.* Ordinarily in this Fourth Week it is more suitable to make four exercises a day instead of five than 2 it was in those which preceded. The first exercise should be made shortly after rising in the morning; the second, near the hour of Mass or near the noonday meal, in place of the first repetition; the third, at the hour of 3 Vespers, in place of the second repetition; the fourth, before the evening meal, should be an application of the senses to the preceding exercises of the day. The retreatant ought to note and dwell reflectively on the principal places where he or she has experienced greater interior motions and spiritual relish.

228 1 *Third Note*. Although a fixed number of points, such as three or five, is presented as the subject matter in all the contemplations, the person who is contemplating may prepare more or fewer points, according to what is found 2 better. Before the contemplation is begun, however, it is highly profitable to determine and choose a definite number of points to be used.

229 1 *Fourth Note*. During the Fourth Week, among the ten Additional Directives, changes should be made in the second, sixth, seventh, and tenth.

2   The second will become: Upon awakening, I will think of the contemplation I am about to make, and endeavor to feel joyful and happy over the great joy and happiness of Christ our Lord [221].

3   The sixth. I will call into my memory and think about things which bring pleasure, happiness, and spiritual joy, such as those about heavenly glory.

4   The seventh. I will avail myself of light or the pleasant features of the seasons, such as the refreshing coolness in summer or the sun or heat in winter, as far as I think or conjecture that this will help me to rejoice in Christ my Creator and Redeemer.

5   The tenth. In place of penance, I will attend to temperance and moderation in all things. However, an exception must be made here if the Church has pre-scribed days of fast and abstinence, unless there is some proper excusing cause.

230 *1* **CONTEMPLATION TO ATTAIN LOVE**[117]

2 *Note.* Two preliminary observations should be made.

First. Love ought to manifest itself more by deeds than by words.[118]

231 *1* Second. Love consists in a mutual communication between the two persons. That is, the one who loves gives and communicates to the beloved what he or she has, or a part of what one has or can have; and the 2 beloved in return does the same to the lover.[119] Thus, if the one has knowledge, one gives it to the other who does not; and similarly in regard to honors or riches. Each shares with the other.

3 *The usual Preparatory Prayer.*

232 *1* *The First Prelude.* A composition. Here it is to see myself as standing before God our Lord, and also before the angels and saints, who are interceding for me.

233 *1* *The Second Prelude* is to ask for what I desire. Here it will be to ask for interior knowledge of all the great good I have received, in order that, stirred to profound gratitude, I may become able to love and serve the Divine Majesty in all things.[120]

234 *1* *The First Point.*[121] I will call back into my memory the gifts I have received—my creation, redemption, and 2 other gifts particular to myself. I will ponder with deep affection how much God our Lord has done for me, and how much he has given me of what he possesses, and consequently how he, the same Lord, desires to give me even his very self, in accordance with his divine design.

3 Then I will reflect on myself, and consider what I on my part ought in all reason and justice to offer and give to the Divine Majesty, namely, all my possessions, and myself along with them. I will speak as one making an

offering with deep affection, and say:

4   "Take, Lord, and receive all my liberty, my memory, my understanding, and all my will—all that I have and
5 possess. [|] You, Lord, have given all that to me. I now give it back to you, O Lord. All of it is yours. Dispose of it according to your will. Give me love of yourself[122] along with your grace, for that is enough for me."[123]

235 1 *The Second Point.* I will consider how God dwells in creatures; in the elements, giving them existence; in the plants, giving them life; in the animals, giving them sensation; in human beings, giving them intelligence;
2 and finally, how in this way he dwells also in myself, giving me existence, life, sensation, and intelligence; and even further, making me his temple, since I am created
3 as a likeness and image of the Divine Majesty. Then once again I will reflect on myself, in the manner described in the first point, or in any other way I feel to be better. This same procedure will be used in each of the following points.

236 1 *The Third Point.* I will consider how God labors and works for me in all the creatures on the face of the earth;
2 that is, he acts in the manner of one who is laboring. For example, he is working in the heavens, elements, plants, fruits, cattle, and all the rest—giving them their existence, conserving them, concurring with their vegetative and sensitive activities, and so forth. Then I will reflect on myself.

237 1 *The Fourth Point.* I will consider how all good things and gifts descend from above; for example, my limited power from the Supreme and Infinite Power above; and so of justice, goodness, piety, mercy, and so forth—just as the rays come down from the sun, or the rains from
2 their source.[124] Then I will finish by reflecting on myself, as has been explained. I will conclude with a colloquy and an Our Father.

[SUPPLEMENTARY MATTER]

238 *1* ## THREE METHODS OF PRAYING.[125]

THE FIRST METHOD.

2 This first method of praying takes as its subject matter the ten commandments, the seven capital sins, the three faculties of the soul, and the five senses of the body.

3 This method of praying is intended to present a structural form,[126] a method, and exercises, so that those praying may prepare themselves, benefit from the exercises,[127] and make their prayer acceptable.[128] That is its aim rather than to give a form or method of prayer properly so called.[129]

239 ### 1. On the Ten Commandments[130]

1 First of all, something should be done which is the equivalent of the Fifth Note[131] of the Second Week [131]. That is, before entering into the prayer, I should briefly recollect myself in spirit, either seated or pacing to and fro, as I find better; and I should consider where I am *2* going and for what. This same Additional Directive [75, 131] will be used for all three of these Methods of Praying [250, 258].

240 *1* *A Preparatory Prayer.* For example, I will ask God our Lord that I may be able to know how I have failed *2* against the ten commandments. Similarly I will ask for grace and aid to amend myself for the future. I will beg, too, for a complete understanding of the commandments, in order to keep them better for greater glory and praise of the Divine Majesty.

241 1 For the First Method of Praying, a suitable procedure for the first commandment is to consider and think over in
2 what I have kept it and in what I have failed, measuring this reflection by the time required to recite three Our
3 Fathers and three Hail Marys. If I discover my faults within this time, I will ask forgiveness and pardon for
4 them and say an Our Father. Then I will follow the same procedure with each of the ten commandments.

242 1 *First Note*. It should be observed that if one begins reflection on a commandment which he or she has no
2 habit of violating, one need not dwell long on it. But if one considers a commandment which she or he breaks often, sometimes more and sometimes less, accordingly more or less time should be taken in considering and
3 scrutinizing this commandment. The same procedure should be used with the capital sins.

243 1 *Second Note*. After finishing the examination of all the commandments in the manner described above, I should accuse myself accordingly and beg grace and help to
2 amend myself for the future. Then I should finish with a colloquy, according to the subject matter.

244 1 **2. On the Capital Sins**

2 With regard to the seven capital sins,[132] after the Additional Directive [75, 239], the preparatory prayer should
3 be made in the manner already described [240]. The only change is that the subject matter here consists of the sins to be avoided, whereas there it was the commandments
4 which should be observed. Likewise the same procedure and measuring of the time should be followed, and a colloquy made.

245 1 To know better the faults springing from the capital sins, one should consider their contrary virtues. Through this, to avoid the faults better a person should propose and

strive by holy exercises to acquire and retain the seven virtues contrary to these sins.

246 1 ### 3. On the Three Powers of the Soul

2 In regard to the three powers[133] of the soul, the same procedure and measuring of time should be observed as with the commandments, by following the additional directive [239] and making the preparatory prayer and colloquy [240-243].

247 1 ### 4. On the Five Senses of the Body

2 In regard to the five senses of the body, the same procedure will always be observed, but the subject matter will be different.

248 1 *Note.* If I wish to imitate Christ our Lord in the use of my five senses, I should commend myself to the Divine Majesty in the preparatory prayer, and after the consideration of each sense, recite a Hail Mary and an Our Father.

2   If I wish to imitate Our Lady in the use of these senses, I should commend myself to her in the preparatory prayer, and ask her to obtain for me that grace from her Son. Then after the consideration of each sense I should recite a Hail Mary.

249 1 ### THE SECOND METHOD OF PRAYING CONSISTS IN CONTEMPLATING THE MEANING OF EACH WORD OF A PRAYER.

250 1 *The Same Additional Directive* is followed as in the First Method [239].

251 1 *The Preparatory Prayer* will be made in conformity with the person to whom the prayer is addressed.

252 1 *The Second Method of Praying*[134] is practiced as follows. One may sit or kneel accordingly as one feels better disposed or finds greater devotion, but should keep the eyes closed or intent on one place, and not allow them to wander. Then the person should say the word "Fa-
2 ther," and continue to consider the word as long as meanings, comparisons, relish, and consolations connect-
3 ed with it are found. The same procedure should be continued with each word of the Our Father, or of any other prayer which one wishes to use in this manner.

253 1 *First Rule.* The person will remain for an hour in this manner of praying, going through the whole of the Our Father. At the end he or she should say a Hail Mary, Creed, Soul of Christ, and Hail Holy Queen, vocally or mentally in the customary way.

254 1 *Second Rule.* If one is contemplating the Our Father and finds in one or two words matter which yields thought,
2 relish, and consolation, | one should not be anxious to move forward, even if the whole hour is consumed on what is being found. At the end of the hour the rest of the prayer will be recited in the customary way.

255 1 *Third Rule.* If one has dwelt for a full hour on one or two words of the Our Father and on another day wishes to return to this prayer, one should recite the word or
2 words in the customary way, then begin the contemplation on the word immediately following, and proceed according to what was stated in the second rule.

256 1 *First Note.* It should be noted that if the Our Father has been finished in one or several days, one should use the same method with the Hail Mary and then with other prayers, in such a way that one is always engaged for a certain time on one of them.

257 1 *Second Note.* When the prayer is finished, one should

turn to the person to whom it is directed and ask for the virtues or graces for which greater need is felt.

258 1
THE THIRD METHOD OF PRAYING
IS TO PRAY
ACCORDING TO RHYTHMIC MEASURES.

2 *The Same Additional Directive* will be followed as in the first and second methods of praying [239, 250].

3 *The Preparatory Prayer* will be the same as in the second method of praying [251].

4 *In this Third Method of Praying,* with each breath taken in or expelled, one should pray mentally, by saying a word of the Our Father, or of any other prayer which is recited. This is done in such a manner that one word of the prayer is said between one breath and 5 another. In between these two breaths one reflects especially on the meaning of that word, or on the person to whom the prayer is being recited, or on one's own lowliness, or on the distance between that person's 6 dignity and our lack of it. The same procedure and rule will be used on the words of the Our Father; and the other prayers—the Hail Mary, Soul of Christ, Creed, and Hail Holy Queen—will be recited in the usual manner.[135]

259 1 *First Rule.* When one wishes to pray again on another day or at another hour, one should say the Hail Mary according to the rhythmic measures, and the other prayers in the customary way. The same procedure may be used with the other prayers.

260 1 *Second Rule.* One who wishes to spend a longer time in this prayer according to rhythmic measures, may use it with all the prayers mentioned above, or on some of them. The same order of rhythmic breathing explained [in 258] should be used.

THE MYSTERIES
OF THE LIFE OF CHRIST OUR LORD

261 *1*

2 *Note.* In all the following mysteries,[136] all the words enclosed in quotation marks[137] are from the four Gospels, 3 but not the other words. For each mystery, at least in most instances, three points are given, to make it easier to meditate and contemplate on them.

[THE INFANCY AND HIDDEN LIFE]

262 *1*

THE ANNUNCIATION TO OUR LADY
St. Luke 1:26-38[138]

2 *First Point.*[139] The angel, St. Gabriel, greets Our Lady and announces to her the conception of Christ our Lord: 3 "The angel entered the place where Mary was, greeted her, and said: 'Hail, full of grace. You will conceive in your womb and give birth to a Son.'"

4 *Second Point.* The angel confirms what he said to Our Lady by telling her about the conception of St. John the Baptist: "And behold, Elizabeth, your relative, has also conceived a son in her old age."

5 *Third Point.* Our Lady replied to the angel: "Behold the handmaid of the Lord. Be it done to me according to your word."

263 *1*

THE VISITATION OF OUR LADY TO ELIZABETH
St. Luke 1:39-56

2 *First Point.* When Our Lady visited Elizabeth, St. John the Baptist, still in his mother's womb, perceived the 3 visitation Our Lady made. "When Elizabeth heard the salutation of Mary, the infant leaped for joy in her

4 womb. And Elizabeth, filled with the Holy Spirit, cried out with a loud voice and said: 'Blessed are you among women, and blessed is the fruit of your womb.'"

5 *Second point.* Our Lady breaks into her canticle, exclaiming: "My soul magnifies the Lord!"

6 *Third Point.* "Mary abode with Elizabeth about three months; and then she returned to her own house."

264 1 ## THE NATIVITY OF CHRIST OUR LORD
St. Luke 2:1-14

2 *First Point.* Our Lady and her spouse St. Joseph journey from Nazareth to Bethlehem: "Joseph also went up from Galilee to Bethlehem, to express his obedience to Caesar, with Mary his espoused wife, who was with child."

3 *Second Point.* "And she brought forth her first-born Son, and wrapped him up in swaddling clothes, and laid him in a manger."

4 *Third Point.* "There was . . . a multitude of the heavenly army saying: 'Glory to God in the heavens.'"

265 1 ## THE SHEPHERDS
St. Luke 2:8-20

2 *First Point.* The birth of Christ our Lord is made known to the shepherds by an angel: "I bring you good news of great joy, for this day is born to you the Savior of the world."

3 *Second Point.* The shepherds go to Bethlehem: "They came with haste; and they found Mary and Joseph and the Infant lying in the manger."

4 *Third Point.* "The shepherds returned, glorifying and praising God."

266 1 ## THE CIRCUMCISION
St. Luke 2:21

2 *First Point.* They circumcised the child Jesus.

3   *Second Point.* "His name was called Jesus, which was called by the angel before he was conceived in the womb."

4   *Third Point.* They handed the child back to his mother, who felt compassion because of the blood which was flowing from her Son.

267 *1*
THE THREE KINGS
St. Matthew 2:1-12

2 *First Point.* The three kings, guided by the star, came to adore Jesus, saying: "We have seen his star in the East, and have come to adore him."

3   *Second Point.* They adored him and offered him gifts: "Falling prostrate on the ground they adored him and offered him gifts: gold, frankincense, and myrrh."

4   *Third Point.* "Having received an answer in sleep that they should not return to Herod, they went back by another way to their own country."

268 *1*
THE PURIFICATION OF OUR LADY AND THE PRESENTATION OF THE INFANT JESUS
St. Luke 2:22-38

2 *First Point.* They carry the infant Jesus to the temple, to present him to the Lord as the first-born son, and they offer for him "a pair of turtledoves and two young pigeons."

3   *Second Point.* Simeon, coming to the temple, "took him into his arms" and said: "Now you dismiss your servant, O Lord, in peace."

4   *Third Point.* Afterwards Anna, "coming in, confessed to the Lord and spoke of him to all who looked for the redemption of Israel."

269 *1*   THE FLIGHT INTO EGYPT
                      St. Matthew 2:13-18

2 *First Point.* Herod wanted to kill the infant Jesus and therefore slew the Innocents. But before their death an angel warned Joseph to flee into Egypt: "Arise, and take the child and his mother, and flee into Egypt."

3 *Second Point.* He arose by night, and departed for Egypt.

4 *Third Point.* He remained there until the death of Herod.

270 *1* HOW CHRIST OUR LORD RETURNED FROM EGYPT
                      St. Matthew 2:19-23

2 *First Point.* The angel tells Joseph to return to Israel: "Arise, and take the child and his mother, and go into the land of Israel."

3 *Second Point.* He arose and went into the land of Israel.

4 *Third Point.* Because Archelaus, son of Herod, was reigning in Judaea, he retired to Nazareth.

271 *1* THE LIFE OF CHRIST OUR LORD FROM THE AGE
                      OF TWELVE TO THIRTY
                      St. Luke 2:51-52

2 *First Point.* He was obedient to his parents, and "Jesus advanced in wisdom, and age, and grace."

3 *Second Point.* It seems that he practiced the trade of carpenter, as St. Mark seems to indicate [6:3]: "Is not this, surely, the carpenter?"

272 1
CHRIST'S VISIT TO THE TEMPLE
AT THE AGE OF TWELVE
St. Luke 2:41-50

2 *First Point.* Christ our Lord at the age of twelve went up from Nazareth to Jerusalem.

3   *Second Point.* Christ our Lord remained in Jerusalem, and his parents did not know it.

4   *Third Point.* After three days, they found him seated among the doctors and conversing with them. When his
5 parents asked him where he had been, he replied: [|] "Did you not know that I ought to be concerned with my Father's business?"

[THE PUBLIC LIFE]

273 1
HOW CHRIST WAS BAPTIZED
St. Matthew 3:13-17

2 *First Point.* Christ our Lord, after his farewell to his Blessed Mother, came from Nazareth to the river Jordan, where St. John the Baptist was.

3   *Second Point.* St. John baptized Christ our Lord; and when he sought to excuse himself because he thought himself unworthy to baptize him, Christ said to him: "Allow it now, for thus it is fitting for us to fulfill all righteousness."

4   *Third Point.* The Holy Spirit descended upon him, and the voice of the Father came from heaven and testified: "This is my beloved Son, in whom I am well pleased."

274 1
HOW CHRIST WAS TEMPTED
St. Luke 4:1-13; St. Matthew 4:1-11

2 *First Point.* After he had been baptized, he went into the desert, where he fasted forty days and forty nights.

3   *Second Point.* He was tempted by the enemy three

times. "The tempter came to him and said: 'If you are the Son of God, command that these stones be made bread. Cast yourself down from here. I will give you all these kingdoms if you will adore me.'"

4   *Third Point.* "Angels came and ministered to him."

275 1   **THE CALLING OF THE APOSTLES**

2 *First Point.* It seems that St. Peter and St. Andrew were called three times; first, to some knowledge, as is evident
3 from St. John [1:35-42]; second, to follow Christ to some extent, but with an intention to return to the possession of what they had left behind, as St. Luke tells us [5:1-11];
4 third, to follow Christ our Lord forever [St. Matthew 4:18-30; St. Mark 1:16-18].

5   *Second Point.* He called Philip [St. John 1:43], and Matthew, as St. Matthew himself tells us [9:9].

6   *Third Point.* He called the other Apostles, although the Gospels do not mention the particular instances.

7   Three other things too should be considered: first, how they came from a rude and lowly condition of
8 living; second, the dignity to which they were so gently
9 called; and third, the gifts and graces by which they were raised above all the Fathers of the New Testament and the Old.

276   **THE FIRST MIRACLE, WORKED AT THE MARRIAGE**
1   **FEAST IN CANA OF GALILEE**
                      St. John 2:1-12

First Point. Christ our Lord was invited with his disciples
2 to the wedding feast.

Second Point. His Mother points out to her Son the
3 shortage of the wine, "They have no wine." Then she orders the waiters, "Do whatever he tells you to do."

Third Point. "He changed the water into wine, and he
4 manifested his glory, and his disciples believed in him."

277 *1* ## HOW CHRIST OUR LORD CAST THE SELLERS OUT OF THE TEMPLE
St. John 2:13-25

2 *First Point*. He drove all the sellers out of the temple with a whip made of cords.

3   *Second Point*. He overturned the tables and spilled the money of the rich money changers who were in the temple.

4   *Third Point*. To the poor people who sold doves, he gently said: "Take these things hence, and do not make my Father's house a marketplace."

278 *1* ## THE SERMON ON THE MOUNT
St. Matthew 5:1-48

2 *First Point*. To his beloved disciples he speaks apart about the eight beatitudes: "Blessed are the poor in spirit, the meek, the merciful, they who mourn, those who hunger and thirst for justice, the clean of heart, the peacemakers, and those who suffer persecution."

3   *Second Point*. He exhorts them to make good use of their talents: "So let your light shine before others that they may see your good works and glorify your Father who is in heaven."

4   *Third Point*. He shows that he is not a transgressor of the Law, but the one who has come to fulfill it, by explaining the precepts: Do not kill, or commit adultery, or swear falsely; and love your enemies: "I say to you, 'Love your enemies, do good to those who hate you.'"

279 *1* ## HOW CHRIST OUR LORD CALMED THE STORM
St. Matthew 8:23-27

2 *First Point*. While Christ our Lord was on the lake, asleep, a great tempest arose.

3   *Second Point*. His frightened disciples awaken him; and he reprehends them for their little faith: "Why are you afraid, O you of little faith?"

4   *Third Point.* He commanded the winds and the sea to cease, and the sea grew calm. The disciples marveled at this, and asked: "What sort of man is this, for even the winds and the sea obey him?"

280 *1*   ## HOW CHRIST WALKED ON THE WATERS
St. Matthew 14:22-33

2 First Point. While Christ our Lord remained on the mountain, he ordered his disciples to go before him in the little boat. Then he dismissed the multitude and began to pray alone.

3   Second Point. The little boat was tossed by the waves. Christ came toward it, walking on the waters; and the disciples thought they saw a ghost.

4   Third Point. Christ said to them, "It is I, do not fear." At his command St. Peter came to him, walking on the water. He doubted, and began to sink. But Christ our Lord saved him, and reprehended him for his little faith. Then he entered into the boat and the wind ceased.

281 *1*   ## HOW THE APOSTLES WERE SENT TO PREACH
St. Matthew 10:1-15

2 First Point. Christ calls his beloved disciples, and gives them power to drive devils out of human bodies and to heal all kinds of infirmities.

3   Second Point. He teaches them about prudence and patience: "Behold I am sending you like sheep in the midst of wolves. Therefore be shrewd as serpents and simple as doves."

4   Third Point. He tells them how they are to go: "Do not seek to possess gold or silver; freely have you received, freely give." And he gave them the matter to preach: "Go and preach, saying, 'The kingdom of heaven is at hand.'"

282 *1* THE CONVERSION OF MAGDALEN
St. Luke 7:36-50

2 First Point. Magdalen enters where Christ our Lord is seated at table in the house of the Pharisee. She was bringing an alabaster jar full of ointment.

3 Second Point. Staying behind the Lord at his feet, she began to wash them with her tears, and to wipe them with the hair of her head. She kissed his feet, and anointed them with ointment.

4 Third Point. When the Pharisee accuses Magdalen, Christ speaks in her defense: "Many sins are forgiven her, because she has loved much." And he said to the woman: "Your faith has made you safe; go in peace."

283 *1* HOW CHRIST OUR LORD
FED FIVE THOUSAND PERSONS
St. Matthew 14:13-21

2 First Point. When evening was near, the disciples ask Christ to dismiss the multitude of those who are with him.

3 Second Point. Christ our Lord commanded the disciples to bring him some loaves, and ordered the crowd to sit down at the table. He blessed and broke the loaves and gave them to his disciples, and the disciples gave them to the multitude.

4 Third Point. They ate and were filled, and they took up what remained, twelve full baskets.

284 *1* THE TRANSFIGURATION OF CHRIST
St. Matthew 17:1-13

2 First Point. Christ our Lord took his beloved disciples Peter, James, and John and was transfigured, and his face shone like the sun, and his garments became white as snow.

3 Second Point. He conversed with Moses and Elijah.

4   *Third Point.* When St. Peter proposed that they should make three tents, a voice sounded from heaven, saying,
5 "This is my beloved Son; listen to him." His disciples heard this voice and fell on their faces through fear, and Christ our Lord touched them and said to them, "Arise and do not be afraid. Do not tell the vision to anyone until the Son of Man is risen from the dead."

285 1   **THE RESURRECTION OF LAZARUS**
                        St. John 11:1-44

2 *First Point.* Martha and Mary inform Christ our Lord about the illness of Lazarus. After he heard this news he remained where he was for two days, to make the miracle more evident.
3   *Second Point.* Before raising him he asks the two sisters to believe, saying: "I am the resurrection and the life; those who believe in me, even though they die, will live."
4   *Third Point.* He raises him, after he has wept and prayed; and the manner in which he raised him was by his command: "Lazarus, come forth."

286 1   **THE SUPPER IN BETHANY**
                        St. Matthew 26:6-13

2 *First Point.* Our Lord eats supper in the house of Simon the leper, together with Lazarus.
3   *Second Point.* Mary pours the perfumed oil on the head of Christ.
4   *Third Point.* Judas murmurs, saying, "To what purpose is this waste of perfumed oil?" But he again excuses Magdalen, with the words: "Why do you trouble this woman? For she has done a good thing for me."

PALM SUNDAY
St. Matthew 21:1-11

287 *1*

2 *First Point.* Our Lord sends for the ass and the colt, saying, "Untie them, and bring them here to me; and if anyone should say anything to you, reply, 'The master has need of them.' Then he will let them go."

3 *Second Point.* He mounted the ass, which was covered with the cloaks of the Apostles.

4 *Third Point.* The people come out to meet him, and spread their cloaks and branches of trees on the road, and shout: "Hosanna to the Son of David! Blessed is he who comes in the name of the Lord. Hosanna in the highest!"

CHRIST'S PREACHING IN THE TEMPLE
St. Luke, Chapter 19; also 21:37-38

288 *1*

2 *First Point.* During each day he was teaching in the temple.

3 *Second Point.* When he had finished preaching, since there was no one to receive him in Jerusalem, he returned to Bethany.

[THE PASSION]

THE SUPPER
St. Matthew 26:17-30; St. John 13:1-17

289 *1*

2 *First Point.* He ate the paschal lamb with his twelve Apostles, and he foretold his death to them: "Amen, I say to you that one of you will betray me."

3 *Second Point.* He washed his disciples' feet, even those of Judas. He began with St. Peter; and Peter, thinking of the Lord's majesty and his own lowliness, was reluctant

4 to consent. "Lord," he asked, "are you going to wash my feet?" But Peter failed to understand that the Lord was

giving an example of humility, and therefore the Lord said: "I have given you an example, so that as I have done, so you also should do."

5   *Third Point*. He instituted the most holy sacrifice of the Eucharist, as the greatest sign of his love. "Take and eat," he told them. When the supper was finished, Judas went out to sell Christ our Lord.

290 1 **THE MYSTERIES ENACTED FROM THE SUPPER TO THE GARDEN, INCLUSIVELY**
St. Matthew 26:30-46; St. Luke 22:39-46;
St. Mark 14:26-42

2 *First Point*. Our Lord, after finishing the supper and singing a hymn, went to Mount Olivet with his disciples, who were full of fear. He left eight of them in Gethsemane, and said, "Sit here while I go over there and pray."

3   *Second Point*. Accompanied by St. Peter, St. James, and St. John, he prayed three times to the Lord, saying, "My Father, if it is possible, let this cup pass from me; yet, not as I will, but as you will." And being in agony, he prayed the longer.

4   *Third Point*. He came to a fear so great that he said, "My soul is sorrowful even unto death," and he sweated blood so copiously that St. Luke says, "His sweat became like drops of blood falling on the ground." This supposes that his clothes were already full of blood.

291 *1* **THE MYSTERIES ENACTED FROM THE GARDEN TO THE HOUSE OF ANNAS, INCLUSIVELY**
St. Matthew 26:47-56; St. Luke 22:47-53;
St. Mark 14:42-53; St. John 18:1-22

2 *First Point.* Our Lord allowed himself to be kissed by Judas, and to be arrested like a thief by the crowd, to whom he said, "You have come out as against a robber with swords and clubs to seize me. Day after day I was *3* teaching in the temple, and you did not arrest me." And when he asked, "Whom are you seeking?" his enemies fell to the ground.

4 *Second Point.* St. Peter wounded a servant of the high priest; and the meek Lord said to him, "Put your sword back into its sheath." Then he healed the servant's wound.

5 *Third Point.* Abandoned by his disciples, he is dragged before Annas, where St. Peter, who had followed him from afar, denied him once, and a blow was given to Christ by a servant who said to him, "Is this the way you answer the high priest?"

292 *1* **THE MYSTERIES FROM THE HOUSE OF ANNAS TO THE HOUSE OF CAIAPHAS, INCLUSIVELY**
St. Matthew 26:57-68; St. Mark 14:53-72;
St. Luke 22:54-65; St. John 18:24-27

2 *First Point.* They take him bound from the house of Annas to that of Caiaphas, where St. Peter denied him twice. When our Lord looked at him, he went out and wept bitterly.

3 *Second Point.* Jesus remained bound all that night.

4 *Third Point.* Besides this, those who held him prisoner mocked him, struck him, blindfolded him, slapped him, *5* and asked him: | "Prophesy for us: Who it is that struck you?" They also uttered similar blasphemies against him.

293 1   FROM THE HOUSE OF CAIAPHAS TO THAT
OF PILATE, INCLUSIVELY
St. Matthew 27:1-26; St. Luke 23:1-5; St. Mark 15:1-15

2 *First Point.* The whole multitude of the Jews bring Christ to Pilate, and before him they accuse him, saying: "We have found this man misleading our people. He forbids payment of taxes to Caesar."

3   *Second Point.* Pilate, after having examined him again and again, says, "I find no guilt in him."

4   *Third Point.* Barabbas the robber was preferred before him. "They cried: 'Not this man, but Barabbas.'"

294 1 FROM THE HOUSE OF PILATE TO THAT OF HEROD
St. Luke 23:6-12

2 *First Point.* Pilate sent Jesus the Galilean to Herod, the tetrarch of Galilee.

3   *Second Point.* Through curiosity Herod questioned him at length, but he gave him no answer, even though the scribes and priests unceasingly accused him.

4   *Third Point.* Herod and his soldiers mocked him and clothed him in a white garment.

295 1 FROM THE HOUSE OF HEROD TO THAT OF PILATE
St. Matthew 27:26-30; St. Luke 23:11-23;
St. Mark 15:15-20; St. John 19:1-11

2 *First Point.* Herod sends him back to Pilate, and because of this they become friends, although previously they have been enemies.

3   *Second Point.* Pilate took Jesus, and scourged him. Then the soldiers wove a crown out of thorns, and placed it on his head, and they clothed him in a purple cloak; and they came before him and said, "Hail, king of the Jews!" And they struck him repeatedly.

4   *Third Point.* Pilate brought him out into the presence of all. So Jesus came out, wearing the crown of thorns

and the purple cloak, and Pilate said to them: "Behold the man." When the priests saw him, they cried out: "Crucify, crucify him!"

296 1   **FROM THE HOUSE OF PILATE
TO THE CROSS, INCLUSIVELY
St. John 19:13-22**

2 *First Point.* Pilate, seated like a judge, handed Jesus over to be crucified, after the Jews had denied him as their king: "We have no king but Caesar."

3   *Second Point.* He carried the cross on his shoulders, and as he could not carry it, Simon of Cyrene was compelled to carry it behind Jesus.

4   *Third Point.* They crucified him in the middle between two thieves, and placed this title above him: "Jesus of Nazareth, King of the Jews."

297 1   **THE MYSTERIES ON THE CROSS
St. John 19:23-37**

2,3 *First Point.* | He spoke seven words on the cross; he prayed for those who were crucifying him; he forgave the thief; he commended St. John to his mother and his

4 mother to St. John; he said with a loud voice, "I thirst," and they gave him gall and vinegar; he said that he was forsaken; he said, "It is finished"; he said, "Father, into your hands I commend my spirit."

5   *Second Point.* The sun was darkened, the rocks were split, the tombs were opened, the veil of the temple was torn in two from top to bottom.

6   *Third Point.* They blaspheme him, saying, "You who would destroy the temple of God, come down from the cross." His garments were divided. His side was pierced by the lance, and water and blood flowed out.

298 1   **THE MYSTERIES FROM THE CROSS**
                TO THE SEPULCHER, INCLUSIVELY
                     St. John 19:38-42

 2 *First Point.* He was taken down from the cross by Joseph
    and Nicodemus in the presence of his sorrowful Mother.
 3   *Second Point.* His body was carried to the tomb,
    anointed, and buried.
 4   *Third Point.* Guards were stationed.

                        [THE RISEN LIFE]

299 1   **THE RESURRECTION OF CHRIST OUR LORD,**
                  AND HIS FIRST APPARITION

 2 *First Point.* He appeared to the Virgin Mary. Although
    this is not stated in Scripture, still it is considered as
    understood by the statement that he appeared to many
 3 others. For Scripture supposes that we have understand-
    ing, as it is written: "Are even you without understand-
    ing?" [Matt. 15:16].

300 1   **THE SECOND APPARITION**
                      St. Mark 16:1-11

 2 *First Point.* Very early in the morning Mary Magdalen,
    Mary the mother of James, and Salome go to the tomb,
    saying: "Who will roll back the stone for us from the
    entrance to the tomb?"
 3   *Second Point.* They see the stone rolled back, and the
    angel, who says, "You seek Jesus of Nazareth. He is
    already risen; he is not here."
 4   *Third Point.* He appeared to Mary, who remained near
    the tomb after the other women had departed.

301 *1*
THE THIRD APPARITION
St. Matthew 28:8-10

2 *First Point.* These Marys went away from the tomb with fear and great joy, eager to announce the resurrection of the Lord to the disciples.

3 *Second Point.* Christ our Lord appeared to them on the way, and greeted them: "Hail to you." They approached, placed themselves at his feet, and adored him.

4 *Third Point.* Jesus says to them, "Do not be afraid. Go, tell my brothers to go into Galilee, and there they will see me."

302 *1*
THE FOURTH APPARITION
St. Luke 24:9-12, 33-34; St. John 20:1-10

2 *First Point.* When St. Peter had heard from the women that Christ had risen, he got up and ran to the tomb.

3 *Second Point.* Entering the tomb, he saw only the burial cloths with which the body of Christ our Lord had been covered, and nothing else.

4 *Third Point.* While St. Peter was thinking on these things, Christ appeared to him. Because of this the Apostles said, "The Lord is truly risen and has appeared to Simon."

303 *1*
THE FIFTH APPARITION
St. Luke 24:13-35

2 *First Point.* He appears to the disciples, who were going to Emmaus, and were conversing about Christ.

3 *Second Point.* He upbraids them, showing from the Scriptures that Christ had to die and to rise again: "Oh, how foolish you are and slow of heart to believe all the things which the prophets have spoken. Was it not necessary that Christ should suffer these things and thus enter into his glory?"

4 *Third Point.* At their urging he remained there and

was with them until he gave them Communion and then disappeared. They returned and told the disciples how they had recognized him in the Communion.

304 1
THE SIXTH APPARITION
St. John 20:19-23

2 *First Point.* The disciples were assembled "through fear of the Jews," except St. Thomas.

3   *Second Point.* Jesus appeared to them when the doors were locked. He stood in their midst and said, "Peace be with you."

4   *Third Point.* He gives them the Holy Spirit, saying to them, "Receive the Holy Spirit; whose sins you forgive are forgiven them."

305 1
THE SEVENTH APPARITION
St. John 20:24-29

2 *First Point.* St. Thomas, unbelieving because he was absent from the preceding apparition, says, "Unless I see, I will not believe."

3   *Second Point.* Eight days after that Jesus appears to them, although the doors are locked, and he says to St. Thomas, "Put your finger here and see the truth, and do not be unbelieving, but believe."

4   *Third Point.* St. Thomas believed, and said, "My Lord and my God." Christ says to him, "Blessed are those who have not seen and have believed."

306 1
THE EIGHTH APPARITION
St. John 21:1-17

2 *First Point.* Jesus appears to seven of his disciples who were fishing, after they had caught nothing during the whole night. They cast forth the net at his bidding, and "were unable to pull it in because of the number of the fish."

3   *Second Point.* Through this miracle St. John recognized him and said to St. Peter, "It is the Lord." Thereupon St. Peter jumped into the sea and came to Christ.

4   *Third Point.* He gave them part of a roasted fish and a honeycomb to eat. He asked St. Peter three times about his love for him, and then he entrusted his sheep to him: "Feed my sheep."

307 *1*

THE NINTH APPARITION
St. Matthew 28:16-20

2 *First Point.* At the command of the Lord the disciples go to Mount Tabor.

3   *Second Point.* Christ appears to them and says, "All power in heaven and on earth has been given to me."

4   *Third Point.* He sent them to preach throughout the whole world, saying: "Go, therefore, and teach all nations, baptizing them in the name of the Father and of the Son and of the Holy Spirit."

308 *1*

THE TENTH APPARITION
1 Corinthians 15:6

2 "After that he appeared to more than five hundred brethren at once."

309 *1*

THE ELEVENTH APPARITION
1 Corinthians 15:7

2 After that he appeared to James.

310 *1*

THE TWELFTH APPARITION

2 He appeared to Joseph of Arimathea, as may be piously meditated, and as we read in the Lives of the Saints.

311 *1*

THE THIRTEENTH APPARITION
1 Corinthians 15:8

2 After his Ascension he appeared to St. Paul, "Last of all,
3 as to one born out of due time, he appeared to me." He
4 appeared also in soul to the holy ancestors in limbo; and
after he had freed them, and taken up his body again, he
appeared to the disciples on many occasions, and
discoursed with them.

312 *1*

THE ASCENSION OF CHRIST OUR LORD
Acts 1:1-12

2 *First Point.* After Christ our Lord had manifested himself
for forty days to the Apostles, giving many proofs and
signs and speaking about the Kingdom of God, he
commanded them to wait in Jerusalem for the Holy Spirit
who had been promised them.

3 *Second Point.* He led them out to Mount Olivet, and
in their presence he was lifted up, and a cloud took him
from their sight.

4 *Third Point.* While they are looking up to heaven the
angels say to them, "Men of Galilee, why are you
standing there looking up at the sky? This Jesus who has
been taken up from you into heaven will return in the
same way as you have seen him going into heaven."[140]

[RULES
FOR THE DISCERNMENT OF SPIRITS][141]

313 *1*   RULES TO AID US TOWARD
PERCEIVING AND THEN UNDERSTANDING,[142]
AT LEAST TO SOME EXTENT,
THE VARIOUS MOTIONS[143] WHICH ARE CAUSED[144]
2   IN THE SOUL[145]: THE GOOD MOTIONS
THAT THEY MAY BE RECEIVED,
AND THE BAD THAT THEY MAY BE REJECTED.
These rules are more suitable for the First Week.[146]

314 *1* *The First Rule.* In the case of persons who are going from one mortal sin to another, the enemy ordinarily proposes to them apparent pleasures. He makes them
2 imagine delights and pleasures of the senses, in order to hold them fast and plunge them deeper into their sins and vices.

3   But with persons of this type the good spirit uses a contrary procedure. Through their good judgment on problems of morality[147] he stings their consciences with remorse.

315 *1* *The Second.* In the case of persons who are earnestly purging away their sins, and who are progressing from good to better in the service of God our Lord, the procedure used is the opposite of that described in the
2 First Rule. For in this case it is characteristic of the evil spirit to cause gnawing anxiety, to sadden, and to set up obstacles. In this way he unsettles these persons by false reasons aimed at preventing their progress.

3   But with persons of this type it is characteristic of the good spirit to stir up courage and strength, consolations, tears, inspirations, and tranquility. He makes things easier and eliminates all obstacles, so that the persons may move forward in doing good.

316 1 *The Third*, about spiritual consolation.[148] By [this kind of] consolation I mean that which occurs when some interior motion is caused within the soul through which it comes 2 to be inflamed with love[149] of its Creator and Lord. As a result it can love no created thing on the face of the earth in itself, but only in the Creator of them all.

3   Similarly, this consolation is experienced when the soul sheds tears which move it to love for its Lord— whether they are tears of grief for its own sins, or about the Passion of Christ our Lord, or about other matters directly ordered to his service and praise.

4   Finally, under the word consolation I include every increase in hope, faith, and charity, and every interior joy which calls and attracts one toward heavenly things and to the salvation of one's soul, by bringing it tranquility and peace in its Creator and Lord.

317 1 *The Fourth*, about spiritual desolation.[150] By [this kind of] desolation I mean everything which is the contrary of 2 what was described in the Third Rule; for example, obtuseness of soul, turmoil within it, an impulsive motion toward low and earthly things, or disquiet from 3 various agitations and temptations. These move one toward lack of faith and leave one without hope and without love. One is completely listless, tepid, and unhappy, and feels separated from our Creator and Lord.

4   For just as consolation is contrary to desolation, so the thoughts which arise from consolation are likewise contrary to those which spring from desolation.

318 1 *The Fifth*. During a time of desolation one should never make a change. Instead, one should remain firm and constant in the resolutions and in the decision which one had on the day before the desolation, or in a decision in which one was during a previous time of consolation.

2   For just as the good spirit is chiefly the one who guides and counsels us in time of consolation, so it is the evil spirit who does this in time of desolation. By follow-

ing his counsels we can never find the way to a right decision.

319 *1* *The Sixth.* Although we ought not to change our former resolutions in time of desolation, it is very profitable to make vigorous changes in ourselves against the desola-
 2 tion, ¹ for example, by insisting more on prayer, meditation, earnest self-examination, and some suitable way of doing penance.

320 *1* *The Seventh.* When we are in desolation we should think that the Lord has left us to our own powers in order to test us, so that we may prove ourselves by resisting the
 2 various agitations and temptations of the enemy. For we can do this with God's help, which always remains
 3 available, even if we do not clearly perceive it. Indeed, even though the Lord has withdrawn from us his abundant fervor, augmented love, and intensive grace, he still supplies sufficient grace for our eternal salvation.

321 *1* *The Eighth.* One who is in desolation should strive to preserve himself or herself in patience. This is the counterattack against the vexations which are being
 2 experienced. One should remember that after a while the consolation will return again, through the diligent efforts against the desolation which were suggested in the Sixth Rule.

322 *1* *The Ninth.* There are three chief causes for the desolation in which we find ourselves.

     The first is that we ourselves are tepid, lazy, or negligent in our spiritual exercises. Thus the spiritual consolation leaves us because of our own faults.

 2   The second is that the desolation is meant to test how much we are worth and how far we will extend ourselves in the service and praise of God, even without much repayment by way of consolations and increased graces.

3   The third is that the desolation is meant to give us a true recognition and understanding, so that we may perceive interiorly that we cannot by ourselves bring on or retain great devotion, intense love, tears, or any other spiritual consolation, but that all these are a gift and
4 grace from God our Lord; and further, to prevent us from building our nest in a house which belongs to Another, by puffing up our minds with pride or vainglory through which we attribute to ourselves the devotion or other features of spiritual consolation.

323 1 *The Tenth.* One who is in consolation should consider how he or she will act in future desolation, and store up new strength for that time.

324 1 *The Eleventh.* One who is in consolation ought to humble and abase herself or himself as much as possible, and reflect how little she or he is worth in time of desolation when that grace or consolation is absent.
2   In contrast, one who is in desolation should reflect that with the sufficient grace already available he or she can do much to resist all hostile forces, by drawing strength from our Creator and Lord.

325 1 *The Twelfth.* The enemy conducts himself like a woman. He is weak when faced by firmness but strong in the face of acquiescence.[151]
2   When she is quarreling with a man and he shows himself bold and unyielding, she characteristically loses
3 her spirit and goes away. But if the man begins to lose his spirit and backs away, the woman's anger, vindictiveness, and ferocity swell almost without limit.
4   In the same way, the enemy characteristically weak-
5 ens, loses courage, and flees with his temptations | when the person engaged in spiritual endeavors stands bold and unyielding against the enemy's temptations and
6 goes diametrically against them. But if, in contrast, that person begins to fear and lose courage in the face of the

7 temptations, there is no beast on the face of the earth as fierce as the enemy of human nature when he is pursuing his damnable intention with his surging malice.

326 1 *The Thirteenth.* Similarly the enemy acts like a false lover, insofar as he tries to remain secret and undetected.
2 For such a scoundrel, speaking with evil intent and trying to seduce the daughter of a good father or the wife of a good husband, wants his words and solicita-
3 tions to remain secret. But he is deeply displeased when the daughter reveals his deceitful words and evil design to her father, or the wife to her husband. For he easily infers that he cannot succeed in the design he began.
4 In a similar manner, when the enemy of human nature turns his wiles and persuasions upon an upright person, he intends and desires them to be received and
5 kept in secrecy. But when the person reveals them to his or her good confessor or some other spiritual person who understands the enemy's deceits and malice, he is
6 grievously disappointed. For he quickly sees that he cannot succeed in the malicious project he began, because his manifest deceptions have been detected.

327 1 *The Fourteenth.* To use still another comparison, the enemy acts like a military commander who is attempting
2 to conquer and plunder his objective. The captain and leader of an army on campaign sets up his camp, studies the strength and structure of a fortress, and then attacks at its weakest point.
3 In the same way, the enemy of human nature prowls around and from every side probes all our theological,
4 cardinal, and moral virtues. Then at the point where he finds us weakest and most in need in regard to our eternal salvation, there he attacks and tries to take us.

[RULES MORE SUITABLE
FOR THE SECOND WEEK][152]

328 1 ### RULES FOR THE SAME PURPOSE,
WITH A MORE PROBING
DISCERNMENT OF SPIRITS.
These rules are more suitable for the Second Week.[153]

329 1 *The First Rule.* It is characteristic of God and his angels, by the motions they cause, to give genuine happiness and spiritual joy, and thereby to banish any sadness and turmoil induced by the enemy.

2   It is characteristic of the enemy to fight against this happiness and spiritual consolation, by using specious reasonings, subtleties, and persistent deceits.

330 1 *The Second.* Only God our Lord can give the soul consolation without a preceding cause. For it is the prerogative of the Creator alone to enter the soul, depart from it, and cause a motion in it which draws the whole person

2 into love of His Divine Majesty. By "without [a preceding] cause" I mean without any previous perception or understanding of some object by means of which the consolation just mentioned might have been stimulated, through the intermediate activity of the person's acts of understanding and willing.[154]

331 1 *The Third.* With or by means of a preceding cause,[155] both the good angel and the evil angel are able to cause consolation in the soul, but for their contrary purposes.

2 The good angel acts for the progress of the soul, that it may grow and rise from what is good to what is better.

3 The evil angel works for the contrary purpose, that is, to entice the soul to his own damnable intention and malice.

332 1 *The Fourth.* It is characteristic of the evil angel, who

takes on the appearance of an angel of light, to enter by going along the same way as the devout soul and then
2 to exit by his own way with success for himself. That is, he brings good and holy thoughts attractive to such an upright soul and then strives little by little to get his own way, by enticing the soul over to his own hidden deceits and evil intentions.

333 1 *The Fifth.* We should pay close attention to the whole train of our thoughts. If the beginning, middle, and end are all good and tend toward what is wholly good, it is
2 a sign of the good angel. But if the train of the thoughts which a spirit causes ends up in something evil or diverting, or in something less good than what the soul
3 was originally proposing to do; or further, if it weakens, disquiets, or disturbs the soul, by robbing it of the peace,
4 tranquility, and quiet which it enjoyed earlier, ⏐ all this is a clear sign that this is coming from the evil spirit, the enemy of our progress and eternal salvation.

334 1 *The Sixth.* When the enemy of human nature has been perceived and recognized by his serpent's tail and the
2 evil end to which he is leading, it then becomes profitable for the person whom he has tempted in this way to examine the whole train of the good thoughts which the evil spirit brought to the soul; that is, how they began,
3 ⏐ and then how little by little the evil spirit endeavored to bring the soul down from the sweetness and spiritual joy in which it had been, and finally brought it to his
4 own evil intention. The purpose is that through this experience, now recognized and noted, the soul may guard itself in the future against these characteristic snares.

335 1 *The Seventh.* In the case of those who are going from good to better, the good angel touches the soul gently, lightly, and sweetly, like a drop of water going into a
2 sponge. The evil spirit touches it sharply, with noise and

disturbance, like a drop of water falling onto a stone.

3   In the case of those who are going from bad to worse, these spirits touch the souls in the opposite

4 manner. The reason for this is the fact that the disposition of the soul is either similar to or different from the

5 respective spirits who are entering. When the soul is different, they enter with perceptible noise and are

6 quickly noticed. When the soul is similar, they enter silently, like those who go into their own house by an open door.

336 1 *The Eighth.* When the consolation is without a preceding cause there is no deception in it, since it is coming only

2 from God our Lord, as was stated above [330]. However, the spiritual person to whom God gives this consolation ought to examine that experience with great vigilance and attention. One should distinguish the time when the

3 consolation itself was present ⎸ from the time after it, in which the soul remains still warm and favored with the gifts and aftereffects of the consolation which has itself

4 passed away. For often during this later period we ourselves act either through our own reasoning which springs from our own habits and the conclusions we draw from our own concepts and judgments, or through

5 the influence of either a good or an evil spirit. In this way we form various projects and convictions which are

6 not coming immediately from God our Lord. Hence these need to be very carefully examined before they are fully accepted or carried into effect. [156]

337 *1*   **IN THE MINISTRY OF DISTRIBUTING ALMS**[157]
     THE FOLLOWING RULES OUGHT TO BE FOLLOWED.

338 *1*   *The First Rule.* If I make the distribution to my relatives
     or friends or persons for whom I feel affection, there are
     four things which I ought to observe. They have been
     treated in part above [184-187] in the matters on which
     an election is made.

   2   First of all, that love which moves me and brings me
     to give the alms should descend from above, from the
   3 love of God our Lord, in such a way that I perceive
     beforehand that the love, whether greater or less, which
     I have for the persons is for God, and that God may
     shine forth in the reason for which I have greater love
     for these persons.

339 *1*   *The Second Rule.* I will imagine a man whom I have
   2 never seen or known. Desiring all perfection for him in
     his ministry and state of life, I will consider how I would
     wish him to use a good norm in his manner of distribut-
     ing alms, for the greater glory of God and the perfection
   3 of his soul. Then I, acting in the same way and neither
     more nor less, will keep the rule and norm which I
     would desire and judge proper for this other person.

340 *1*   *The Third Rule.* I will consider, as if I were at the point
     of death, what procedure and norm I will at that time
   2 wish I had used in the discharge of my administration.
     Then, guiding myself by that norm, I will apply it in the
     acts of my distribution.

341 *1*   *The Fourth Rule.* Imagining how I will find myself on
     judgment day, I will think well how at that time I will
     wish that I had carried out this office and duty of my
   2 ministry. The rule which I will then wish I had used is
     what I will follow now.

342 1 *The Fifth Rule.* When I perceive myself inclined and affectionately attached to others to whom I want to 2 distribute alms, I should delay and think over the four rules mentioned above [184-187]. I should examine and 3 test my affection by means of them, and not give the alms until, in conformity with those rules, my disordered affection has been completely removed and banished.

343 1 *The Sixth Rule.* There is clearly no fault in accepting the goods[158] of God our Lord in order to distribute them, when one has been called by our God and Lord to that 2 ministry of distributing alms. However, there is place for doubt about culpability and excess in regard to the amount one should take and apply to oneself from what 3 one holds for distribution to others. Hence one can reform one's way of living in his state, by means of the rules mentioned above [338-342].

344 1 *The Seventh Rule.* For the reasons already mentioned and many others, in regard to our own persons and household arrangements, it is always better and safer to 2 curtail and reduce our expenses. The more we do this, the more do we draw near to our high priest, model, and 3 rule, who is Christ our Lord. In conformity with this the Third Council of Carthage (at which St. Augustine was present) decided and ordered that the furniture of the bishops should be inexpensive and poor.
4   The same consideration should be applied to all the styles of living, in accordance with the condition and 5 state of the persons under consideration. For example, in the state of marriage we have Sts. Joachim and Anne. 6 They divided their possessions into three parts, gave the first to the poor, the second to the ministry and service of the temple, and kept the third for their own support and that of their family.[159]

345 1   **TOWARD PERCEIVING AND UNDERSTANDING
SCRUPLES
AND THE INSINUATIONS OF OUR ENEMY,
THE FOLLOWING NOTES[160] ARE HELPFUL.**

346 1   *The First Note.* People commonly apply the word scruple
to something which comes from our own judgment and
free will, for example, when I take something that is not
2 sinful and freely build it up into a sin. This happens, for
instance, if someone accidentally steps on a cross made
by straws and afterwards forms the judgment that he or
she has sinned. This, strictly speaking, is an erroneous
judgment and not a scruple in the proper sense of the
term.

347 1   *The Second Note.* After I have stepped on that cross, or
after I have thought or said or done something else
similar, there comes to me from without the thought that
I have sinned; but on the other hand I think I have not
2 sinned. However, in all this I feel disturbed, that is, at
one moment I doubt and at another I do not. This is a
scruple in the proper sense of the term, and a temptation
brought on by the enemy.

348 1   *The Third Note.* The first scruple, that described in the
first note, should be strongly abhorred, since it is totally
erroneous. But the second, described in the second note,
can for a limited period of time be profitable to a person
2 performing spiritual exercises. For it greatly purifies and
cleanses a soul, and separates it far from every sem-
blance of sin, in accordance with Gregory's maxim: "It is
characteristic of good souls to see a fault where none exists."[161]

349 1   *The Fourth Note.* The enemy considers attentively
whether one has a lax or a delicate conscience.
        If a conscience is delicate, the enemy strives the

harder to make it delicate even to an extreme, in order to
2 trouble it more and eventually thwart it. For example, if
he sees that a person does not consent to any sin,
whether mortal or venial or even merely an appearance
3 of deliberate sin, since he cannot make the person fall
into what even appears to be sinful, he brings him or her
to judge as sinful something in which no sin exists; for
example, in some unimportant word or thought.

4   But if the person has a lax conscience, the enemy
5 works to make it still more lax. For example, if the soul
previously made little or nothing of venial sins, he tries
to bring it to similar unconcern about mortal sins; and if
previously it did have some concern about them, he now
tries to lessen the concern or to banish it.

350 1 *The Fifth Note.* A person who desires to make progress
in the spiritual life ought always to proceed in a manner
2 contrary to that of the enemy. In other words, if the
enemy seeks to make a soul lax, it should try to make
3 itself more sensitive. In the same way, if the enemy seeks
to make a soul too sensitive, in order to entice it to an
extreme, the soul should endeavor to establish itself
staunchly in a correct mean and thus arrive at complete
peace.

351 1 *The Sixth Note.* Sometimes a good soul of this type
wishes to say or do something which, in conformity with
the Church or the mind of our superiors, contributes to
2 the glory of God our Lord. But this person gets a
thought or temptation from without not to say or do it.
Specious reasons of vainglory or other similar things are
brought up. In such a case we ought to raise our minds
3 to our Creator and Lord; and if we see that it is for his
due service, or at least not opposed to it, we ought to act
diametrically against the temptation. We should reply as
St. Bernard did: "I did not begin because of you, and
neither will I desist for you." [162]

[RULES FOR THINKING, JUDGING, AND FEELING WITH THE CHURCH][163]

352 *1* ## TO HAVE THE GENUINE ATTITUDE[164]
WHICH WE OUGHT TO MAINTAIN
IN THE CHURCH MILITANT,[165]
WE SHOULD OBSERVE THE FOLLOWING RULES.[166]

353 *1* *The First Rule.* With all judgment of our own put aside, we ought to keep our minds disposed and ready to be obedient in everything to the true Spouse of Christ our Lord, which is our holy Mother the hierarchical Church.[167]

354 *1* *The Second.*[168] We should praise confession to a priest, reception of the Most Blessed Sacrament once a year, and much more once a month, and still more every week, always with the required and proper conditions.

355 *1* *The Third.* We should praise frequent attendance at Mass; also, chants, psalmody, and long prayers inside
2 and outside the church; and further, the schedules setting the times for the whole Divine Office, for prayers of every kind, and for all the canonical hours.

356 *1* *The Fourth.* We should strongly praise religious institutes, virginity and continence, and marriage too, but not as highly as any of the former.

357 *1* *The Fifth.* We should praise the vows of religion, obedience, poverty, chastity, and vows to perform other works
2 of supererogation which conduce to perfection. We should remember, too, that just as a vow is made in regard to matters which lead towards evangelical perfection, so vows ought not to be made with respect to

matters that withdraw one from it, such as to enter business, to get married, and the like.

358 1 *The Sixth*. We should praise relics of saints, by venerating the relics and praying to the saints. We should extol visits to stational churches, pilgrimages, indulgences for jubilees and crusades, and the lighting of candles in churches.

359 1 *The Seventh*. We should praise precepts of fast and abstinence, for example, in Lent, on ember days, vigils, Fridays and Saturdays; also penances, not only interior but also exterior.

360 1 *The Eighth*. We ought to praise church buildings and their decorations; also statues and paintings, and their veneration according to what they represent.

361 1 *The Ninth*. Lastly, we should praise all the precepts of the Church, while keeping our mind ready to look for reasons for defending them and not for attacking them in any way.

362 1 *The Tenth*.[169] We ought to be more inclined to approve and praise the decrees, recommendations, and conduct of
     2 our superiors[170] [than to speak against them]. For although in some cases their acts are not or were not praiseworthy, to speak against them either by preaching in public or by conversing among the ordinary people would cause more murmuring and scandal than profit.
     3 And through this the people would become angry at
     4 their officials, whether civil or spiritual. However, just as it does harm to speak evil about officials among the ordinary people while they are absent, so it can be profitable to speak of their bad conduct to persons who can bring about a remedy.

363 1 *The Eleventh.* We ought to praise both positive theology
and scholastic theology.[171] For just as it is more characteristic of the positive doctors, such as St. Jerome, St.
Augustine, St. Gregory, and the rest to stir up our
affections toward loving and serving God our Lord in all
2 things, so it is more characteristic of the scholastic
teachers, such as St. Thomas, St. Bonaventure, the Master
3 of the Sentences, and so on to define and explain for our
times the matters necessary for salvation, and also to
4 refute and expose all the errors and fallacies. For the
scholastic teachers, being more modern, can avail
themselves of an authentic understanding of Sacred
5 Scripture and the holy positive doctors. Further still they,
being enlightened and clarified by divine influence,
make profitable use of the councils, canons, and decrees
of our Holy Mother Church.

364 1 *The Twelfth.* We ought to be on our guard against
comparing those of us who are still living with the
blessed of the past.[172] For no small error is made when
2 one says, ǀ for example, "He knows more than St. Augustine," or "He is another St. Francis, or even more," or
"He is another St. Paul in goodness, holiness, and the
like."

365 1 *The Thirteenth.*[173] To keep ourselves right in all things,
we ought to hold fast to this principle: What seems to
me to be white, I will believe to be black if the hierarchi-
2 cal Church thus determines it.[174] For we believe that
between Christ our Lord, the Bridegroom, and the
Church, his Spouse, there is the one same Spirit who
3 governs and guides us for the salvation of our souls. For
it is by the same Spirit and Lord of ours who gave the
ten commandments that our Holy Mother Church is
guided and governed.

366 1 *The Fourteenth.* It is granted that there is much truth in
the statement that no one can be saved without being

2 predestined and without having faith and grace. Never-theless great caution is necessary in our manner of speaking and teaching about all these matters.

367 1 *The Fifteenth.* We ought not to fall into a habit of speaking much about predestination. But if somehow the topic is brought up on occasions, it should be treated in such a way that the ordinary people do not fall into an
2 error, as sometimes happens when they say: "Whether I am to be saved or damned is already determined, and this cannot now be changed by my doing good or evil."
3 Through this they grow listless and neglect the works which lead to good and to the spiritual advancement of their souls.

368 1 *The Sixteenth.* In the same way we should take care that we do not, by speaking and insisting strongly about faith
2 without any distinction or explanation, give the people an occasion to grow listless and lazy in their works — either before or after their faith is informed by charity.

369 1 *The Seventeenth.* Similarly, we ought not to speak so lengthily and emphatically about grace that we generate
2 a poison harmful to freedom of the will. Hence one may speak about faith and grace as much as possible, with God's help, for the greater praise of the Divine Majesty;
3 but not in such ways or manners, especially in times as dangerous as our own, that works and free will are impaired or thought worthless.

370 1 *The Eighteenth.* It is granted that we should value above everything else the great service which is given to God because of pure love. Nevertheless we should also
2 strongly praise fear of the Divine Majesty. For not only is filial fear something pious and very holy, but so also is servile fear. Even if it brings a person nothing better or more useful, it greatly aids him or her to rise from
3 mortal sin; and once such a one has risen, one easily

attains to filial fear, which is wholly acceptable and pleasing to God our Lord, since it is inseparably united with love of him.

THE END

LIST OF ABBREVIATIONS

ENDNOTES ON THE *EXERCISES*

APPENDICES I AND II

SELECTED BIBLIOGRAPHY

EDITORIAL NOTE

INDEX

LIST OF ABBREVIATIONS

AHSJ	*Archivum Historicum Societatis Iesu.* Periodical, Rome
AldamIntro	Aldama, A. M. de, *An Introductory Commentary on the Constitutions* (St. Louis, 1989)
Autobiog	The *Autobiography* of St. Ignatius
BibThSpEx	Cusson, G., *Biblical Theology and the Spiritual Exercises* (St. Louis, 1988)
Cons	*The Constitutions of the Society of Jesus,* by St. Ignatius, in any text
*Cons*MHSJ	*Constitutiones et Regulae Societatis Iesu,* 4 vols. The critically edited texts in the series Monumenta Historica Societatis Iesu (Rome, 1934-1948)
ConsSJComm	*The Constitutions of the Society of Jesus.* Translated, with an Introduction and a Commentary, by G. E. Ganss, S.J. (St. Louis, 1970)
DalmIgn	Dalmases, C. de, *Ignatius of Loyola: Founder of the Jesuits. His Life and Work* (St. Louis, 1985)
DalmMan	Dalmases, C. de, *Ejercicios Espirituales. Introducción, texto, notas y vocabulario* por Cándido de Dalmases (1987). The critically edited Spanish text in the form of a manual for practical use
DeGuiJes	De Guibert, J., *The Jesuits: Their Spiritual Doctrine and Practice* (St. Louis, 1986)
Directory	The official *Directory of the Spiritual Exercises* issued by Aquaviva in 1599
DirSpEx	*Directoria Exercitiorum Spiritualium (1540-1599)* (Rome, 1955)
DSpir	*Dictionnaire de spiritualité* (Paris, 1937–)
Dudon	Dudon, Paul. *Saint Ignatius of Loyola* (Milwaukee, 1949)
EppIgn	*S. Ignatii Epistolae et Instructiones.* 12 volumes in MHSJ (Rome, 1903-1911)
FN	*Fontes Narrativi.* 4 volumes in MHSJ (Rome, 1923-1960)

IgnCLWS	*Ignatius of Loyola, The* Spiritual Exercises *and Selected Works.* Ed. George E. Ganss. No. 72 in The Classics of Western Spirituality (Mahwah, 1991).
LettersIgn	*Letters of St. Ignatius.* Trans. W. J. Young (Chicago, 1959)
LeturIñg	Leturia, Pedro de. *Iñigo de Loyola* (Chicago, 1965)
MHSJ	Monumenta Historica Societatis Iesu. The series of critically edited historical sources of the Jesuits, 124 volumes
MonNad	*Epistolae et Monumenta Patris H. Nadal.* 6 vols in MHSJ
n or nn	note(s), or footnote(s), or endnote(s)
no or nos	number(s)
NCathEnc	*New Catholic Encyclopedia* (New York, 1967)
NDicTh	*The New Dictionary of Theology* (Wilmington, 1987)
Obrascompl	*Obras completas de San Ignacio.* 4th ed. (Madrid, 1982)
OxDCCh	*Oxford Dictionary of the Christian Church* (1974)
PG	Patrologia Graeca. Ed. Migne
PL	Patrologia Latina. Ed. Migne
SpDiar	The *Spiritual Diary* of St. Ignatius, 1544-1545
SpEx	The *Spiritual Exercises* of St. Ignatius, in any text
*SpEx*MHSJ19	*Exercitia Spiritualia S. Ignatii . . . et Eorum Directoria* (1919), in MHSJ
*SpEx*MHSJ69	*Sti. Ignatii . . . Exercitia Spiritualia. Textuum antiquissimorum nova editio* (Rome, 1969). The critical text of the *Exercises*, edited by C. de Dalmases as volume 100 in the series MHSJ. It is a revision of *SpEx*MHSJ19 (1919).
ST	*Summa theologiae* of St. Thomas Aquinas

ENDNOTES ON THE *EXERCISES*

The Introductory Explanations

1. *Anotaciones*: In Spanish as in English, the word "annotation" means a jotting or note added by way of commentary or explanation; e.g., a marginal note. In Ignatius' *Exercises*, however, a collection of such notes or explanations serves as the introductory chapter to his book. Hence we translate the word by the more descriptive term "introductory explanations." Originally these twenty sections were probably mere notes which Ignatius jotted down while his experience with the Exercises was growing. In time he gathered them together at the beginning of the *Exercises*, without troubling himself to find a more descriptive title. The Exercises properly so called begin only at section 21 below.

These introductory explanations elucidate the nature and purpose of the Exercises (1); the procedure in general (2-3); their division and duration (4); the basic dispositions required in the exercitant (5); the director's dealings with the exercitant in his or her most vital experiences (6-17); the adaptations of the Exercises to different classes of retreatants (18-20).

Explanations 3, 5, 11, 12, 13, 16, 20 deal with the exercitant's dispositions, and 1, 2, 4, 6-10, 14, 15, 17, 18, 19 are addressed chiefly to directors (see Iparraguirre in *Obrascompl*, 4th ed. [1982], p. 15).

2. Disordered affections: tendencies, attachments, etc., which are not ordered according to the principles in the Foundation (23). See note 20 below.

3. History: Usually it is the gospel narrative of the topic contemplated. For other cases see n. 63 on 102 below and n. 76 on 150, below.

4. The good spirits may be God or an angel, the evil spirits are devils. For Ignatius these spirits are always persons, intelligent beings. Discernment of spirits is a means to discernment of the will of God, on which see n. 156 on 336 below. For Ignatius' experiences and reflections from which his teachings on discern-

ment of spirits (313-336) evolved, see *Autobiog*, esp. 8, 19-20, 26.

5. Just as a 16th century Spaniard would speak or write respectfully of "His Majesty King Charles I," so did Ignatius write "His Divine Majesty" (*su divina majestad*) as one of his favorite titles of God. This title sprang spontaneously from his heart and with lapidary brevity expressed the deep reverence he habitually felt for his Creator. It is a title of God ubiquitous in his letters and other writings, occurring some twenty-three times in the *Exercises* alone. Much the same can be said of a favorite title of St. Teresa of Avila for God, "His Majesty." It occurs almost on every other page of her *Interior Castle*, and often two or three times on a page. To introduce a change in this phrase of Ignatius risks losing the nuance of reverence so deep in his personality. However, after calling attention to this feature, we shall usually soften the phrase to "the Divine Majesty" because of the considerations discussed on pp. 11-12 above.

6. *Mociones*: "Motions" is here Ignatius' technical term, taken from scholasticism, to designate the interior experiences, such as thoughts, impulses, inclinations, urges, moods, consolations, desolations, and the like. For further explanations see n. 100 on 182 and n. 143 on 313 below.

7. *El que da los ejercicios* and *al [= a+el] que se ejercita* literally mean "he who gives the Exercises" and "he who exercises himself"; and *en su ánima*, "in his or her soul": Ignatius gave the Exercises to both women and men. In the circumstances of his lifetime the directors were Jesuits and therefore men. But in his concept of possible directors Ignatius included women. To Paolo Achille, a Jesuit who lacked time to give the Exercises to some nuns, he wrote on June 19, 1555: "Perhaps some way could be found to give this aid [the Exercises] to the nuns without spending too much time—if the Exercises should be given diligently to one nun among them and she would give them afterwards to the others" (*EppIgn*, 9:220; see also *DeGuiJes*, p. 125, footnote 71).

8. Ignatius' mention of the purgative and illuminative "life" (*vida*) clearly refers to the classic doctrine of the three ways (*viae*) or stages of growth in the spiritual life: the purgative, illuminative, and unitive ways. Early Directories too apply that doctrine to the *Exercises*; e.g., González Dávila, and the official *Directory* of 1599, ch. 11, nos. 2, 3; 18, no. 3; 37, no. 1; 39. Ignatius could

have learned this doctrine already at Montserrat from Cisneros' *Book of Exercises for the Spiritual Life,* or from other books during his studies. Only here does he himself mention this doctrine in the *Exercises.* On it see *IgnCWS,* pp. 61-63; *DeGuiJes,* pp. 605-609, and in the index, pp. 686, 691, s.v. Stages; Ways.

9. The term "benefice" originally meant a grant of land for life as a reward (*beneficium*) for services. As canon law developed, the term came to imply an ecclesiastical office which prescribed certain spiritual duties or conditions ("spiritualities") for the due discharge of which it awarded regularly recurring revenues ("temporalities"). See *OxDCCh,* p. 156; *NCathEnc* 2:305. The system was obviously subject to abuses of neglecting the spiritual ministration. But Ignatius regarded benefices as such as good, objects about which one should be indifferent, i.e., impartial (16, 169, 171, 178, 181).

10. In 18, 19, and 20 Ignatius indicates the chief manners in which the Exercises can be adapted to various classes of people in their various circumstances, through a great variety of ways and means. Hence many forms of retreats naturally evolved. The ideal, the closed retreat of 30 days, is treated in 20; the "Exercises in Everyday Life," an open retreat near to that ideal, in 19; and in 18 "light exercises" (18:10), a retreat either closed or open which aims at whatever is possible in the circumstances.

11. Ignatius' term *pecados mortales* is here translated by "capital sins" because it refers to the traditional teaching on seven capital vices, commonly listed (with variations) as pride, anger, avarice, gluttony, lust, envy, and sloth. They are not necessarily sins in themselves; e.g., there can be righteous anger. But they are sources (*capita*) from which sins easily flow. In Ignatius' day (as in ours) they were often called "mortal" or "deadly" sins, although this terminology is rather inaccurate because in concrete instances they may be mortal or venial sin or no sin at all. Ignatius uses *pecados mortales* to mean the capital sins in 18, 238, 244, and 245, and to mean mortal sins which bring eternal damnation in 33, 44, 48, 52, 57, 165, 314, 370, where we translate the phrase by "mortal sins" (see *DalmMan,* p. 200).

12. G. Cusson, *The Spiritual Exercises Made in Everyday Life: A Method and a Biblical Interpretation* (St. Louis, 1989) is a directory which sprang from his extensive experience in the practice of the "Exercises Made according to Annotation 19." Materials

arranged for directing or making such retreats can be found in the loose-leaf book of another experienced director, Joseph A. Tetlow, *Choosing Christ in the World: Directing the Spiritual Exercises according to Annotations Eighteen and Nineteen. A Handbook* (St. Louis, 1989).

THE FIRST WEEK

13. In the manuscript of the Autograph text *A* the words *primera semana* appear above 21, in the form of a running head. But their position here presents a difficulty: Should the Foundation (23) be considered as a part of the First Week which, Ignatius stated in 4 above, is devoted to the consideration of sins? To this controverted question an affirmative answer can be given, for these reasons. In about 1536 at the time of Helyar's retreat, the Foundation seemingly was still among the Introductory Explanations (*anotaciones*) used to prepare exercitants for the retreat before it began. It was merely recalled by a brief explanation on the morning of the first day, on which the exercise on sin was to begin in the afternoon. However, the Foundation contained a vision which focused the exercitant's attention on God's whole plan of creation and salvation as it was evolving in history, and it also presented the vital principle of indifference, the hinge on which the election depends. As this importance was gradually discovered the Foundation was made into an exercise within the retreat itself. In his Dictated Directory Ignatius himself advised keeping the exercitant "on the consideration of the Foundation and on the particular and general examens for three or four days or even more" (*SpEx*MHSJ19, p. 791). Thus it began to be divided into points and became a part of the First Week, even though the announced topic of that Week had been "sins" (4). Furthermore, in texts P^1 and P^2 of the First Latin Version, the title *primera semana* is found above 21-22. By 1556 the Foundation was the first exercise within the retreat itself. Hence we place the words "the First Week" before section 21. See *BibThSpEx*, pp. 47-51.

The End of the Exercises

14. To "overcome oneself" is the "negative" purpose of the Exercises: a preliminary removal of obstacles, such as sin or disordered inclinations to it. This is usually a first step indispensable to spiritual progress. To this negative end Ignatius

immediately adds the genuine, positive, and inspirational aim of the Exercises, eternal salvation. New and enriching aspects of this goal, especially those known from divine revelation, emerge as the exercitant goes through the Exercises, and even subsequently as he or she goes through life in the light of them. In Ignatius' thinking, to "order one's life" is to bring its details into accordance with the Principle and Foundation about to be given in 23.

And yet, what is the essential end of the *Exercises*? Although Ignatius' succinct statement in 21 seems clear at first reading, it has given rise to extensive discussions. With some oversimplification to get to the heart of the matter, the chief writers can be divided into two schools, "electionists" (e.g., L. de Grandmaison) and "perfectionists" (e.g., L. Peeters). De Grandmaison maintained in 1921: The end is to prepare a spiritually minded person to make a wise election of a state of life in which he or she can serve God best. The text as it stands is clearly directed to that end. Peeters objected in 1931: The end and culminating point of the Exercises can only be a union with God which is most intimate and total. An answer unifying both these extremes was written by Joseph de Guibert shortly before his death in 1942 and posthumously published in 1953: Those two ends are complementary, not mutually exclusive. If we consider Ignatius' printed text of 1548 and his process in writing it while winning companions from 1534 onward, the end expressed *in his text* is to facilitate a good election; and that is the supposition which best enables us to interpret the wording of Ignatius' text itself. However, if we consider the uses which he himself made of his text, we see that he gave the exercises to persons whose election was already made (e.g., Xavier and Favre), and that his objective was to lead them to intensive union with God. He found the principles in the text leading to an election to be equally suitable for guiding exercitants to lofty union with God; but he did not trouble himself to state this explicitly by stylistic revisions in the text itself. He left it to directors to adjust the text and its principles flexibly to the personalities and needs of each exercitant. On this discussion, see *DeGuiJes*, pp. 122-132, esp. 126; also, ch. 13, esp. pp. 531-532); on its extent and history, see Cusson, in *BibThSpEx*, pp. 80-93.

15. That is, to avoid coming to a decision through attachments, inclinations, urges, likes, or dislikes which are not in

accord with the norms for the proper use of creatures given below in 23:7.

In this Ignatian usage such affections are propensities and not mere emotions. Affective attachments to good objects, procedures, or persons can be great helps in the spiritual life. But they can become disordered and consequently dangerous or even sinful.

16. Or, "the other person may be saved" [from error or blame]. The Spanish text is ambiguous and can be translated either way.

To profit from the Exercises, an exercitant must be reasonably open to their content and to the director. A retreatant who is suspicious or hostile and searching for heresy or Illuminism would lack the desirable openness. Ignatius is here asking for fairness. If something is unclear, let the exercitant ask about it. On the suspicions rife in the era of the Illuminati which are reflected in this presupposition, see Hervé Coathalem, *Ignatian Insights: A Guide to the Complete Spiritual Exercises* (Taichung [Taiwan], 1971), p. 59.

The Principle and Foundation

17. By its clear statement of the purpose of human existence on earth this Principle and Foundation orients the retreatant for his or her work during the Exercises and for living after they are finished. It is both the starting point of the *Exercises* and a premise from which flow conclusions of the greatest importance for the spiritual life. It briefly presents God's plan of creating human beings who can use their freedom wisely to work out their spiritual growth and eternal self-fulfillment: their happiness by glorifying God both on earth and in the beatific vision. In this way it sketches the worldview of Christian faith as the background against which everything else in the *Exercises* and in life should be viewed. It opens the way for the retreatant to see his or her place and role in God's plan of salvation as it evolves in history.

The official *Directory* of 1599 regards the Foundation as "the basis of the whole moral and spiritual edifice" (ch. 12, no. 1). The principles enunciated here, and also their implications, underlie and govern all of Ignatius' thought—both later in the *Exercises* (especially in the directives for an election [169-189]) and also in his *Constitutions* (see, e.g., 622,a; also 616, 633),

Spiritual Diary, and Letters, where they reoccur constantly as occasions for their application arise. Dalmases approvingly quotes the great expert Luis de la Palma's *Camino espiritual . . . de los Ejercicios* (1626): "It is called a *principle* because in it are contained all the conclusions which are later explained and specifically expounded; and it is called a *foundation* because it is the support of the whole edifice of the spiritual life" (*DalmMan*, p. 57).

We can with profit elaborate La Palma's metaphor of the "whole edifice of the spiritual life." If we consider Ignatius' spiritual doctrine in the *Exercises* as a Gothic cathedral, this Principle and Foundation comprises four pillars supporting all their thought content, particularly that in the Election and the Rules for Discernment. These pillars are (1) a goal which attracts and inspires an exercitant toward making her or his life meaningful: salvation, glorifying God in the beatific vision and being happy by doing it; (2) the means to this goal, creatures rightly and wisely used; (3) a vital preliminary attitude: keeping oneself "indifferent," that is, with decision or choice suspended until the true reasons for a wise choice appear; and (4) the norm for choice among the options one faces: that which is likely to result in greater glory or praise to God (which entails one's own greater self-fulfillment and happiness). This result, the praise of God both on earth and in the beatific vision, is Ignatius' supreme end, and therefore the keystone of the arch which all the four pillars support.

Each of these four principles is made more meaningful as the *Exercises* proceed. For example, the end of human beings, baldly called "salvation" here in 23, is formulated as "to come to perfection" in 135; "to praise God and save one's soul" in 169, 177, 179, 181; "the praise and glory of God" in 167, 179, 180, 189, 240. For Ignatius "salvation" often connoted also "perfection."

In his *Powers of Imagining: Ignatius de Loyola* (Albany, 1986), pp. 101-103, Professor Antonio T. de Nicolas maintains that *principio* in the Foundation cannot be correctly translated as "principle" but should be turned by "origin," for "origins have nothing to do with cognition and cognitive skills"; that therefore, since English translations other than his own use the word principle, "they share a cognitive bias absent in the saint" and are "totally wrong." In support of his opinion he offers his theory on the use of the imagination in Ignatius. But he does not bring up considerations based on study or discussion of the structure, coherence, and consistency of Ignatius' thought. This writer finds the reasons advanced unconvincing and disagrees with his opinion. It overlooks the conclusions which Ignatius himself continually draws from the Principle and Foundation throughout the *Exercises* (especially, for example, in the Election [169-189]), in the *Constitutions,* and the close reasoning in the Deliberation on Poverty which Ignatius so carefully repeated even during the eminently affective mystical experiences recorded in his *Spiritual Diary*). That opinion attributes error not only to the English translations but also to the best versions in French and German, and it sets itself in opposition to the tradition (mentioned above) of Spanish interpreters of the Foundation from La Palma to Dalmases. Careful reasoning is characteristic of all Ignatius' writings, and to make the Exercises according to his directions requires a well-balanced union of logical reasoning, imagination, affectivity, and decisions.

For further considerations on the Foundation, see the Appendix II below, pp. 208-214, Toward the Deeper Study of the Foundation.

18. Ignatius quite surely meant the triune God as known from revelation. See the paragraph on *Dios nuestro Señor* under "Reason or Faith" in Appendix II, on p. 209 below.

19. "To save one's soul": That is, to save and perfect or develop one's whole self into the eternal life (John 17:3) of the beatific vision (1 Cor. 13:12; 1 John 3:21). From parallel passages we know that by "salvation" Ignatius meant also continual spiritual progress; e.g., *SpEx,* 20: "as much progress as possible"; 135: "to arrive at perfection"; *Cons,* 3: to labor for "the salvation and perfection" of one's neighbors; 813: "to reach their ultimate and supernatural end." See also pp. 208-210 below.

Anima, a Latinism constantly used by Ignatius instead of the Spanish word *alma,* means the rational soul (*DalmMan,* p. 190). However, very often (as here) Ignatius uses the scholastic term *anima* to mean the person, the whole self considered as a compound of body and soul. This sense of *anima* occurred already in classical Latin (e.g., *Aeneid* xi:24; Horace, *Satires* i, 5, 41), the Latin Vulgate (e.g., Gen. 2:7, Matt. 16:26, 1 Cor. 15:45), and subsequently with great frequency in all the languages of Christian Europe throughout the Middle Ages to and including the present (see, e.g., Blaise, *Dictionnaire des auteurs chrétiens,* s.v. "*anima,*" 4; *Webster's Ninth New Collegiate Dictionary* (1986), s.v.

"soul," 3, "a person's total self"). Throughout Christianity this has been the figure of synecdoche by which Christians named the part (soul, *anima*) to express the whole self, the living human being (*homo*). Simultaneously, while reciting the Creed, they were professing their belief in the resurrection of the body. Their outlook was therefore manifestly a Christian dualism or anthropology and not the viewpoint of some Neoplatonists or others who depreciated the body as evil or as "the tomb of the soul." Awareness of this usage is a key which is necessary for accurate interpretation of virtually all Christian writers throughout the history of spirituality.

Indifference

20. "Indifferent": undetermined to one thing or option rather than another; impartial; unbiased; with decision suspended until the reasons for a wise choice are learned; still undecided. In no way does it mean unconcerned or unimportant. It implies interior freedom from disordered inclinations. It is a key technical term of Ignatius' spirituality. To his examples of indifference it is often wise to add some which are fully under the control of our free will, such as: whether to become a physician or a banker; whether to read a book or go to a lecture. Ignatius' own examples often fall outside our power to choose.

21. Is the necessity of using creatures rightly, as is stated in 23:5, a necessity of precept or of counsel? Pierre Bouvier maintains that it is one of counsel. In *L'interprétation authentique de la méditation fondamentale* (Bourges, 1922), pp. 9-55), he presents the following analysis. The Foundation contains two principles or premises and two conclusions, which in turn become premises for further conclusions throughout the rest of the *Exercises*.

23:2 *Principle 1.* Human beings are created to serve God and save their souls.

23:3 *Principle 2.* The other created things are means to help them attain this end.

23:4 *Conclusion 1.* From this it follows that we must use these things to the extent that they help us to this end, and free ourselves from them to the extent that they hinder us from it.

23:5 *Conclusion 2.* To attain this it is necessary to make

> ourselves indifferent to all created things left to our free will, and to desire and choose those more conducive to the end.

First of all, we should notice, in regard to things commanded or forbidden under pain of mortal or venial sin there is necessity of precept and we may not be indifferent about them. Ignatian indifference pertains only to neutral things, those neither good nor bad in themselves. Among these, however, some are more suitable for our end than others and yet we are not commanded to choose them, e.g., to give an alms unnecessarily large. Here, therefore, the necessity can be one only of counsel; and the necessity asserted by Ignatius in his two conclusions of 23:4 and 5 is also one of counsel. In these statements an unexpressed condition is understood:

23:4 *Conclusion 1.* From this it follows that [if we wish to tend toward perfection] we ought to use these things to the extent that they help us to our end and free ourselves from them to the extent that they hinder us.

23:5 *Conclusion 2.* To attain this it is necessary, [if we wish to tend toward perfection], to make ourselves indifferent, and to choose the things more conducive to the end.

Ignatius is manifestly thinking chiefly about the fit and generous exercitants of *SpEx*, 20 who desire "to make all the progress possible."

22. This is Ignatius' chief criterion for choosing among options. It stimulates toward generosity, the "magis." But in his spirituality, we should remember, generosity should be under the control of "discreet charity," the discretion of a prudent person. One should be generous but also content with one's own physical and spiritual limitations, various circumstances, and the measure of grace which God gives. See *BibThSpEx*, p. 71. To find the golden mean requires careful and sometimes long discernment.

The Examinations of Conscience

23. These examinations of conscience (24-44) represent instructions which, adjusted to personal needs, were to be given to exercitants early in the retreat. Examinations of conscience had forerunners among the Pythagoreans and Stoics and were practiced in the Christian tradition from early times. Ignatius practiced reflective self-examination to an extraordinary degree (see *DeGuiJes*, pp. 39-40, 66-68). In his *Exercises* he gave the practice two structures and methods which were original and have been widely used ever since. The Particular Examination (24-31) is concentrated on a single objective, such as correcting a sin, or one's predominant fault, or a group of non-sinful defects. Thus during the Exercises it can well be focused on the failings or negligences connected with the periods of prayer, or the Additional Directives, or the like. The General Examination (32-44) and its method (43) are aimed at self-purification and also at preparation for confession. On the General Examination see *DSpir*, 4: cols. 1789-1837; on the Particular Examination, cols. 1838-1849.

24. In Ignatius' day breakfast was very light and was not taken by all. In summer the main meal (*comida*, dinner) was taken at 10:00 A.M. and supper (*cena*) at 6:00 P.M.; in winter at 11:00 and 7:00 (*DalmIgn*, p. 267).

25. The g probably means the first letter of the Italian *giorno*, day. The seven letters "g" indicate the days of the week. To count the faults dots are entered for each day, on the top line for the morning and on the bottom line for the evening.

26. In the 1500s the ordinary faithful confessed only once a year, but in an extraordinarily detailed manner. Penitents prepared themselves, sometimes for several days, by reading books called "confessionals," which had long lists of sins. Their use entailed a review of the catechism and much moral theology. The accusation of sins was unusually long, went into more details and circumstances than necessary, and was sometimes made in writing. Ignatius' own confession at Montserrat is an example. It was made in writing and lasted three days (*Autobiog*, 17). In 32-44 he sketches aids to help exercitants prepare for confession.

27. Cassian made virtually this same observation in his Conference 2 on Discrimination of Spirits: "There are three sources of our thoughts. They come from God, the devil, and ourselves" (PL 49: col. 508). However, the source from which Ignatius drew his own statement is unknown.

28. The Latin Vulgate translation adds this clarification: "with evil intention or serious harm to the person's reputation" (*DalmMan*, p. 65).

29. Here too the Vulgate adds: "Among sins of speech could be listed those of ridiculing, insulting, and the like, which the giver of the Exercises can develop as he deems necessary" (ibid.).

30. *Conciencia* can mean consciousness as well as conscience. An insightful and widely used article on this exercise is George A. Aschenbrenner, "Consciousness Examen," *Review for Religious* 31 (1972): 13-21.

The Meditations of the First Week

31. Here begin the exercises properly so called of the First Week, "on the sins" (4). This Week engages the exercitant in the purification of the soul from sin and inclinations to it. Sin is the attempt to frustrate God's plan of creation which has been pondered in the Principle and Foundation. Ignatius presents a global view of sin, its history, our role in that history, and Christ's role in it (see 53; also *BibThSpEx*, pp. 136-165). Ignatius starts with the sins of the angels and of our first parents and comes down to the exercitant's own personal sins. Thus he induces the retreatant into viewing his or her sins and future role against that background of God's plan of salvation unfolding in the history of salvation. He or she learns how evil functions in its effort to impede the divine salvific plan, and how to cope with evil in one's own life.

"Meditation"

In this first meditation, too, Ignatius explains in detail "meditation," the first of his two chief methods of prayer which he teaches in the *Exercises*. It is discursive mental prayer especially suited to "beginners" (*incipientes*) in the purgative way or stage of spiritual growth, who usually need to reason out principles and to form basic convictions. He shows them how to proceed by using their mental powers of memory, intellect, and will. He will similarly teach his second fundamental method, "contemplation" as he uses the term, early in the Second Week in 101-117 below.

32. The preparatory prayer and preludes, each lasting a minute or so at the beginning of a prayer period, are means of recollecting oneself and performing the prayer in a better, reverential manner. Throughout the *Exercises* Ignatius considers them to be of great importance.

33. "Intentions, actions, and operations": Taken together, these three words mean "all my physical and mental efforts during this prayer period." Ignatius prescribes this same preparatory prayer before all the prayer periods in the Exercises. Intention is the directing of the will to an end. "Actions" can be understood as exterior activities, and "operations" as interior or mental activities (*DalmMan*, p. 69).

34. *Composición*, used 13 times in the *Exercises*, means for Ignatius the mental act of putting things together. This act is done by the exercitant in order to put herself or himself into the right disposition for praying. The manner of doing this and the things to be put together vary according to context and often involve use of the imagination. In *SpDiar*, 144, after struggling with distractions Ignatius wrote, "I composed myself" for Mass. This chance remark has turned out to be a commentary which clearly shows the purpose of his *composición*.

35. *Todo el compósito*: The description of human beings as composed of body and soul was commonplace terminology of the scholasticism which Ignatius studied at Paris for 3 1/2 years; and philosophers and preachers alike often spoke of the "corruptible body." Mark 1:13 states that Christ was in the desert for forty days, tempted by Satan "among the beasts." It is easy to see how these ideas, so commonplace in his day, had a direct influence on Ignatius. In his search for a vivid image to make the abstract thought of this prelude more concrete and by it to stir up the shame and confusion he counsels the retreatant to pray for in the second prelude immediately below, he imaginatively combined the above notions, probably without reflecting where he first learned them. His image was effective for his purpose.

However, it has also led some persons to find in his image a

Neoplatonic or other exaggerated dualism which regarded the separate existence of the soul as the ideal and the body as a prison of the soul. If such influences existed, they were far weaker than those from the Bible and scholasticism. On them see W. Ong, "St. Ignatius' Prison Cage and the Existentialist Situation," *The Barbarian Within* (New York, 1954), pp. 242-259. See also n. 19 on 23 above.

36. "What I want and desire": In this Prelude the retreatant focuses on what he or she hopes to obtain in the prayer period, and asks God for what he or she genuinely wants (see, e. g., 48, 55, 65, etc.). Throughout the Exercises Ignatius brings in this prayer of desire in the second or third prelude. Genuine desire is of great importance in his spirituality. On it see E. E. Kinerk, "Eliciting Great Desires: Their Place in the Spirituality of the Society of Jesus," *Studies in the Spirituality of Jesuits* 16 (Nov. 1984); also *BibThSpEx*, Index II, p. 375 s.v. "desire." On the preludes, see A. Brou, *Ignatian Methods of Prayer* (Milwaukee, 1949), pp. 94-108.

37. On this method of meditation or discursive mental prayer, see Brou, *Ignatian Methods*, pp. 109-122; L. Classen, "The Exercise with the Three Powers of the Soul" in *Ignatius, His Personality and Spiritual Heritage*, ed. F. Wulf (St. Louis, 1977), pp. 237-271; J. de Guibert, *The Theology of the Spiritual Life* (New York, 1953), pp. 195-197; A. Tanquerey, *The Spiritual Life* (Baltimore, 1930), pp. 319-315. Other Exercises which are meditations begin in 45, 55, 65, 136.

38. Ignatius took this statement from Ludolph's *Vita Jesu Christi*, I, ch. 2, no. 3, which states: "Adam was formed in the area of Damascus near Hebron." Hebron is twenty miles south of Jerusalem, in a valley named Damascus.

On the updated theological doctrine expressed through the story of Adam and Eve see John L. McKenzie, *Dictionary of the Bible* (Milwaukee, 1965), s.v. "Adam," p. 12, "fall," pp. 271-273, and "sin," 817-821, esp. on original sin, pp. 818-821; see also, *NDicTh*, s.v. "original sin"; and, in *The New Jerome Biblical Commentary* (1989), J. A. Fitzmyer, pp. 1,402-1,403 on original sin; p. 1,400 on the Redemption; and pp. 1397-1,398 on the effects of the Christ event, justification.

39. The colloquy is another constant element in Ignatian methods of prayer. On it see Brou, *Ignatian Methods*, 119-121.

Although it is especially fitting as the conclusion of prayer, it may be made at any time during it. See the *Directory* of 1599, ch. 15, no. 5.

40. In this colloquy the exercitant is led directly to Christ, whose presence is supposed throughout the entire First Week. The exercitant may turn to him at any time. On the Christology of the First Week, see *BibThSpEx*, pp. 161-163; H. Rahner, *Ignatius the Theologian* (New York, 1965), pp. 53-93.

41. The preceding meditation showed the exercitant the whole history of sin, from the angels to some soul lost forever; this second exercise shows to the retreatant her or his own place, actual and potential, in that history. Ignatius did not use "one's own" in his title, but that is clearly what he meant. It is attested by the whole context and by the many times he uses the first person throughout this exercise, e.g., *mis* in the second prelude, *he habitado* in 56, *yo* and *me* in 58.

42. *Proceso*, literally, a trial in court or its record. Ignatius' figure is that of an arraignment in a law court, when the list of charges against the accused is read. He further develops this figure in 74 below.

43. The descriptions given here and in 63 make clear that the repetitions are not a mere reviewing of the preceding meditation or contemplation, but rather an affective assimilation, a deepening personalization of one's previous interior experiences.

44. *Mundo*. Three meanings of "world" occur in the *Exercises*: (1) the inhabited earth; (2) all human beings; (3) any person or thing hindering one's advance to God, as here in 63 (*DalmMan*, p. 201).

45. These three petitions are a résumé of the fruit of the meditation, now reviewed in intimate conversations with Mary, Jesus, and the Father.

46. The prayer Soul of Christ (*Anima Christi*), found in one form already in a manuscript of about 1370, was widely used in the 16th century and Ignatius presupposes its text as known. But today it is not so well known. Hence many modern editors print it at the beginning of the *Exercises*. Its author is unknown. In missals it has often been printed in the thanksgiving after Communion, until recently with the title "The Prayer of St.

Ignatius." This description probably arose because he popularized the prayer through his *Exercises* (*DSpir* 1: cols. 670-671). The text is on p. 20 above.

47. To 71 the Latin Vulgate translation adds: "If the director thinks it expedient for the exercitant's spiritual profit, other meditations can be added here, for example, on death, other penalties of sin, judgment, and the like; one should not think them forbidden, even though they are not listed here." To give them has been customary in and since Ignatius' day, particularly in retreats preached to groups. Their use is not equally frequent today.

48. *Adiciones*, literally "Additions." To bring out what they clearly are in this context, we translate this vague term by "additional directives." They inculcate practices, an environment, and a mental attitude to enable the exercitant to keep his or her attention focused undistractedly on the effort to commune intimately with God and to find what is being sought. However, they are means rather than ends and should be varied and adapted to circumstances and personalities.

49. This is another key principle of great importance in all Ignatian methods of prayer. On it see also 2:3,4 and 121-126, 254 below; Coathalem, pp. 120-121; and esp. W. Longridge, *The Spiritual Exercises . . . with a Commentary* (London, 1919), pp. 71-72; 258-262. Through its prudent application any portion of an Ignatian prayer period may, with God's grace, lead to increasingly simplified mental prayer. For example, the satisfying pause in a contemplation (according to Ignatius' meaning in 101-117) may become the gateway into acquired contemplation and even into infused contemplation if God should grant it. (For an explanation of this traditional terminology, see *IgnCLWS*, pp. 60-63.) All of Ignatius' statements on the repetitions and application of the senses (121-126) are relevant here, as also his letters of Sept. 20, 1548, to Borgia (*LettersIgn*, pp. 180-181), and of Sept. 11, 1536, to Teresa Rejadell (ibid., p. 24). The psychological wellspring motivating use of this key principle is genuine desire, (on which see n. 36 on 48 above). See also note 66 on 76, below.

50. *Partes inferiores*: literally, "the lower parts," that is, the sensory faculties and appetites. In scholastic terminology, the one soul has three powers: intellective, sensitive, and vegetative. The "inferior parts" of the soul are those faculties or powers in

regard to which the soul depends directly on the bodily senses for their operation. See St. Thomas, *ST* 3, 14, 1; 46, 7; also *DalmMan*, p. 204; and n. 59 on *sensualidad* in 97 below. Christ in his Passion experienced pain in the "inferior parts" or faculties of his human soul. The "higher parts" or faculties are the memory, intellect, and will.

THE SECOND WEEK
The Kingdom of Christ

51. This bracketed title, "The Contemplation of the Kingdom of Jesus Christ," is taken from text *V*, the Latin Vulgate. By his very use of this Vulgate with approval from 1548 to 1556 Ignatius has given an indication of what he understood this exercise as a whole to be; and "the Kingdom" has remained its common designation ever since. In the Autograph text, *A*, Ignatius himself wrote no title for this complete exercise. "The Call of the Temporal King" has occasionally been taken to be such a title, but in fact it applies only to the less important Part I. This exercise is within the Second Week, but it is somewhat like an introductory chapter to it. For in 101 Ignatius calls the Incarnation the first Exercise on the First day (see the *Directory*, ch. 19, no. 1).

52. With the exercises of the purgative way now completed, the exercitant here advances into the more constructive work of the illuminative and unitive ways, especially by contemplating Christ in the Second, Third, and Fourth Weeks. The present exercise, made on a transitional day of relative repose with only two prayer periods prescribed, is Ignatius' introduction to the rest of the retreat. He gives here an inspirational bird's-eye view of Christ as King, his Kingdom, and his mission as they will be contemplated in detail throughout these Weeks. This exercise functions as a second Foundation for the rest of the Exercises (*Directory* of 1599, ch. 19, no. 1), to which it gives an explicit Christological orientation. Its purpose is to stir up enthusiasm, generosity, and desire to follow Christ in love and to accept his invitation to share in his saving mission (91:4; 98). This thrust becomes especially clear in the suggested offering to which it leads: Eternal Lord, I offer myself to labor with you in your mission, no matter what the cost.

53. This is an echo of Matt. 9:35 and 10:5. The word "castles"

is an anachronism. Those which Ignatius saw were built by the crusaders. However, Christ did see Herod's grandiose constructions.

54. This parable (92-94) is merely an aid to the reality in the Second Part and should be meditated with relative brevity. There have been many interpretations of it and many comparisons with other leaders. Cusson aptly views the parable as a résumé of Ignatius' own experience with its fantasies and dreams. Before his conversion he eagerly pursued worldly glory by serving dukes and through them Ferdinand V or Charles I; but he transferred his enthusiastic loyalty to the Eternal King (*BibThSpEx*, pp. 180-181). Similarly, an exercitant can take his or her past life with its dreams and fantasies and think of dedicating them to Christ by answering his call.

55. This meditation has a coloring of crusader mentality which is easily seen in the parable. On crusade spirituality in Ignatius, see Hans Wolter in *Ignatius, His Personality*, ed. Wulf, pp. 97-134.

56. The parallel announced here is not fully carried out. In Part I, the parable, we have (1) the king, (2) his call, and (3) the response. But in the more important application in Part II, the corresponding points are (1) the King *and* his call, (2) the first response of the wholeheartedly dutiful, and (3) a second response which includes the first and raises it to greater heights: that of those eagerly generous to give distinguished service. As the second prelude makes clear, the chief focus of this contemplation is on these two degrees of generosity in the responses to Christ's call. The states of life are not explicitly treated until 135, although they are foreshadowed along the way, as can be seen in the offering in 98.

57. This is an invitation from Christ to accept a role with himself in his saving mission, the spreading of his Kingdom— which in its concrete reality is exercised through his Church, his Kingdom and Mystical Body (1 Cor. 12:11-31; Eph. 1:23; Col. 1:18). See *BibThSpEx*, pp. 205-213. The reign of a king who has no organized kingdom seems rather anomalous. Especially in Matthew's Gospel (e.g., 13:36-43, 16:18, 18:17) the "reign of God" (*regnum*) is shown to subsist in an organized society, the Church (*ecclesia*, 16:18, 18:17), whose nature is further described by parables (13:24-30, 36-43, 47-50). See McKenzie, *Dictionary of the*

Bible, s.v. "kingdom," p. 480, and s.v. "Matthew," p. 556. The "reign of God," however, extends more widely than the organized kingdom, the Church.

58. This is an example of the Ignatian principle of counterattack (*agere contra*), which is inculcated also in 13, 97, 325, 350, 351. We not only stand firm against the temptation or desolation but also try to turn the seemingly bad situation into an occasion for greater generosity, praise, and service of God. On this, see Jules Toner, *A Commentary on St. Ignatius' Rules for the Discernment of Spirits* (St. Louis, 1982), pp. 160-162; 198-199.

59. *Sensualidad* is a term of scholasticism, meaning the appetitive faculty of the sensitive part of the soul, i.e., the soul as operating through the senses (see n. 50 on 87). Aquinas states that "the motion of sensuality is a certain inclination of the bodily senses, since we desire things which are apprehended through the bodily senses" (*ST* 1, 81, 1, ad 1). Hence by *sensualidad* Ignatius means basically the sense appetites, and in the present context the sensitivities, sensibilities, or inclinations of one's human nature. Though the term is sometimes applied to excess in food, drink, or sex, it does not of itself imply excess. It easily comes to mean the likes and dislikes of our human nature, which are often emotional. In 87 and here in 97 it refers to our human nature with its emotions, e.g., attachments, longings, inclinations, etc. They may be rightly ordered in accordance with the Principle and Foundation, or they may be ill ordered by being opposed to a greater good or by being sinful. For many a retreatant the sensitivities will be repugnances, human desires which tend to lower generosity.

60. Actual poverty is the lack of material goods; spiritual poverty is detachment from them whether one has them or not. It also includes our emptiness before God and need of him for spiritual progress. For details, see n. 72 on 146 below. To reason them out is more appropriate there in the discursive meditation rather than in the colloquy here.

61. A slavishly literal translation, "The First Day *and* First Contemplation," is misleading and misses what Ignatius really means. The first day has four more contemplations, including the Nativity (110-126).

"Contemplation"

In this and the following exercise on the Nativity Ignatius gives his most detailed explanation of "contemplation" as he uses this term in the *Exercises*. It is his second basic method of mental prayer and consists in attending to the persons, their words, and their actions, largely by use of the imagination. In general, contemplation is viewing or gazing and it stimulates reflections and emotions. Since this method leads to reflections it can be and often is discursive mental prayer. Ordinarily, however, it is an easier and more affective kind of prayer, especially suitable for the contemplation of scenes from the Gospels. On it see Brou, *Ignatian Methods*, pp. 130-145; *DeGuiJes*, pp. 133-137, 548, 607; Tanquerey, *The Spiritual Life*, nos. 991, 467-468; Longridge, pp. 257-262. Contemplation in this sense prepares for but is somewhat different from what many writers on ascetical or mystical theology term "acquired contemplation" or "infused contemplation" (on which see *IgnCLWS*, pp. 62-63; *DeGuijes*, pp. 605-609, and the index, s.v. Contemplation, Stages, Ways).

62. After viewing the fall of Adam and his descendants in the First Week, Ignatius here moves into the next great stage in the history of salvation: the Incarnation, Nativity, and subsequent hidden life.

Three Time Periods.
The First of Them: Days 1 through 3 (101-134)

At this point it is important for those reading or studying the *Exercises* to attend to the structure which Ignatius prescribed for the exercises performed within the remainder of the Second Week. His text itself, though applicable to persons in any state, is in its structure directly adjusted to the ideal case of a generous exercitant who is deliberating about the choice of a state of life in a closed retreat. For such a one the coming exercises will be divided into three time periods, all of them preparatory to the election or decision, which often is made at some time in the third period.

The first period, with five contemplations a day, will consist of three days devoted to contemplations on the Incarnation and hidden life, to bring the exercitant to growing affective attachment to Christ in his poverty and humility. The second period will consist of one day, the fourth. It starts with the brief Preamble to the Consideration of States of Life (135), followed by the discursive and other mental prayer in the Two Standards and Three Classes of Persons (135-157). These meditations aim to make sure of the attitude proper for a sound election, especially the indifference in case it has been weakened by subtle temptations or self-deceit. The third period consists of days 5 to 8 or up to day 12, devoted to contemplation on the life of Christ and simultaneous considerations on the election. See n. 83 below on 158.

63. *Historia*: In the 1500s this word meant "a narration and exposition of past events" to which an author sometimes added his or her own explanations or comments (Covarrubias, *Tesoro* [1611], p. 692). For Ignatius it means "the authentic basis" of the gospel narrative, which is sometimes supplemented by imagined details; and (2) it is sometimes the preliminary explanation of a topic—given here in 102 by use of the imagination. His usage of the word is nuanced according to contexts.

64. *Se haga hombre*: This venerable phrase, stemming from John 1:14 and occurring in the Creeds, really means the Second Person should become "also a human being." Before the Incarnation he possessed the divine nature and operated by it. After it he remained divine but possessed also a human nature and operated by it.

65. "Interior knowledge" is not limited to someone's external features such as age, height, etc., but goes farther to items such as his or her scale of values, opinions on the meaning of life, ideals, and the like. It is intimate and easily becomes suffused with love. It has been beautifully described as the knowledge of the heart. See Coathalem, p. 148.

The Application of the Senses

66. The application of the senses is another method of mental prayer. It has a long previous history (*DSpir*,1, cols, 822-826) but is described here for the first time in the *Exercises*. In it there is less reasoning and drawing of conclusions, and a more restful manner of absorbing in an affective and more passive way the fruit of the previous contemplations of the day. It is "not discursive, but merely rests in the sensible qualities of things, such as the sights, sounds, and the like, and finds in them

enjoyment, delight, and spiritual profit" (*Directory* of 1599, ch. 20, no. 3). It can become a transition from meditation into contemplation (ibid. col. 810). Many exercitants, coming from the previous contemplations with warm devotion, find their love nourished by these sensible objects (ibid., no. 4). This method is less fatiguing than meditation or contemplation, and is therefore done in the evening when the exercitant is presumably tired. In his letter of Sept. 11, 1536, to Teresa Rejadell Ignatius makes observations applicable here (*LettersIgn*, p. 24).

Polanco pointed out in his Directory (nos. 65-66, in *DirSpEx*, pp. 300-302) that "senses" in *SpEx* 121 can be interpreted to mean either (1) the bodily or imaginative senses or (2) the mental or "spiritual" senses. The first interpretation, he states, is more suitable for use with retreatants less experienced in prayer, and the second (which is based on St. Bonaventure's *Ascent of the Mind to God*) for those more experienced.

In points 1 and 2 Ignatius writes of the imaginative senses, sight and hearing, not exclusively but as joined to the intellect and will. In point 3 he passes on to the "spiritual senses," the intellect and will as functioning especially through their intuitive activities. In their operation they stimulate pious affections, and sometimes discover features somewhat similar to those perceived by the imaginative senses. On this topic see Coathalem, pp. 153-158; *DeGuiJes*, p. 246; Brou, *Ignatian Methods*, pp. 146-167; H. Rahner, *Ignatius the Theologian* (New York, 1968), pp. 181-213; *DSpir* 1: cols. 810-828, esp. 826-828; other references in *Obrascompl*, p. 236.

What Ignatius says about application of the senses (121-126), and—far more important—the use of his key principle of dwelling on any relished experience in prayer "until I am fully satisfied, without any anxiety to go on" (76, with n. 49 above), open the way into the contemplation or loving gaze which is termed "active" or "acquired"; and also, if God should so will, into that contemplation called "passive" or "infused" or "mystical." (For an explanation of this classical terminology, see *IgnCLWS*, pp. 61-63; or *DeGuiJes*, pp. 605-609, 640, 686.)

For many and perhaps most persons, progress in mental prayer includes a growth toward simplicity. They advance through discursive meditation and prayer increasingly affective into the loving gaze called contemplation. In real life, of course, these forms of prayer are mingled together with great spontaneity; there are overlappings and veerings back and forth. Since

Ignatius' *Exercises* sprang in no small measure from the notes which he prepared for his conversations with lay persons whom he was encouraging to intensive spiritual living; and since, too, many of these were deliberating about choice of a state of life, it was natural for him to begin by teaching them discursive meditation. They needed, sometimes to purify themselves from sin, and virtually always to clarify their convictions and learn norms and habits for sound choice. Hence in the *Exercises* he explained in detail methods of discursive meditation (45-54), affective contemplation (101-117), and application of the senses (120-126). By these, especially as supplemented by his key principle in 76 and 254, he led retreatants into contemplation either acquired or infused if God should so will; but in the *Exercises* he did not treat this contemplation in any detail.

In this he is an interesting contrast to St. Teresa. She was speaking or writing chiefly for the sisters of her own contemplative order, usually persons of advanced spiritual experience. Hence she devoted most of her time and space to contemplation —seemingly with a hope that through this preparation God would grant to many of her sisters mystical gifts similar to her own. In these circumstances she naturally gave comparatively little space to discursive meditation or affective prayer with multiple acts. Much the same can be said of St. John of the Cross, since he too was writing especially for Teresa's nuns or his own Carmelite friars.

Ignatius was a mystic who received from God lofty gifts of infused contemplation and accompanying mystical phenomena, as his *Spiritual Diary* amply reveals. By his Letters too he directed and encouraged other mystics such as St. Francis Borgia. Nevertheless he also thought that such gifts are not necessary for all; and experiences such as those with Onfroy and Oviedo (*DeGuiJes*, pp. 87-88) made him fear illusions in some who alleged that they were mystics. One can sincerely and successfully attain advanced spiritual growth even if God does not grant infused gifts. De Guibert aptly quotes Brou's summary statement of Ignatius' thought and practice pertaining to mystical contemplation and phenomena. "First, a profound esteem for these 'very holy gifts' of God, but an esteem which does not go so far that it makes the mystical states a necessary condition of attaining perfection; second, a great reserve in speaking about these states; and third, a fear of illusions" (*DeGuiJes*, p. 562).

The Second Time Period: Day 4 (135-157)

67. *Estados,* in this context, means the states of life, as the Vulgate shows by translating it *statuum seu generum vitae diversorum.* Section 135 is a brief transitional introduction to the second period of the Second Week, ordinarily occurring on its fourth day. Attention is now turned to the election expected to come some days later, probably near the end of the third period (days 5 to 8, but perhaps up to day 12 [161]). During those deliberations the exercitant is likely to experience subtle temptations, both from the devil with his deceits and from his or her own human weakness, likes, dislikes, or self-deceit. Here much reasoning becomes necessary. To help the retreatant to the right dispositions for making a sound choice of a state of life or for serious pursuit of spiritual progress in whatever state one will be in, on day 4 Ignatius presents two exercises containing much discursive mental prayer: the Two Standards (136) and the Three Classes of Persons (149).

68. The states of life have been divided in many ways. In 134 and 135 Ignatius uses only two states, the observance of the commandments and that of the search for evangelical perfection —i.e., life in the world and religious life. That division, used by Christ with the rich young man (Mark 1:17-27), was common almost till the present time and was practical for the ideal retreatant whom Ignatius' text envisaged. But in modern times many have found those two categories unsatisfactory, and a gradually growing opinion found expression in Vatican Council II: "All Christians in any state or walk of life are called to the fullness of Christian life and to the perfection of love" (On the Church, no. 40). This more comprehensive teaching updates Ignatius' views but does not conflict with them. In fact, he equivalently states the new doctrine at the end of 135: "to come to perfection in whatsoever state of life God may grant us to elect." One practical division for retreatants deliberating about a state of life today is: the states of (1) marriage; (2) single persons in the world; (3) diocesan priesthood; (4) religious life as a priest, brother, or sister. For an exemplification of its use in counseling, see G. E. Ganss, "Prudence and Vocations," *Review for Religious,* 22 (1962): 434-442; also, "'Active Life' or 'Contemplative Life'?" ibid., 22 (1963): 53-56.

The Two Standards

69. *Banderas*, "standards" in the sense of flags or banners around which the followers of the respective leaders rally. This justly famous meditation, to which Ignatius attached great importance, is very imaginatively presented. It seems to be original with Ignatius, though the theme of opposition between the forces of good and evil is frequent throughout the centuries. St. Paul counseled: "Put on the armor of God so that you may be able to stand firm against the tactics of the devil. For our struggle is not with flesh and blood but with the principalities, ... the evil spirits in the heavens" (Eph. 6:11). Augustine viewed history as a struggle between the City of God, the sum total of human beings and angels who are living according to God's directing laws, and the City of This World, the sum total of human beings and angels who live according to their own desires rather than his. In the Lives of the Saints which Ignatius read at Loyola in 1521, Jacobus de Voragine wrote a paragraph (quoted in *IgnCLWS*, p. 18) describing Augustine's City of God: "He also treats of the two cities, Jerusalem and Babylon, and their kings," Christ and the devil. Jacobus' paragraph and Ignatius' Two Standards have much the same tenor of thought. It is at least possible that Ignatius read that paragraph and found in it the germ of his Two Standards. As is shown in *IgnCLWS*, p. 18, both the Kingdom and the Two Standards were part of the nucleus of the primitive *Exercises*.

70. The aim of this meditation, as the third prelude clearly shows, is to study the tactics of the two leaders, Christ and Lucifer.

71. Pride, the capital "sin," is a source of myriad other offenses (see n. 11 on 18 above). These steps in 146 are examples of the devil's tactics, particularly suited for tempting a person who is deliberating about self-dedication to God. Satan also has innumerable other tactics; and each exercitant does well to think of those which might be used against himself or herself. With obvious changes the same holds true of the tactics of Christ in 146 below.

72. *Pobreza actual*, "actual poverty," is that really existing, and not merely potential (*DalmMan*, pp. 189, 202); the actual lack of material goods. *Pobreza spiritual*, "spiritual poverty," is that of

the "poor in spirit" of the beatitude (Matt. 5:3). Des Freux's Latin translation of 98 in the Vulgate, "with poverty of spirit as well as of things" (*cum paupertate tum spiritus tum rerum*), makes clear Ignatius' meaning in both these terms, so important for his spirituality. See also n. 60 on 98 above.

In Old and New Testament times the vast majority of people were poor and had a very low standard of living. Only a few were rich and there was virtually no middle class. Christ wanted his followers to have poverty of spirit, that is, interior detachment from material goods, whether they possessed them or not, so that they might have heavenly riches (Matt. 6:19-21, 13:22). He also spoke of the religious value of the actual poverty of the devout poor and taught them how to view it, e.g., in his discourse on Providence (Matt. 6:25-33). Such actual poverty (today termed also real, material, or effective) can be a sign of and means to interior detachment when it is inspired by trust in God. What matters above all, Christ concludes, is to seek to cooperate with God's plan of salvation: "Seek first the kingdom of God and his righteousness, and all these things will be given you besides" (Matt. 6:33). (See Léon-Dufour, *Dictionary of Biblical Theology*, p. 437.)

The term actual poverty can also mean the vowed poverty of a religious institute. In 147 Des Freux translates *pobreza actual* by *in rerum expoliatione*, "the deprivation of one's goods"; and in 157 by *in rerum abdicatione*, "the renouncing of one's goods," a canonical term for vowed poverty. Hence for one deliberating about entering religious life there is in 146 and 147 at least a hint or connotation of canonical poverty. Ignatius left it to the exercitant to take whichever meaning was more useful to him or her at the time.

However, to learn the full profound scope of what poverty means for Ignatius, we must go beyond the *Exercises* and consider his use of *pobreza* in his *Constitutions*, Letters, and other writings. Then we see it as the profoundly humble attitude of a person who "has emptied his or her self of the love of earthly things" and "filled that self with God and his gifts" (*EppIgn* I:575, cited in Iparraguirre, *Vocabulario de Ejercicios Espirituales: Ensayo de Hermenéutica Ignaciana*, p. 183). Iparraguirre treats this at length, largely by citations from Ignatius (ibid. pp. 184-190). Cusson writes about this as the "absolute poverty of our spiritual condition" (*BibThSpEx*, p. 215; see also the Index, s.v. "Poverty"). To sum up, in its profound sense for Ignatius, poverty is our total emptiness before God and our dependence on him for any and all spiritual progress.

73. Humility is the opposite of pride, hence characteristic of Christ as the opposite of Satan. Further, humility is a first step toward any and all virtues. Ignatius will soon develop this traditional teaching further in his three ways of being humble (165-168).

The Three Classes of Persons

74. This meditation is about three persons, each of whom is typical of a class or group of others who think and act in a similar manner, namely, (1) the postponers; (2) the compromisers; and (3) the wholeheartedly indifferent, those open to whatever option will after deliberation turn out to be the better. Each of these three is endeavoring to discard an attachment for something which, though legitimate, is an obstacle to a greater good and is therefore somewhat disordered. The object of this attachment escapes being sinful, but it is not "what is more conducive" to salvation and perfection (23).

The aim of the meditation is to help the exercitant toward embracing what is better for herself or himself; in other words, to prepare one's dispositions for the coming deliberations on the election, by confirming and perfecting the indifference acquired in the Foundation. Thus he or she will become open to learn and embrace whatever will be discovered to be more to God's glory—as the title and second prelude explicitly indicate. The election is expected to come, not in this meditation, but a few days later, i.e., during or after the deliberations treated in 169-189.

Unfortunately Ignatius' Spanish text of this meditation is overly terse, uses a puzzling vocabulary, and becomes a prime example of his sometimes unpolished style. It has been a source of disagreement among translators from the First Latin Version to the present day. Time after time they must choose one of several meanings, each of which is possible. Moreover, although the principles of indifference and choice which he is exemplifying are reasonably clear and already known from the Foundation, there is danger that a retreatant will spend more time and energy in efforts to figure out precisely what Ignatius means to say than in grasping and applying the spiritual principles which he is confirming here. Our translation hopes at least to minimize this unfortunate danger and to make the principles stand out prominently.

75.   The first of the above-mentioned difficulties occurs already in 149, which serves as the title. The Autograph, *A*, has *tres binarios de hombres*, which means literally "three binaries of persons," i.e., at first sight "three pairs"; and in each of the three points it has *binario* in the singular, e.g., "the first pair." But what did Ignatius really mean by *binario* here? For clues we turn to the early translations. We meet great variety. In the First Latin version used in Paris in the 1530s, the translator (probably Ignatius himself) also has in the title, 149, "meditation on the three pairs of persons" (*meditatio trium binariorum hominum*) and in the first point, 153, "the first pair" (*primus binarius*). In the Latin Vulgate of 1548, translated under Ignatius' eyes and approved by his continual use, Des Freux translated *binario* in the title by the collective noun *classis*: "on the three classes or groups of persons, that is, how they differ" (*de tribus hominum classibus seu differentiis*). In the points 153-155 he uses "the first class" (*prima classis*). All this makes clear that Ignatius' thought is manifestly about groups or classes or kinds of persons, each one of whom has the characteristics common to its class and is typical of it.

Since the Spanish text of the *Exercises* was not printed until 1615 and the early Jesuits used only the Latin Vulgate from 1548 to 1615, the "three classes of men" became the common designation of this meditation in the early Directories and virtually all treatises on the *Exercises* from 1548 until the present. Hence like Des Freux, in our title (149) we translate *binarios* by "classes" (see Iparraguirre in *Obrascomp*, p. 240, n. 98).

However, we gain much further light on what *binario* meant to Ignatius by considering his environmental background at the University of Paris. In the 15th and 16th centuries (as also today) moralists in solving their cases of conscience used fictitious typical persons and called them a "pair" (*binarius*, Spanish *binario*); e.g., Titius and Bertha in a marriage case, or Titius and Caius in one about justice (*DalmMan*, p. 191; *Obrascompl*, p. 240). The Latin *binarius, a, um* means a person or thing belonging to a group of two (e.g., *binarius homo* in 149 of the First Latin Version). It can also be used as a noun to mean one such person, e.g., Titius or Bertha. Further, Ignatius' own term here (the singular *binario* in the Spanish and *binarius* in text *P*[1]) can be a Latinism of his, like his constant use of *ánima* instead of *alma*. Hence his Spanish *binario* and his Latin *binarius* can mean one such typical person (e.g., Titius) or a pair of them (e.g., Titius and Caius of the Parisian moralists). In either case Ignatius in this exercise was writing about three persons each of whom is typical of a class or category. He was setting up a case in spirituality to exemplify his spiritual principles about indifference and decision. Against this background, we translate *binarios* in 148 as "typical persons"; and in 153, 154, and 155 we translate *binario* as a "person typical of a class."

This translator agrees with Gueydan and his team of experts who also interpret *binario* as singular, a *"homo binarius"* (*Exercices*, p. 87). In 149 they translate the title by *"méditation des trois hommes,"* and in 153 *el primer binario* by *"le premier homme."*

When Ignatius is writing about the exercitant in the second and third preludes and in the note after the meditation, he uses the first person: "that I may desire and know" (151), "I will ask for the grace" (152), "when we feel an inclination against actual poverty" (157). But when he is writing about the typical persons in the points (153-155), he uses the third person (*el primo binario, primus binarius*), possibly because some exercitants might more easily reason objectively about some person other than themselves.

76. *Historia*: Moralists use fictitious typical persons to set up and solve "cases of conscience." Here Ignatius' "history" is an exposition which sets up a comparable "case of spirituality," that about the three persons typical of their respective classes. See also n. 63 on 102 above.

77. That is, although it is licit to keep the money, the motive for retaining it is mingled with an attachment or inclination prompted by self-love rather than the love of God. Therefore this attachment is not yet fully ordered according to the principles of indifference and choice contained in the Foundation (23). This lack of indifference, though not sinful, is a danger or impediment to a greater good.

78. "What is better" (in 149), "more pleasing to the Divine Goodness" (151), "what is more to the glory of the Divine Majesty and the salvation of my soul" here in 152, and "to serve God our Lord better" in 155 are all variant expressions equivalent to Ignatius' norm of choice in the Foundation (23), "what

is more conducive to the end for which we are created." Similar variations of that principle and norm will occur throughout his treatment of the election below in 169-189.

79. *Afecto*: attachment or affection. In 153, 154, 155, and 157 it means also an inclination or propensity (*DalmMan*, p. 189) and could be so translated. Gueydan, *Exercices*, pp. 97-98, translates it by the synonym "*inclination*."

80. Notice the future tense. Ignatius is preparing the retreatant's dispositions for the coming election, for which the deliberations will take place from day 5 onward. He or she is not expected to conclude the election in this meditation. Notice also that this person is not depending on human willpower alone; there is question both of God's impulses on the will through actual graces and of the individual's free decision.

81. This obscure and extensively discussed statement has caused great trouble to commentators and translators. Fortunately, however, in the statement which immediately follows the debated sentence Ignatius makes his thought fully clear. This stands and suffices even if we fail to solve the puzzles in the preceding words.

The obscurity in the first statement arises from *in afecto*, "in affection." That is, in Dalmases' opinion, one is, on one's own part, disposed or willing to relinquish everything (*DalmMan*, p. 103). Roothaan conjectured that *afecto* is an error for *efecto*; one imagines one has given up everything in fact. But all the Spanish manuscripts have *afecto*, and the Latin P^1 has *affectu*. The translation of this passage in the Latin Vulgate seemed excessively free, and a committee appointed by General Congregation V in 1596 to harmonize it with the Autograph gave the interpretation "one carries on like one who has relinquished everything in affection" (*SpEx*MHSJ69, p. 252). Our addition of "[In other words]" in 155:3 is based on *scilicet* in that committee's report.

82. Notice that persons of this third class are perfect examples of the indifference of the Foundation. That, too, is the grace begged in the third prelude (152): "to choose what is more to the glory of the Divine Majesty." What Ignatius teaches in this third point is taught by him also in 16 and 179.

The Third Period: Days 5 through 8 and up to 12 (158-189) Concurrent Deliberations and Contemplations

83. Here on day 5 the third period of the Second Week begins and runs flexibly through days 5 to 7 or up to day 12 (see n. 62 on 101 above). During this period two interacting series of exercises will be carried on parallel to each other: (1) contemplations on the public life of Christ, merely mentioned in 161-164 but with their details presented in 273-287; and (2) considerations on the directives and methods of making a good election (169-189). Early in the period the director will explain the Three Ways of Being Humble (165-168), and more gradually the principles and methods for making a sound election (169-189). Thus the affective spirit of the contemplations and the colloquies on the Three Ways will provide the atmosphere for the deliberations about the election.

84. Notice in 156 through 161 that although there are four or five prayer periods per day, on days 5 to 7 or up to day 12 Ignatius assigns for each day only one gospel topic. Probably his purpose is to avoid too great a multiplicity of thoughts while the exercitant is deliberating about the election.

Three Ways of Being Humble

85. I.e., throughout each whole day during the remaining days while the deliberations on the election are taking place. This protracted pondering will tend to put the retreatant's heart into the indifference which was intellectually perceived in the Foundation and Three Classes, and to keep one from shrinking back if one comes face to face with a choice of something for which repugnance is felt. The love for Christ will be so strong that it will outweigh the repugnance (*Obrascompl*, p. 243).

86. This title is in the manuscript of text *A*, but only as a running head. *Maneras*, manners or ways, could be translated also as kinds, or modes, or degrees, or species; its many varied translations already in Ignatius' day are presented just below.

Ignatius' concept of Three Ways of Being Lovingly Humble is an important characteristic of his spirituality. He presents it, not in the form of a meditation or contemplation, but as a consideration which is to pervade the exercises, and also the time between them, on all the coming days devoted to the election. His aim is to bring the exercitant to great openness to God and to a loving desire to be as like to Christ as possible. He also wants to induce the retreatant to review the principles of the Foundation from the new viewpoint of her or his love of God which has been growing through the contemplations. Here too, as in the Three Classes above, his severely terse style and his terminology have led to interpretations of his doctrine too numerous to be given in detail. A glance at the historical background of the topic and the terms he and his associates used in discussing it are great helps toward discovery of his genuine meaning.

St. Benedict in his Rule explained humility as the opposite of pride (*RB 1980: The Rule of St. Benedict in Latin and English with Notes*, ed T. Fry [Collegeville, 1981], pp. 191-201; ch. 7:1, 2). To reach the summit of humility a monk, knowing himself to be lowly, must climb Jacob's ladder and by twelve steps (*gradus*) arrive at the top, step twelve, by which he attains to perfect *love* of God (ibid., 67). St. Bernard praised this teaching, wrote his own book on *The Steps of Humility*, and in his Sermon 26 (PL, 183: col. 610) observed that humility consists in subjection of our will to that of God. St. Thomas Aquinas too praised Benedict's doctrine, but remarked that the degrees (*gradus*) of humility are variously enumerated by different authors, some having three (*ST* 2-2, 161, 6). For Thomas too humility consists in the subjection of the person to God (ibid., 162, 5). Ignatius is clearly writing in this same tradition of thought and terminology, but we do not know the immediate sources from which he derived his terse treatment here in 165-168, seemingly his own formulation for his own purposes.

In the Autograph text, *A*, Ignatius used in 164 *tres maneras de humildad*, which can be translated accurately as "three kinds" or "three manners" of humility, or "three ways of being humble." The Latin version used in Paris in 1534 calls them *tres species humilitatis*, "three species of humility," and the Vulgate of 1548 *tres modos*, "kinds" or "sorts" of humility. Another interpretative key of great value comes to us from Pedro Ortiz, the doctor of Scripture and ambassador to the papal court who in 1538 made the Exercises for forty days under Ignatius' personal direction at Monte Cassino. In his notes, which no doubt reflect his conversations with Ignatius about the topic, he terms them degrees of *love*: "Three kinds and degrees *of love* of God and desire to obey and imitate and serve His Divine Majesty" ("tres maneras y grados *de amor* de Dios y deseos de obedecer y imitar y servir a su Divina Majestad" [*SpEx*MHSJ69, p. 635; see also *BibThSpEx*, pp. 264-265; italics ours]).

All this put together indicates clearly that Ignatius is dealing successively with *three ways or manners of being lovingly humble*. They can be accurately called kinds, or modes, or ways, or species, or degrees. Particularly his third degree, like Benedict's twelfth step, is a humility permeated with great love, an *humildad amorosa*. Ignatius' first and second degrees are concerned with obedience to God's laws. The third degree, like St. Benedict's twelfth step, rises above law into love.

In Ignatius' *Spiritual Diary* loving humility (*humildad amorosa*) will emerge as the climax of the spiritual and mystical journey which Ignatius records there. The whole second copybook, March 13, 1544, through February 27, 1545, is devoted to this Stage VI of his journey: Walking along a new path, that of loving humility, reverence, and affectionate awe (see the Introduction, in *IgnCLWS*, pp. 233-234, and the texts, ibid., pp. 259-270). To walk habitually along that path was considered by Ignatius as the chief lesson which the Divine Schoolmaster was teaching him in the whole mystical journey recorded in our extant fragment of his *Diary*.

87. *Siendo igual*: This participial phrase is equivalently a conditional clause (if), or a temporal clause (when), or a proviso (provided that). It is a hinge on which the rest of the thought in the sentence depends—although Ignatius placed it last where it comes too late to the mind and its importance is often missed. To make perception of his whole thought easier we have transposed it to the beginning of the sentence. This, however, brought conflict with the new computer-verse numbers and forced us to place the verse recently numbered 2 before that numbered 1. Hence our English sentence moves into verse 2, then back into 1, then again into 2.

88. A person whose attitude is that of the second way of being humble (1) has the indifference of the Foundation and (2) is speaking the language of right reasoning.

89. A person whose attitude is that of the third way of being humble (1) has indifference and (2) is speaking the language of love. His or her attitude is, "I love Christ and want to be as like to him as possible, no matter what the cost." This too is what

she or he has been praying for in the third preludes of the contemplations on the mysteries of Christ, e.g., in 104, 113. Lovers are willing and sometimes even desire to labor or suffer for the beloved, because by such labor or suffering they manifest their love, or increase it, or prove it. They choose the suffering, not as if it were a good or end in itself, but as a means to a higher good. See also note 15 on *Cons*, 101 in *IgnCLWS*, pp. 454-455. Ignatius' Christocentric teaching on love of the Cross is virtually identical with that about the Third Way of Being Lovingly Humble.

The Election

90. *Elección:* The English word "election," in its basic meaning of an act or process of electing, choosing, or selecting (*Webster's New International Dictionary*, unabridged, a Merriam Webster, 1976), accurately translates Ignatius' Spanish term. Among its synonyms, "election implies an end or purpose which requires exercise of judgment" (*Webster's Ninth Collegiate Dictionary* [1986], p. 692). The synonyms "choice," "selection," or "decision" could also be used here. But the term "election" so permeates all the literature on Ignatian spirituality from his day till now that we think it better to retain this traditional term.

91. *Que*, literally "which." But the relative clause is adversative, as the particle *tamen* in the First Latin Version reveals.

92. This Introduction to the Making of an Election supplements the brief Introduction to the Consideration of the States of Life given in 135. Ignatius' characteristic insistence on clarity about ends and means is prominent here in 169; it clearly reminds a retreatant of the Foundation (23). Clarity about what is end and what is means is the indispensable hinge on which a sound election turns. This clarity about the end is a prominent trait of Ignatius' spirituality.

93. This word "consideration" is taken from text P^1. P^2 uses "Note," and V "Introduction." A has nothing. The deliberations envisaged in 170-178 are expected to take place outside the prayer periods but also to be carried into them.

94. Although the main structure of Ignatius' text chiefly concerns a person deliberating about election of a state of life (see *DeGuiJes*, pp. 126), here in 170 (as also in 178 and 189 below)

he broadens the horizon of his text itself and states that the principles for an election may be applied to anything important to the spiritual life and not sinful. As Polanco wrote, "it may be made about a state of life or any other matters" (*SpEx*MHSJ19, p. 30; quoted in *BibThSpEx*, p. 90).

95. The three favorable "Times" are situations or occasions of spiritual experiences. The call mentioned in the First Time (see Matt. 9:9; Acts 9:6, 15; 22:21; 26:17-18), precisely as it is described here, is rare in practice. But experiences more or less similar to it do occur and bring to a person a great peace of soul along with a sense of God's presence and illumination.

96. In the Second Time or situation the retreatant reflects on the "motions" experienced in his or her soul and tries to learn, by applying the rules for the discernment of spirits (313-336) and perhaps from counsel of a director, which motions come from God or a good angel, and which from an evil spirit. One may be stirred by strong experiences of consolation or desolation which manifest the trend of God's call. But there is some danger of illusion or self-deception; hence the need of discernment. Furthermore, in these experiences the will often precedes the intellect. Consequently it is prudent to supplement it by the reasoning in the third time, when the intellect is operating in tranquility under the influence of ordinary grace. On the three times, see Coathalem, pp. 187-190; also, the *Directory*, chs. 26 and 27. The deliberations for the election are ordinarily carried on outside the prayer periods, but also within them where they are made the object of prayer and colloquies. Hence the director should take care not to overburden by too many prayer periods a retreatant who is engaged in an election (see *Directory*, ch. 31, no. 2).

97. In this third time or situation, exemplified in Ignatius' Deliberation on Poverty, the exercitant considers the pros and cons which the question has in regard to attainment of her or his end, the greater service of God. Ordinarily the role of the will and affections is more predominant in the second time, and the role of the intellect in the third time. The two procedures supplement each other. Ignatius in his own practice combined the activities of the second and third times, as his *Spiritual Diary* abundantly shows. See also *DeGuiJes*, s.v. "election," p. 644.

98. In the Foundation (23), Ignatius stated, "I must *make*

myself indifferent," i.e., acquire indifference; but here he writes, "I must *find* myself indifferent," i.e., must ask, "Have I retained the indifference I established in the Foundation and Three Classes?"

99. A prime example of Ignatius' own use of this procedure is found in his Deliberation on Poverty. By putting the pros and cons on paper a person gains clarity of formulation and readier perception of the cumulative weight of each group.

100. Here in 182 *moción racional* and the contrasting *moción sensual* are both cases where *moción* means a change or experience in the soul arising from its own activity (*SpEx*, 32). *Moción rational* is an experience arising from the soul's intellectual activity; and *moción sensual* arises from sensitive human nature (see *DalMan*, pp. 200, 204). This meaning of *moción* should be carefully distinguished from its other meaning (found, e.g., in 6, 313, and 314): an experience in the soul caused by God, an angel, or a devil (see also n. 6 on 6 and n. 143 on 313 below).

101. *Deliberación* is here used by Ignatius in the sense of *determinación*, conclusion (*DalmMan*, p. 193). The Vulgate translates this passage by "conclude the election" (*electionem concludere*).

102. The Second Method calls the affections and imagination into play more than the first, in which the stress is on reasoning.

103. *Forma y medida*: Our translation interprets *forma* here as a manner of doing something, hence, a procedure or method; and *medida* (basically "a measuring rod") as a norm or criterion. In the *Exercises, forma* sometimes means the scholastic "form" as distinct from "matter" (105:2, i.e., a procedure informing the subject matter, and 119), and at other times "a manner of proceeding," a method, or a means (204:1,3; see also 104). Both *forma* and *medida* have many meanings, and translators have understood them differently in many instances. See Gueydan, *Exercices*, pp. 82 and 143; also nn. 126 and 129 on 238 below.

104. I.e., toward reforming one's life in whatever state of life one may be. The suggestions and spirit of this section are especially applicable to those who make annual retreats and aim at spiritual renewal rather than an election of a state of life or another matter of similar importance.

105. To understand this terse directive, stated in a somber negative manner, we must view it against the background from which it springs: Ignatius' desire to bring as much glory and service to God as possible. Rightly ordered self-love, self-will, and self-interest are good qualities, gifts of God which are often obligatory. Hence we should have, recognize, and esteem these gifts, since humility should be based on truth. However, they tend to excess and hence must be continually reexamined and readjusted according to the principles of the Foundation; else they lead to sin or at least hinder greater good. By now a generous retreatant will want to bring God as much glory as possible, and the divestment advised is a means to that end and an attack on the excess. It is a positive procedure.

THE THIRD WEEK

106. In the view of many commentators, after the election or reformation of life has been concluded, the purpose of the last two Weeks is to confirm the exercitant by contemplation of Christ's sufferings in the Third Week and his joy in the Fourth (see, e.g., the *Directory* of 1599, ch. 35, no. 1). Other writers from the time of La Palma (1611) onward find this true but incomplete. Hitherto Ignatius has had the exercitant contemplating God's plan of salvation unfolding in history through the Incarnation, Nativity, and public life. That plan reaches its high point on earth in Christ's redemptive death and resurrection, and the aim of the last two Weeks is the exercitant's profound and intimate association with Christ as he goes through suffering and death into the joy and glory of the risen life (Rom. 6:3-11; Col. 3:1, 2). In this interpretation the Third and Fourth Weeks pick up and develop Christ's call in the Kingdom (95): The disciple "must labor with me, so that through following me in the pain he or she may follow me also in the glory." The retreatant's inspiring task is participation in the whole of the paschal mystery, as described by Vatican Council II: "the work of Christ our Lord in redeeming mankind and giving perfect glory to God. He achieved this task principally by the paschal mystery of his blessed passion, resurrection from the dead, and glorious ascension" (On the Liturgy, nos. 5,6). For more on this view see, e.g., Coathalem, pp. 194-197, 209-212; and esp. Cusson, *BibThSpEx*, pp. 219-222, 233-235, 278-279, 287-292. Ignatius did not use the term "paschal mystery"; but the reality it expresses

is manifestly the very substance of what he proposes for contemplation in the Third and Fourth Weeks.

107. Points 4, 5, and 6 are not necessarily successive new points, but rather viewpoints which can be brought into play on any of the contemplations previously indicated in points 1, 2, and 3.

For some personalities, to spend two full weeks merely contemplating the persons, their words, and actions begets fatigue and desolation. One important solution to this problem, to which these points 4, 5, and 6 (196-198 and 223-224 below) open the way, is to go through the Passion in empathy with Christ not only in regard to its physical activities but also in connection with their significance in God's redemptive plan. That plan is the preeminent message by which the exercitant should be guided during the Exercises; it shines through all the single events suggested for contemplation, and Ignatius wants the retreatant prayerfully to penetrate it as deeply as possible. We today, profiting by modern discoveries in theology, Scriptural exegesis, spirituality, and the like, can often see features of that plan not known to him. But just as he used the best sources he could in his day, our using those of our day is fully in accord with his own example and practice. The subject of our prayer can be not only the gospel events of the Passion and risen life, but also their good effects in our own soul and in the history of salvation. This approach is discussed at length in Cusson's *BibThSpEx*, esp. pp. 278-281; see also 39-43, 219-233, (esp. 220 and 224), 296-301; *DeGuiJes*, pp. 539-543, 564; David Stanley, *A Modern Scriptural Approach to the Spiritual Exercises,* and his *"I Encountered God!" The Spiritual Exercises with the Gospel of St. John* (St. Louis, 1986); and many other writers.

108. The subject matter: i.e., the material being contemplated. Implied, however, is the exercitant's intellectual, emotional, or spiritual disposition resulting from the varying subject matter. See *DalmMan*, p. 200; Calveras, *Vocabulario* on *SpEx*, 4, 48, 49, 74, 105, 109, 204, 225, 226.

109. Text *A* has "Two Classes," an error which is corrected by the "Three" in *V*.

Rules

110. *Reglas.* This is the first of five sets of such directives which Ignatius terms "Rules" in the *Exercises*: those on eating (210-217), on discernment of spirits I (313-317) and II (328-336), on distributing alms (337-344), and on maintaining a genuine filial attitude in the Church (352-370). Each set of these rules was given, not to all retreatants, but according to the needs and desires of individuals (*Directory*, ch. 38, no. 1). In all these cases it is important to attend to what he means by "rules." The classical Latin *regula* has many meanings: (1) a measuring rod and then (2) a pattern, model, example, measure of right and wrong, and hence sometimes (3) an obligation or law. In ecclesiastical Latin *regula* (and the Spanish *regla*) often meant a rule imposing an obligation. But by "rules" in the five sets just mentioned Ignatius cannot mean rules imposing an obligation, since an exercitant has no obligation even to make the Exercises. Therefore he has other meanings according to contexts, such as directives, guidelines, norms, suggestions, or models, as when he wrote that Christ is "our model and rule" (*regla* in 344).

111. By this time the exercitant, growing in eagerness to serve God well, is aware that the human appetites for food and drink are good but tend toward excess, a disorder that must be controlled by the virtue of temperance. Appropriately Ignatius offers directives for an examination of one's situation, correction of possible disorders, and formulation of a plan for the better use of these appetites. His suggestions should be properly adapted to the needs and circumstances of each person, and to modern knowledge of a nutritious diet. Rules 1 through 4 deal with what one eats or drinks; rules 5 through 8 suggest ways of drawing greater spiritual profit from eating or drinking.

The structural connection of these rules with the Third Week is not readily apparent. They are applicable about equally well, with appropriate changes, to all Four Weeks. Why, commentators wonder, did Ignatius place them here? Perhaps, as the *Directory* indicates (ch. 35, no. 13), because there was room for them here; the First and Second Weeks were already crowded with new instructions which the exercitant had to learn. Others think that they were placed here because of the connection with the Last Supper (191-198) and to encourage mortification during the atmosphere of the contemplations on Christ's Passion.

Another possible reason is to start the readjustment of one's manner of living immediately, within the context of the Exercises.

112. On May 12, 1556, two months before Ignatius died, he wrote to A. Adrianssens a letter of prudent advice on eating and drinking for the preservation of health (*LettersIgn*, p. 421). It serves as an excellent commentary on these rules, bringing out the spirit from which they sprang.

THE FOURTH WEEK

113. Ignatius now takes up the risen life, the next stage of the paschal mystery. Already in 4 above he stated that the Fourth Week was to be about the "Resurrection and Ascension." Rather surprisingly, however, he does not use the title "The Resurrection" for his first contemplation. Nevertheless that is the topic he has in mind, as is clear from 299 below in the Mysteries of Christ's Life, to which he refers us and to which we must go to find his customary points—in this instance, one sole point. There he describes this same contemplation by a more accurate title: "The Resurrection of Christ Our Lord. His First Apparition"—as he states also here in the first prelude (219). The appearance to Mary is a part of the Resurrection, and because of his tender love of her it is the first point which occurs to his mind to contemplate. All these items form one more example of Ignatius' unconcern for stylistic niceties. In general, during this Week he focuses, not on the Resurrection itself, but on the apparitions of the risen Christ communicating his joy as well as his graces and spiritual consolations to humankind now redeemed. The exercitant too shares abundantly in the graces of Christ's life-giving Resurrection.

114. *Infierno*, i.e., as in the Apostles' Creed, "He descended into hell"; it is probably associated with the Hebrew notion of Sheol, the abode of the dead. See 1 Peter 3:19, 4:6; and on these verses McKenzie, *Dictionary of the Bible*, p. 104, s.v. "descent."

115. Christ's apparition to Mary is not found in Scripture, but it is an opinion prominent in a long tradition of Christian writers. It is found in ch. 70 of the *Life of Christ* by Ludolph, and Ignatius may have accepted it from him. Ludolph cites testimony from Sts. Ambrose, Anselm, and Ignatius of Antioch. Cusson lists some twenty writers who held this opinion, including

Sedulius, Paulinus of Nola, Albert the Great, Bernardino da Siena, Maldonatus, and Pope Benedict XIV (*BibThSpEx*, pp. 303-304).

116. The third prelude, the grace to be prayed for, also gives a clue to one important purpose of the Fourth Week: intimate association with Christ in his joy. Virtually all commentators hold that the Week pertains chiefly to the unitive way. Beyond that, however, they divide along the same lines as in the Third Week (see n. 106 on 190 above). One group, including the *Directory* of 1599 (ch. 36, no. 1), affirms confirmation of resolutions and union with Christ in his joy. Another group adds also a sharing as great as possible in the fruits of his life-giving Resurrection (see *BibThSpEx*, pp. 309-311).

117. This justly renowned contemplation is aimed directly at increasing the exercitant's love of God, as the second prelude clearly shows. Moreover, the Vulgate translated Ignatius' Spanish title by "Contemplation to Stir Up Spiritual Love of God in Ourselves." Retreatants, however, by increasing their own love of God also open themselves to an increased manifestation of God's love toward them. This exercise is the conclusion and apt climax of the spiritual experience of the Exercises. Love of God is the greatest of the virtues (1 Cor. 13:13); and it includes love of our neighbor. Those who think they love God but do not love their neighbor are in error, called "liars" in 1 John 4:20.

A few early commentators, e.g., Miró and Hoffaeus, thought that this Contemplation to Attain Love could well be given in the Third, or Second, or even the First Week. Their opinion was short-lived; although this would bring some profit, it would not be fulfilling the function of this contemplation which Ignatius intended in the structure of the *Exercises*. Consensus soon arose that this Contemplation pertains to the unitive way and is part of the Fourth Week, though it may be either spread through the other mysteries of the Week or made as the last Exercise of the retreat (Polanco in *SpEx*MHSJ19, pp. 825, Nadal, González Dávila, and the *Directory* of 1599 [ch. 36, no. 2]; see also *Bib-ThSpEx*, pp. 312-314).

118. This is typical of Ignatius' practicality. He in no way depreciates affective love of another person with its warmth and consolation; but he also goes farther and points out the necessity of effective love, of doing what is pleasing to the other. The

effective love remains even when the affective love is difficult or absent (as in desolation). Moreover, affective love not carried into practice by effective love easily degenerates into self-interest or self-deceit.

119. This wise observation sets the stage for the movement of the thought throughout the contemplation. Love ordinarily arises from gratitude. The lover gives to the beloved and the beloved, recognizing the giver's goodness, experiences gratitude and increased love for the giver. Through their mutual love their friendship is deepened.

120. This prelude shows both the purpose of the contemplation and its function in the structure of the *Exercises* as a whole. The idea which was common in most of the preludes in the Second Week, "to love Christ more," now becomes to love God more "in all things"—reminiscent of Ignatius' constant concern to "find God in all things" of ordinary everyday life. Another important function of this contemplation is to build a bridge for intensive spiritual living in everyday life after the Exercises have ended (*Obrascompl*, pp. 327; *BibThSpEx*, pp. 326-332).

121. The four points overlap somewhat; they view the gifts of God from many angles rather than in a logical order. Some find it helpful to contemplate God in point 1 as the giver of all gifts; in 2 as present in all the creatures and conserving their existence; in 3 as cooperating in their activities; and in 4 as the preeminent Source of all the good present in creatures. This offering, the "Take and Receive" (*Suscipe*), is one of the most famous of Ignatius' prayers and one regularly associated with him.

122. *Vuestro amor y gracia,* literally, "your love and your grace," is what Ignatius wrote in text *A*. But what he really meant seems to be better expressed by De Freux's Latin translation, the Vulgate, which Ignatius used for seven years: *amorem tui solum cum gratia tua,* "Give me only love of yourself along with your grace." This is the grace petitioned in the second prelude (233), "to love and serve the Divine Majaesty in everything." See Gueydan, *Exercices,* p. 140; also, note 117 above.

123. Notice the totality of this offering: The exercitant, in deep fervor from the month of spiritual experience and moved by profound gratitude to increased effective love, offers his or

her whole self back to God, to be guided henceforth by his good pleasure through the rest of one's life.

124. God's immanence in all the created world, which the résumé in point 4 brings out, is an expression of his benevolent love for us. Awareness of this ignites in the human heart gratitude, adoration, and a loving application of one's whole self to serving him as well as possible. As the Exercises close, the exercitant—like Ignatius himself—has viewed the grandeur of the created universe: its origin from God (23), and its being destined by God to return to himself (by contributing to his glorification through the joyful praise of those who have cooperated with his plan of creation and redemption). By starting with a love that descends from God above, the retreatants will view all created reality as being on its way to God through His being praised by those who are saved. These exercitants will find God in all things, and by means of them. They will resonate with words which Ignatius wrote on many other occasions: "May our Lord give us the light of his holy discretion, that we may know how to make use of creatures in the light of the Creator" (*LettersIgn*, p. 421); "All the good which is looked for in creatures exists with greater perfection in God who created them" (*EppIgn*, 5:488; see also *LettersIgn*, pp. 18, 309); "May his holy name be praised . . . , he who has ordained and created them for this end [his own glorification] which is so proper" (*LettersIgn*. p. 83). The whole doctrine is summed up by St. Paul: "For from him and through him and for him all things are. To him be glory forever. Amen" (Rom. 11:36). See *BibTh-SpEx*, pp. 317-319, 326-332.

SUPPLEMENTARY MATTER
Three Methods of Praying

125. The main course of Ignatius' Exercises for thirty days is now complete. The rest of his book consists of appendices, sets of "rules," i.e., directives or suggestions. They are intended to be helpful both for cases which may arise during the retreat and also for carrying its fruits into persevering practice after the Exercises. Not all these sets are suitable for everyone, and they should be communicated according to the needs and devout desires of each exercitant (*Directory*, ch. 3).

The first such set is the present one on the Three Methods of

Praying. Beyond the basic methods of meditation and contemplation in his book he also teaches other methods, surprisingly many. His effort is to find some method suitable for any personality. In 18 above, Ignatius described this First Method of Praying as a "light exercise" which can be given to simple and illiterate persons who are unqualified for the full Exercises. In his *Constitutions* too he states (649) about these three methods that "anyone who has good will seems to be capable of these exercises." The *Directory*, however, points out that although these methods are suitable for beginners, they are also useful for persons very advanced (ch. 37, no. 1). For detailed commentary on these methods see Coathalem 232-238; *Directory*, ch. 37.

126. *Forma*, "structural form": In 204:1,3, Ignatius uses *forma de proceder* to refer to the structural form or model of the second of two chief methods of mental prayer which he uses and teaches throughout the *Exercises*. These two forms are: discursive meditation by use of the memory, intellect, and will (in 45-55) and the more affective contemplation of the persons, words, and actions (in 101-117). Here in 238:3, he is setting up a similar form or framework for another method (*modo*) and exercises (*ejercicios*) or practices for the method. *Forma* has many meanings from which have sprung varying translations.

127. "From these exercises": For this interpretation see Calveras, *Vocabulario*, p. 160. However, in Ignatius' one long Spanish sentence this phrase possibly refers back to the ten commandments and capital sins.

128. *Acepta*: The Vulgate, *V*, adds here "to God." However, the Spanish, *A*, and the Latin, P^1, can also mean "acceptable to the one praying," i.e., to make the prayer a pleasing experience.

129. "Properly so called": In this context these words seem necessary to show that *forma* and *modo* probably refer to the meditation of 45-55 and the contemplation of 101-117. See Gueydan, *Exercices*, p. 143.

130. In text *A* this heading is part of the title in 238 above. We transfer it here where it is more functional in making the thought easier to grasp. The commandments are the first of four subjects suggested under the First Method.

131. Ignatius' manuscript, text *A*, has *tercera adición*, a manifest error for the Fifth Note (*quinta nota*, 131) of the Second

Week. This note adapts the Third Additional Directive of the First Week (75) to the Second Week. See *DalMan*, p. 136.

132. *Pecados mortales, the capital sins*: See n. 11 on 18 above and the list of the capital sins there. The opposite virtues are humility, patience, generosity, temperance, chastity, neighborly love, and diligence.

133. Powers: the faculties of memory, intellect, and will, as in 45-52.

134. The Second Method is similar to the ancient tradition of "prayerful reading" (*lectio divina*) of which St. Benedict wrote in his *Rule*, ch. 48. On *Lectio divina* see D. M. Stanley, *The Exercises with . . . St. John*, pp. 311-327.

135. Ignatius' method of praying according to a rhythmic measure has noteworthy similarity to the "Jesus prayer," which with varying formulations was practiced and taught especially among Greek Fathers such as Diadochus of Photice (d. before 486), Hesychius of Jerusalem, St. John Climacus (d. 649), and others. A short formula such as "Jesus Christ, Son of God, have mercy on me" was recited with every breath to bring about an absorption in the presence of God. A documented history of the spread of this prayer, which had widespread popularity in the 14th century and its apogee in the 17th, is in I. Hausherr, *The Name of Jesus* (Kalamazoo, 1978), pp. 241-347. Particularly interesting are the citations from St. Francis Xavier (p. 343) and the Jesuit general Claudio Aquaviva (p. 334). See also *Westminster Dictionary of Christian Spirituality*, p. 223; *NCathEnc*, 7:971; *DSpir* 8: cols. 1126-1150.

The Mysteries of the Life of Christ

136. "Mysteries" (*misterios*) here means the events or episodes in the life of Christ, the medieval sense of the word as found in the "mystery plays," e.g., on the Nativity. Some of these events are also mysteries in the theological sense, "a religious truth revealed by God that human beings cannot know by reason alone," e.g., the Eucharist in 289. But most of them are not mysteries in this strict theological sense. However, since they involve the actions of the God-Man and build up to his Passion and Resurrection, they implicate the great mysteries strictly so called, such as the Trinity, Incarnation, and Redemption

(*NCathEnc*, 10:148).

Ignatius' aim is to furnish a series of topics for contemplation during the retreat and also, as 162 indicates, to help exercitants to continue such contemplations after the retreat. He presents 51 mysteries from which a director may choose. All are from Scripture, except Christ's appearance first to Mary (299) and to Joseph of Arimathea (310). Almost all of Ignatius' topics are also in Ludolph's Life of Christ and in the same sequence as in Ludolph. This suggests that already at Manresa he drew up at least a preliminary list of these topics from the copybook of his readings at Loyola. However, the present form of these mysteries comes from his years in Paris. His quotations from Scripture are his own Spanish translations from the Latin Vulgate. At Manresa he did not yet know Latin, and Spanish translations of the New Testament were very rare before 1569. The first printed Spanish translation was the Protestant edition at Antwerp in 1543, after Ignatius' revisions of the *Exercises*. See *SpExMHSJ69*, p. 55; *DalmMan*, p. 142; *IgnCLWS*, pp. 12-13, 19-20.

137. The manuscript has parentheses (*parentesis*), the 16th-century usage which modern editions replace by quotation marks.

138. The manuscript has *Lucas en el primero capitolo, littera c.* This too is now replaced by the clearer citations of chapters and verses, the system of Estienne introduced in 1551. Ignatius compressed the sentences of Scripture which he translated from the Latin Vulgate into Spanish, but he kept the sense unaltered. The present English translation is made from Ignatius' Spanish.

139. In these points Ignatius presents for imaginative and reverent contemplation what he regards as the "history" (see n. 63 on 102), the "authentic foundation" (4) which he wished to be the basis of the exercitant's reflections and applications. He obviously meant the *historia* insofar as he was able to know it from theological, devotional, and scriptural writings of his day. Since then, however, the historical character of Christ's words and deeds has been immensely nuanced by modern discoveries in all these fields. If knowledge of these developments does not shine through a modern director's presentation, he or she is likely to receive complaints from retreatants.

Many problems are connected with this situation. Ordinarily, the more theological and scriptural knowledge a director or a retreatant brings to the contemplation of these mysteries, the more fruitful and solidly based will his or her spirituality be. A director, however, should not convert his or her presentation of points into a lecture addressed to the intellect alone; a director's function is to stimulate prayer and warmth which is solidly based. Similarly the retreatant should not, by too much reading during the prayer period, convert it into study rather than prayer. But if a director does much study of this kind before presenting the points, the results will naturally shine through the points. Also, a retreatant can turn the prayerful contemplations made during the Exercises into a stimulus for extensive reading after them which confirms and deepens the fruit of the retreat experience. Cusson sets up these problems well in *BibThSpEx*, pp. 39-43, 220, and 224, and discusses them on pp. 223-242, 278-279, 296-301. On pp. 351-364 he gives an extended bibliography of articles and books on each of Ignatius' mysteries. See also "Keys to Interpretation" in *IgnCLWC*, pp. 59-60; and Stanley, *The Spiritual Exercises with . . . St. John*, pp. xi-xii, xv-xvi.

140. Ignatius did not include Pentecost among these mysteries, possibly because it did not come under their title, "The Mysteries of the Life of Christ our Lord." That he was not opposed to including it appears from this statement of Polanco, who knew his mind so well: ". . . under the heading Resurrection include also the mysteries of the Ascension and Pentecost" (cited in *BibThSpEx*, p. 314, from *SpEx*MHSJ19, p. 825).

Rules for the Discernment of Spirits

141. This short title, not in Ignatius' text *A*, is an editorial addition by which his rules have been commonly known throughout their influential history. It has been added in many editions because Ignatius' own title is so long, compact, and unwieldy. Ignatius here takes up the subtle topic and art of discernment of spirits.

Our short title added to Ignatius' text is a slightly abbreviated translation of the title (probably Ignatius' own) in the First Latin Version, P^1: "Some rules toward discerning the various spirits agitating the soul" (*animam agitantes*). However, it omits many important nuances contained in Ignatius' terse but lengthy title in the Autograph. They require careful study.

First of all, it is important to understand Ignatius' terminology with precision. In his usage, to discern is to see deeply in order to recognize and separate; in other words, to identify and distinguish the good spirits from the bad. The Spanish *discernir* (from Latin *discernere, discrevi, discretum,* to separate, distinguish, discern, discriminate) means to know, judge, comprehend, distinguish, or discriminate. For the substantive form of *discernir* Ignatius uses *discreción* (176, 325) in the sense of *discernimiento (DalmMan,* p. 194), that is, discernment, insight, discrimination. "Keenness of insight" and "skill in discerning or discriminating" *(Webster's Seventh New Collegiate Dictionary* [Merriam-Webster, 1967] are the meanings of the English word "discernment" which are most relevant for accurate understanding of Ignatius' thought here. See Toner, *Commentary,* pp. 18-19.

The history of discernment of spirits extends from the Bible to the present time (see *DSpir* 3: cols. 1222-1291; translation by Innocentia Richards, in *Discernment of Spirits* [Collegeville, 1970]). However, Ignatius' well-known rules are based chiefly on his own experiences and his reflections upon them, as we learn from Câmara's note on *Autobiog,* 7-9, and from ibid. 20-22, 25-26, 54-55, 99-101. Toner's *Commentary* of 352 pages, mentioned just above, presents a deep and excellent analysis of these rules. Briefer but comprehensive and sound is Coathalem, *Ignatian Insights,* pp. 243-278. Another excellent article, focused especially on the structure of these rules, is Michael J. Buckley, "Rules for the Discernment of Spirits," *The Way,* Supplement 20 (Autumn 1973): 19-37; reprinted in *The Way of Ignatius Loyola: Contemporary Approaches to the Spiritual Exercises,* ed. Philip Sheldrake (London and St. Louis, 1991), pp. 219-237. A collection of useful articles on discernment and spiritual direction is found in *Notes on the Spiritual Exercises. The Best of the Review [for Religious],* ed. David L. Fleming (St. Louis, 1983). Ignatius' letters of June 18 and Sept. 11, 1536, to Sister Teresa Rejadell *(LettersIgn,* pp. 18-24; 24-25) show how he applied his principles in practice and are also considered a commentary on these rules. His letter to St. Francis Borgia of Sept. 29, 1548, and of July, 1549, ibid., pp. 179-182, 195-211 are an application of these rules respectively in spiritual direction and in judging cases alleged to be mystical.

142. Toward perceiving and then understanding *(sentir y conocer)*: These words reflect Ignatius' own experiences with discernment of spirits. From *Autobiog* 7-8 we learn the initial experience from which his knowledge of and skill in discern-

ment of spirits gradually grew. First, he noticed that spirits were affecting his soul. Second, little by little through his reflections on these experiences he came to understand them. Some were good and moved him toward good, others bad. Through years of practice he gradually developed his experience into a refined art. This skill, he well knew, takes years to acquire. Here he is primarily helping directors to know what to watch for and say in dealing with retreatants. But through the directors he is also introducing exercitants in the First Week to their first acquaintance with this complex art of interpreting their interior experiences. Such exercitants can hope to understand these "motions" or tactics only to some extent (*en alguna manera*). It is wise for them to seek further help from a director.

143. *Mociones*, motions: In Ignatius' usage this word usually has a technical meaning: the interior experiences in the soul. They can be acts of the intellect (e.g., thoughts, lines of reasoning, imaginings, etc.); or of the will (such as love, hate, desire, fear, etc.); or of affective feelings, impulses, inclinations, or urges (such as peace, warmth, coldness, consolation, desolation, etc.). These can come (1) from ourselves under some control of our free will (32); or (2) from a good spirit (God or an angel); or (3) from an evil spirit. See 6 above with n. 6 and 182 with n. 100.

144. "Are caused": i.e., by good or evil spirits. There are also other motions which arise spontaneously from ourselves under some control of our free will (32 above), but they are not directly treated here. Instead, Ignatius is directly treating only the last two categories just mentioned in endnote 142: the motions which are caused by good or evil spirits for their respective ends. Indirectly, however, the first category, motions arising from ourselves (32), can fall within the scope of his rules, insofar as the good or evil spirits can take these emotions and work on them for their respective ends. See Toner, *Commentary*, pp. 37-38.

Ignatius clearly believed in the existence of angels and devils, and for him the spirits, whether good or evil, are always persons, intelligent beings. A few writers have held that the word "spirits" can be replaced by "motions" (see Coathalem, p. 244). Sometimes their opinion has sprung from modern doubts about the existence of devils or angels. See Toner, *Commentary*, pp. 34-37, 260-270; also, Paul Quay, "Angels and Demons: The Teaching of IV Lateran," *Theological Studies*, 42

(March 1981): 20-45.

145. *Ánima,* soul: i.e., the person. "Soul" is used by synecdoche to mean the person (see n. 19 on 23 above). However, because Ignatius' training in scholastic philosophy is reflected in his writing and helps toward its interpretation, we think it better to retain "soul" as the safer guide to his thought in this subtle material.

146. "More suitable for the First Week": i.e., because cases where they are applicable are more likely to arise during the First Week, though they may arise at any other time. The rules for the First Week are concerned especially with the experience of spiritual desolation and ways of coping with it to avoid deviation from pursuit of the end, salvation. They are particularly applicable to the purgative way. An outline of the treatment in the rules for the First Week, based on Toner, *Commentary,* pp. vi-vii, can be given as follows:

I. Fundamental Principles for discerning spirits: the contrary actions of the good and evil spirits on regressing and progressing Christians (rules 1-2).

    A. Spiritual consolation and desolation (R 3-14)
      1. Their nature (R 3-4)
    B. Responding to the Holy Spirit during desolation (R 5-6)
      1. Accepting the desolation as a test (R 7)
      2. Counterattack by patience (R 8)
      3. Examination of the causes (R 9)
      4. During consolation prepare for desolation (R 10-11)
      5. Style and strategy of the devil (R 12-14)

147. *Por el synderese: Synderesis* is a person's natural ability to judge rightly in moral matters (*DalmMan,* 167). See also *ST,* 1, 79, 12; also 1-2, 94, 1, ad 2.

148. "Spiritual Consolation": Throughout these rules, whenever Ignatius uses the term "consolation" he means spiritual consolation, and only it. There are also many experiences of consolation which are non-spiritual, e.g., some licit (such as a feeling of satisfaction which arises from study) and some illicit (such as anticipatory enjoyment of an intended activity which is grievously sinful). To interpret this as spiritual consolation is erroneous self-deceit. Spiritual consolation always includes a tendency toward an increase of charity.

However, spiritual consolation can have a concomitant overflow or effect on the emotions and senses, e.g., joy. But this is accidental, something that can be present or absent. Consolation which is purely sensible is excluded.

There is a misunderstanding of Ignatius' term "consolation" which arises rather frequently in practice, though it is not found in reputable authors. Any feeling of joy, satisfaction, or peace is taken, often too hastily, as a good spirit's sign of approval for some option. This overlooks the distinction between spiritual and non-spiritual consolation and often leads to false discernment, selfishness, or rationalization of less good conduct. See Toner, *Commentary*, pp. 283-284.

149. This rule 3 is of great importance for judging problems connected with infused contemplation. On this see Coathalem, pp. 257-258, 279-283; for bibliography, *Obrascompl*, p. 279.

150. As with consolation, so too the desolation treated in the *Exercises* always pertains to spiritual desolation, with its possible overflow into the emotions and senses. To interpret non-spiritual desolation as spiritual desolation is to steer oneself into danger of errors, self-deceit, and rationalization.

151. *De grado* here has the meaning of *ante la condescencia* (Calveras, *Vocabulario*, p. 203); i.e., when face to face with one who is submissive. Other translations too are possible. This statement is terse and even the ancient Latin versions turned or paraphrased it differently. Ignatius clarifies the statement by the context below it. The devil cannot work directly on our will, but only indirectly by tempting us through the imagination or senses. If we show ourselves strong, he weakens and retreats. If we show ourselves weak, he grows strong and furious. To expand Ignatius' comparison into a depreciation of women in general goes beyond his text and is also historically erroneous. The 352 pages of his correspondence with women, assembled in Hugo Rahner's *St. Ignatius Loyola: Letters to Women* (New York, 1960), reveal him as a zealous, prudent, and understanding spiritual director of women who highly esteemed them and was similarly esteemed by them in return.

152. This brief title, customary in many editions, is added to Ignatius' text to facilitate references. An outline of the Rules More Suitable for the Second Week, based on Toner, *Commen-*

tary, pp. vi-vii, follows:

II. The evil spirit in time of spiritual consolation (R 1-8)
   A. Deception beginning during spiritual consolation itself
      (R 1-7)
      1. Characteristics of the good and evil spirits (R 1)
      2. Consolation without a preceding cause (R 2)
      3. Consolation with a preceding cause (R 3)
      4. Deception in consolation with a preceding cause
         (R 4)
      5. How to detect such demonic deception (R 5-6)
      6. Learning by reflection on experience (R 6)
      7. Assurance and explanation (R 7)
   B. Deception during the afterglow of spiritual consolation
      (R 8).

153. That is, for cases more likely to arise during the Second Week, especially emotions caused by the evil spirit using his deceptive tactics during the time of the election. This set of rules is especially applicable to the illuminative and unitive ways, and deals chiefly with demonic deceptions during the journey to the goal, the greater glory of God. See endnote 142 on 313 above; also Coathalem, 247-248.

154. Consolation without a previous cause is an invasion of God into the soul without any previous use of its own intellectual, volitional, or sense faculties. It may have been involved in the call of St. Matthew or St. Paul (175), or be similar to what St. Teresa called "the prayer of union" (*Interior Castle,* Mansion V, chs. 1-2), or to the "substantial touch" of St. John of the Cross (Coathalem, pp. 271-272; see also 256-257). Since it comes from God, it obviously cannot contain error. However, if a person (or her or his director) is to be sure that an experience is a genuine case of consolation without antecedent cause, subtle and careful discernment is necessary; and even that may turn out to be inconclusive. Ignatius' remarks are too brief to enable us to know with precision what he truly means by this phrase, or to answer the numerous questions it raises. Many interpretations ancient and modern have arisen but so far no one of them has won general agreement. Four recent opinions of Karl Rahner, Harvey Egan, Hervé Coathalem, and Daniel Gil are discussed by Toner, *Commentary,* pp. 291-313. Great uncertainty remains, in his opinion, about the nature of consolation without preceding

cause, how frequently it occurs, and how it functions in discernment either of spirits or of God's will. Harvey Egan, basing his thought on Karl Rahner, views the matter differently and cites other authors in support of his opinion. See his *The Spiritual Exercises and the Ignatian Mystical Horizon* (St. Louis, 1976), pp. 31-65.

155. That is, by leading us to acts of perceiving, thinking, reflecting emotionally, etc. These acts are antecedent to the consolation and are a means by which the experience is stimulated. Such stimulation might arise, e.g., from one's meditations, contemplations, or reflections, from a book, homily, picture, and the like.

156. At the end of these rules we are in position to observe a matter of great importance. The *Exercises* present two distinct forms of discernment, (1) discernment of the will of God and (2) discernment of spirits, which is a means toward discerning God's will. The principles used in both forms are as useful outside a time of retreat as within. The first procedure, discernment of the will of God, is found chiefly in the directives for making an election (135, 169-189); and the second procedure is principally in the rules for the discernment of spirits (313-336). There is some overlapping in the two procedures, insofar as the suggestions in one are usually applicable also in the other; but the main objective in each set remains distinct. In discerning the will of God, a person asks questions such as: "By which option am I, with my personality and in my circumstances, likely to bring greater glory to God?" or "to serve God better?" or "to increase my supernatural life more and thereby bring him proportionally greater praise through eternity?" While engaged in such deliberations, he or she is likely to receive thoughts and impulses from the good spirit and subtle temptations from the evil spirit. Here recourse to discernment of spirits is needed, and perhaps also consultation with a counselor. Toner's *Commentary* touches on this distinction (pp. 12-15) and gives great help toward acquiring the art of discerning spirits. Similar help toward the more important art of discerning the will of God is found in his later book, *Discerning God's Will: Ignatius of Loyola's Teaching on Christian Decision Making* (St. Louis, 1991).

Rules for Distributing Alms

157. Ignatius' title suggests that these rules are addressed chiefly to ecclesiastical officeholders, e.g., those who possess a benefice or are seeking one, in which they are charged to superintend the distribution of alms. Notice the words "ministry" (337, 339, 343), "the distribution" rather than merely "giving" (338, 342), "office of my administration" (340), "office and duty of my ministry" (341; cf. 343). In this context, the "state" is the clerical state of life. With appropriate adaptations, however, these rules can also serve as guides to non-officeholders, as Ignatius points out in the last rule (341). See *DalmMan*, p. 175; *Obrascompl*, p. 284.

158. That is, the ecclesiastical goods, capital, foundations, gifts, and so forth made to the church. To confer the office on someone is to appoint one also to administer these goods.

159. These incidents are not in the Gospels. But they are found in Ludolph's *Vita Jesu Christi*, Part I, ch. 2, no.7, from which Ignatius probably took them.

The Notes on Scruples

160. Ignatius' title indicates that these are not rules or directives giving norms of conduct; rather, they are simple "notes" toward helping persons who are troubled by scruples. They are also helps for directors or counselors. They manifestly reflect his own experiences with scruples at Manresa, as recounted in *Autobiog*, 22-25, and also his experience in counseling others. They were wise counsels for his day and remain so. But for modern times they are incomplete and need to be supplemented by the many discoveries which have been made in pastoral experience, psychology, psychiatry, and the like. In his day scruples were too readily seen chiefly as an affliction brought on by God or the devil for their respective purposes. Further comments and references can be found in David L. Fleming, *The Spiritual Exercises: A Literal Translation and a Contemporary Reading* (St. Louis, 1978), pp. 227-229.

161. Letter 64, in PL 77: col. 1195.

162. Possibly Ignatius took this quotation from the life of St. Bernard in the *Flos sanctorum*, the Spanish translation of Jacobus'

Legenda aurea published in 1493 (*DalmMan*, 179).

The Genuine Attitude in the Church

163. This is an attempt (admittedly with limited success) to pack the meaning of Ignatius' lengthy title (352) into a short one for handy reference. Longstanding endeavors in the same direction have been "Rules for Thinking with the Church" and "Rules of Orthodoxy." Each of these attempts is accurate but incomplete; for his lengthy title in 352 involves far more than the realm of thought or correct belief.

Ignatius' own title is found in three formulations which illumine one another, in texts *A*, *P*[1], and *V*. They are printed in parallel columns in *SpExMHSJ69*, p. 374-375. Of the three, that in the Autograph, *A*, immediately below in 313, best reveals his whole thought. But it receives clarifications from *P*[1] and *V*, as will be seen in nn. 164 and 165 on 352 below.

The Historical Background of These Rules

These well-known and influential rules on harmonizing our attitude with that of the Church were in the manuscript of the *Exercises* during their revision in Rome (1539-1541), and possibly already during Ignatius' stay in Paris (1528-1535). In either case they reflect the Church's stormy situation which he knew from his experiences both in Paris and Rome. Many people were justly clamoring for the Church's reform. Some of them pointed out the abuses respectfully and properly, but others acted irreverently and dangerously. For example, one group, the Illuminati in Spain and others like them in Paris, was practicing a pseudo-mysticism which ignored doctrinal accuracy and scorned the precisions of scholastic theology. A second group consisted of those openly heretical, such as the "Lutheranizers" (*Lutherizantes*) in Paris. In a grey area in between these two groups was a third, disgruntled Catholics and humanists who often gave reason to doubt whether their faith was still genuinely Catholic. They were critical of the Church, frequently uncharitable, sarcastic, or ambiguous. Erasmus is an example, with his captivating but mordant satires and exaggerations mocking pope, bishops, theologians, priests, and nuns. Two years before Ignatius arrived in Paris an edition of 20,000 copies of his *Praise of Folly* was exhausted. In May, 1526, the Sorbonne requested Parlement to condemn his *Colloquia*. In Rome Ignatius contended with the persecutions stirred up by Landívar and the disguised heretics Mainardi, Mudarra, and Barreda (*Autobiog*, 98).

Most of these practices went contrary to Ignatius' temperament and typical procedures. For him the Church was a mother and a divinely established institution, an embodiment of the Kingdom of Christ. Painfully aware of her defects, he loved her none the less and sought her renewal. But his tactics were quiet, positive, and constructive. They aimed chiefly at interior reform of individuals through conversations and his Exercises, and eventually they blossomed into his Society of Jesus with its educational system, foreign missions, and other ministries.

He placed these rules about the proper attitude of genuine Catholics in the Church at the very end of his *Exercises*, and in them he is not polemical or argumentative. He is content to give calm counsel. He intended the rules especially for an exercitant who for a month had been gazing in love on Christ, contemplating his calls for help in spreading his Kingdom and his example, and was now about to return to ordinary life, perhaps among heretics or weak Catholics. Polanco states in his Directory that these rules are given as antidotes "to those things which the heretics of our time, or those showing affinity to their doctrine, are prone to attack or scorn. . . . Moreover, they serve not only to keep such an exercitant from erring by speaking privately or writing publicly in a manner other than proper, but they also help him to discern whether the statements and writings of others are departing from the Catholic Church's manner of thinking and speaking, and to advise others to be on their guard" (*Directorium Polanci*, no. 112, in *DirSpEx* [Rome, 1955], p. 327). On this topic, see Leturia, "Sentido verdadero en la Iglesia militante," *Estudios*, 2:149-174; also, based chiefly on it, Ganss, "Thinking with the Church: The Spirit of St. Ignatius' Rules," *The Way*, Supplement 20 (1973): 72-82; see also *Studies in the Spirituality of Jesuits*, 7 (January 1975): 12-20.

Many of Ignatius' topics and details are as applicable in our day as in his, but many too are rather obsolete in our vastly changed circumstances. What is most important for any person now is to catch the underlying tenor, the attitude of loyalty which runs all through Ignatius' rules, to devise a similar attitude of one's own, and by it to guide oneself and others to live and work in loving loyalty to the Church, Christ's spouse and our mother.

164. *Sentido* (sense, reason, feeling, and many other meanings) is often used by Ignatius with nuances of his own. Frequently, as here, it means cognition which is basically intellectual but is savored so repeatedly that it becomes also deeply emotional and "satisfies the soul" (*SpEx*, 2). Thus it becomes *a habitual attitude of mind*, a frame of reference instinctively used to guide one's life (Leturia, *Estudios*, 2:153). A genuine or authentic attitude means one proper to a loyal Catholic.

165. Militant, i.e., the Church on earth, with the human defects found in many of her popes, bishops, priests, religious, and other members.

166. Rules, i.e., guidelines, directives, counsels, norms, or suggestions to be prudently applied; but not obligations. See n. 110 on 210 above.

167. This rule is the fundamental principle underlying all the rest. It is developed by three groups of counsels which follow, as the notes on 354, 362, and 365 below will indicate.

Section 353 is astonishingly compact. In no other one place in the *Exercises* does Ignatius so fully reveal his concept of the Church: true spouse of Christ, our mother, and hierarchical. But his concept is richer still. Elsewhere he describes her as Christ's Kingdom to be spread (91-95), the community of the faithful (177), Roman (*SpEx*, 353 in text P^1), and as Christ's mystical body governed on earth by his vicar (*LettersIgn*, 367-372), from whom all authority descends through hierarchically ordered superiors (*Cons*, 7, 603, 666, 736).

168. Group I, rules 2 through 9, gives suggestions for establishing an attitude on the practices, devotions, and way of life of loyal Catholics.

169. Group II, rules 10-12, builds an outlook in regard to superiors in the Church, respectively in regard to jurisdiction, learning, and sanctity. The fundamental principle of this group is in rule 10: Be more inclined to praise than to blame.

170. *Mayores* means, here and in 42, 351, 362, our superiors, as the Vulgate translates it; i.e., the officials or authorities both ecclesiastical and civil (*DalmMan*, 200; Leturia, *Estudios*, 2:164).

171. In the 1500s many humanists and reformers were

reacting against the scholastic teachers and their methods, often with scorn, and putting more stress on Scripture, sometimes taken alone or sometimes along with the Fathers. They set scholastic and positive theology in opposition, but Ignatius saw the good in both and presented the two as complementary. Thus through his *Exercises* (363) and his colleges and universities as guided by his *Constitutions* (351, 353, 366, 446, 464, 467), his attitude exerted for centuries a widespread influence on the teaching and study of theology. On scholastic and positive theology see n. 39 on *Cons*, 366 in *IgnCLWS*, pp. 295 and 460-461.

172. This is a caution against premature admiration of living persons even over canonized saints. In Ignatius' experience, e.g., with Landívar, Mudarra, and Barreda in Rome in 1538, some living preachers were highly esteemed for a while but were disguising their heresy.

173. Group III, rules 13-18, treats of doctrinal topics, some of them controverted often passionately, and a manner of expounding them in the troubled sixteenth century. Again, the group begins with the fundamental principle in rule 13, which is in substance a rephrasing of rule 1 (353).

174. *Determina* (determines, resolves, decides, defines) in this context means "defines." Texts P^1 of about 1534, P^2, and *V*, the Vulgate of 1548, all translate it by *diffiniret* or *definierit*. Notice that Ignatius does not state that we ought to believe that white is black, as he has often been misquoted to state. Instead, he writes that "what *seems to me* to be white," (or more literally, "what I see" [*que yo veo*] "as white,"); and the Latin Vulgate in 1548 translated this by "what appears to *my* eyes as white." In other words, the error would be in my hasty subjective judgment and not in the Church, because the Church is governed by the Holy Spirit and cannot err in her solemn definitions. This statement seems to be an allusion to Erasmus, who had written: "Nor would black be white, if the Roman Pontiff should pronounce it so, a thing which I know he will never do" (*DalmMan*, p. 183, citing Erasmus *Opera* 9 [1706]: 517).

APPENDIX I

SCRIPTURE TEXTS: GOD'S PLAN
AND THE HISTORY OF SALVATION

Ignatius' book, *Spiritual Exercises*, providentially absorbed the most important truths in God's plan of creating free human beings for his own glory and their beatitude. Furthermore, it presented these truths in a chronological sequence which shows this divine design as evolving by stages in the history of salvation. It teaches people how to lead their lives cooperatively with this divine plan and motivates them to do it. For them the *Exercises* are a practical application of this saving plan to their everyday living until they reach their rich self-fulfillment in the beatific vision. Life becomes an opportunity to fulfill the role offered by God during one's lifetime as the divine plan is evolving in history.

To have a synthetic concept of this divine plan of salvation and spiritual growth fresh in memory when we make or study the *Exercises* is a great aid toward gaining a deeper and even a more prayerful insight into their rich message. To provide such a synthesis the following collection of scriptural texts[1] is presented here. They summarize the most relevant features of this plan of God's love, "the mystery of Christ" which so forcefully inspired St. Paul (Rom. 16:25; Eph. 1:8-10, 3:1-21; Col. 2:2,3).

These texts, and the eight brief introductions to them, can well be read in the spirit of the "prayerful reading" (*lectio divina*) commended in chapter 48 of *The Rule of St. Benedict*, or of Ignatius' Second Method of Praying (*SpEx*, 249-252) which is so similar. The introductions stem from the very structure of St. Thomas Aquinas' *Summa of Theology* (all things come from God and through Christ are means to lead human beings back to God), or from any of the manuals of theology since his day, all

---

1. The selections are taken, with some revisions and adaptations, from this writer's appendix in *BibThSpEx*, pp. 335-344. The translations are taken from the New Revised Standard Version of *The Holy Bible* (Nashville: Thomas Nelson, 1989).

of which mirror the Church's long theological reflection on the deposit of faith found in Scripture and Tradition.[2]

God's Plan for the Creation, Redemption, and Glorification of Free Human Beings

1.   Because of God's desire to share his happiness with others, he created the material universe to reveal his existence and goodness to free human beings, and to give them an opportunity to achieve their self-fulfillment or happiness, in this world and the next, by knowing, loving, and praising or glorifying him forever:

> Ever since the creation of the world, his eternal power and divine nature, though they are invisible, have been understood and seen through the things that he has made. So that they [the pagans] are without excuse; for though they knew God, they did not honor him as God or give thanks to him, but became futile in their thinking, and their senseless minds were darkened (Rom. 1:20-21).
>
> For from him and through him and to him are all things. To him be glory forever. Amen (Rom. 11:36; see also 1 Cor. 13:9-12 just below).
>
> Thus says the Lord: . . . Surely I know the plans I have for you, says the Lord, plans for your welfare and not for harm, to give you a future with hope. Then when you call upon me and come and pray to me, I will hear you. When you search for me, you will find me; if you seek me with all your heart, I will let you find me (Jeremiah, 29:10-14).[3]

2.   To give human beings opportunity for a more intensive happiness, one undue or "supernatural" to them, he gave them a special means (termed "life" by St. John and "justice," "grace,"

---

2. For further reading about the divine savific plan see: Léon-Dufour, *Dictionary of Biblical Theology*, s.v. Plan of God, pp. 432-436 and, s.v. Mystery, pp. 374-377; *The New Jerome Biblical Commentary*, Index s.v. Plan of God, p. 1,464 and s.v. *Mysterion*, p. 1,460; *BibThSpEx*, pp. 335-342.

3. In this passage Jeremiah is speaking directy about God's plans to reestablish the Jewish people in Jerusalem after their captivity in Babylon. But all the statements remain equally true if they are applied to his wider salvific plan for the salvation and glorification of any individual person who freely cooperates with it.

"justification," or "life" by St. Paul). Thus they could know him, not only dimly on earth through the creatures which mirror his attributes, but also by direct vision eternally in heaven:

> For [here below] we know in part and we prophesy [or teach] only in part; but when the complete comes, the partial will come to an end. . . . For now we see in a mirror dimly, but then we will see [God] face to face. Now I know only in part; then I will know fully, even as I have been fully known [by God] (1 Cor. 13:9-12).

> See what love the Father has given us, that we should be called children of God; and that is what we are. . . . Beloved, we are God's children now; what we will be is not yet revealed. What we do know is this: when he is revealed to us we will be like him, for we will see him as he is (1 John 3:2).

> I came that they [my sheep] may have life, and have it abundantly (John 10:10).

3. That supernatural life, the necessary means to human-kind's supernatural destiny of seeing God face to face, was lost to the human race through original sin; but God gratuitously restored it:

> Sin came into the world through one man and death through sin, and so death spread to all men because all have sinned. . . . Therefore just as one man's trespass led to condemnation for all, so one man's act of righteousness leads to justification for all (Rom. 5:12, 18, 19).

4. God worked this restoration of supernatural life through the Incarnation and Redemption:

> In the beginning was the Word, and the Word was with God, and the Word was God. . . . And the Word became flesh and lived among us, and we have seen his glory, the glory as of a father's only son, full of grace and truth (John 1:14).

> God so loved the world that he gave his only Son, that everyone who believes in him may not perish but may have eternal life (John 3:16).

5. In Paul's concept of "the mystery," the Redemption was achieved by Christ's life, passion, death, and resurrection; and through baptism "into" him we become closely associated with

him in his life, death, and eternal life:

> Do you not know that all of us who have been baptized into
> Christ Jesus were baptized into [fellowship with him in] his
> death? Therefore we have been buried with him by baptism
> into [this close fellowship with him in] his death, so that, just
> as Christ was raised from the dead by the glory [or resplen-
> dent power] of the Father, we too might walk in newness of
> life [with him]. For if we have been united with him in a
> death like his, we will certainly be united with him in a
> resurrection like his (Rom. 6:3-5).

6. To those who freely cooperate with the divine plan, God
grants the reward of the beatific vision, more joy-filled in
proportion to their devotion and generosity on earth.

> Do not store up for yourselves treasures on earth, where
> moth and rust consume and where thieves break in and
> steal; but store up for yourselves treasures in heaven, where
> neither moth nor rust consumes and where thieves do not
> break in and steal (Matt. 6:19-20).
>
> Each will receive wages according to the labor of each (1
> Cor:3:8)
>
> Whatever your task, put yourselves into it, as done for
> the Lord and not for your masters, since you know that from
> the Lord you will receive the inheritance as your reward;
> you serve the Lord Christ (Col. 3:23-24).
>
> Come, you that are blessed by my Father, inherit the
> kingdom prepared for you from the foundation of the world;
> for I was hungry and you gave me food; . . . (Matt. 15:34).

7. At the end of the world Christ will present to his Father
the Kingdom of all those who believed in him and served God
faithfully, and thus they will attain the purpose for which God
created them:

> For as all die in Adam, so all will be made alive in Christ. But
> each in his own order: Christ the first fruits, then at his
> command those who believe in Christ. Then comes the end,
> when he [Christ] hands over the kingdom to God the Father,
> after he has destroyed every ruler and every authority and
> power [of his enemies]. . . . For God has put all things in
> subjection under his feet. . . . When all things are subjected

to the one who put all things in subjection under him, so that God may be everything to everyone [that is, everything to everybody] (1 Cor. 15:22-28; see also Rom. 8:19-23; Eph. 4:8-10; Apoc. 21:1-4).

8. Similarly, the whole material universe will then fully attain the purpose for which God created it: to mirror forth God's perfections to men and women, and thus be a means enabling them to cooperate freely with his plan by meriting on earth their supernatural end, the beatific vision. However, since they were incapable of reaching it after Adam's fall, the material universe too was by that fall made incapable of helping them to their supernatural destiny. In St. Paul's words, it was subjected to futility—the futility which Christ's Redemption removed:

> I consider that the sufferings of this present time are not worth comparing with the glory that is to be revealed to us. For the creation waits with eager longing for the revealing of the sons of God; for the creation was subjected to futility, . . . [But] the creation itself will be set free from its bondage to decay and obtain the freedom of the glory of the children of God. . . .
> We know that all things work together for good for those who love God, who are called according to his purpose [that is, his plan or design] (Rom. 8:18-21, 28).

Reflections in Later Centuries

The thought contained in the texts of Scripture cited above was part of the deposit of truths which Christ entrusted to his Church to preach to all nations even to the end of the world (Matt. 28:19-20). Ever since then Christian thinkers have been reflecting on those truths and deepening our insights into them. St. Augustine comes to mind, and the many Councils of the Church. By Ignatius' sixteenth century syntheses of those truths (naturally each summation with a character of its own and clothed in trappings of its particular era) were available to him in three influential works: the *Life of Christ* by the Carthusian Ludolph of Saxony, the *Sentences* of Peter Lombard, and the *Summa of Theology* by the Dominican Thomas Aquinas.

A few citations from the first chapter of Book II of Peter Lombard's *Sentences* are highly relevant to our present reflections on God's plan of creation. They too serve as fruitful *lectio divina.*

3. God created the world at the beginning of time. . . . Therefore we should believe that there is no other cause of the created beings . . . than the goodness of the Creator. . . . His goodness is so great that he wills others to be sharers of his eternal beatitude. He sees that his own happiness can be communicated, but in no way diminished. . . .

4. . . . Therefore God made the rational creature which could know the Supreme Good, and by knowing him love him, and by loving him possess him, and by possessing him enjoy him. . . . Consequently, if it is asked why a human being or an angel was created, the brief reply can be given: because of the goodness of God. . . .

6. And if it is asked for what destiny the rational creature was created, the answer is: to praise God, to serve him, and to enjoy him; and in all these activities the rational creature, not God, gains the benefit. For God, being perfect and full of all goodness, cannot be either increased or diminished. . . .

8. And just as human beings were made for God, that is, that they might serve God, so the world was made for human beings, that it might serve them. Hence they were placed in the middle [between the world and God], that they might be both served themselves and in turn give service [to God]; . . . For God willed to be served by men and women in such a way that by that service, not God but they who are doing the serving, might be the ones aided. God further willed that the world should be of service to human beings, and that they might be aided by it.[4]

Did Ignatius read those paragraphs of Peter? We do not have documentary evidence that he did. But other indications make it probable. At Loyola in 1521 he meditated profoundly on Ludolph's *Life of Christ*, which already in its second chapter expounded the reality of God's redemptive plan (though not in our modern terminology), and then through the rest of its pages showed that plan evolving in the history of salvation--all the way to human salvation by praising or glorifying God in the joy

---

4. *Petri Lombardi Sententiarum libri quattuor* (Paris: Migne, 1853), col. 143. Translation mine.

of the beatific vision. That chapter of Ludolph's *Life* was seemingly the source from which Ignatius took the idea that Adam was created in the plain of Damascus (*SpEx*, 51). Moreover, during his mystical illuminations at Manresa in 1522 which brought him a synthesis of his previous knowledge, he tells us that "the manner in which God had created the world was presented to his understanding with great spiritual joy" (*Autobiog*, 29). By now his interest in creation was manifestly strong. Then at Alcalá in 1527 "he studied the Master of the Sentences" (ibid., 57). From 1533 to 1535 in Paris he had to bring to his theological lectures in the Dominican convent on the rue Saint-Jacques a commentary on Peter Lombard's *Sentences*.[5] All this shows that the ideas contained in Peter's statements were part of the academic atmosphere in which Ignatius studied at Alcalá and Paris. Against this background, it is rather hard to think that Ignatius failed to discover and ponder the pages of Peter Lombard cited above. At least he must have been in some way influenced by them. Since their thought is so similar to his own in his Principle and Foundation, his hunger for a few pages such as Peter's would have been natural. It is possible or even probable that his formulation of the Foundation began in the form of his terse notes on those pages.[6] In any case, the thought contained in the above citations from Scripture and from Peter Lombard became Ignatius' heritage. He in turn passed it on, compactly in his Foundation and more extensively in the rest of his *Exercises*.

---

5. *DalmIgn*, p. 122.

6. For more on the intellectual and spiritual formation of Ignatius' worldview, see *IgnCWS*, pp. 12-44.

APPENDIX II

TOWARD THE DEEPER STUDY OF THE FOUNDATION

The Principle and Foundation (23) has long been admired as a compressed synthesis of the most important basic principles which function throughout the rest of the *Exercises*. An introduction to the basic principles and terminology of this Foundation has been given in endnotes 17-22 above.

But the importance of the Foundation extends far beyond the *Exercises*. These same principles which are so tersely expressed in the Foundation were also the mainspring or driving force which guided and inspired all the activities of Ignatius' life. He was constantly applying them in his other writings. They were under God the chief source of his extraordinary vitality and influence. The Foundation contains in germ the substance of his expansive worldview on God, the universe, and the role of free human beings in God's plan of salvation and spiritual growth. Hence for those who wish to study it more deeply it seems advisable to point out some of its additional features which will enrich the rest of one's life.

Reason Alone or Faith?

If the words alone of the Foundation are considered without any context, all the truths in it are such that they could be learned from reason alone, for example, by Plato or Aristotle. This fact is occasionally useful with non-Christian retreatants or in missionary countries. But it has also given rise to different interpretations and controversies. How did Ignatius himself really mean it?

Most commentators now think that he did not restrict the Foundation to natural reason, but intended it to be understood in the light of God's revelation: the divine redemptive plan in the existing supernatural order; and consequently, that a Christology is implicitly present in it. When Ignatius was revising his *Exercises* from 1522 to 1541, he was writing as a Christian for Christian exercitants in his own Christian culture. By the word "God" in the Foundation he meant the triune God as known from revelation, and by "save their souls" he meant the revealed supernatural destiny of the beatific vision. He and his exercitants had no reason to prescind from faith and operate by natural reason alone, like a teacher of philosophy in our twentieth century.

Confirmation of this opinion arises from his use in *SpEx,* 23:2 of the phrase by which he habitually expressed his deep reverence for God: "God our Lord" (*Dios nuestro Señor*). By that phrase he often directly meant Christ; for example, in 53 he calls *Cristo nuestro Señor* our "Creator."[1] Because of Ignatius' terseness in the Foundation we cannot be certain whether his thought here in 23 is focused directly on God as Trinity or on Christ. But in either case Christ is included within the phrase "God our Lord."[2]

In his monograph *L'interprétation authentique de la méditation fondamentale* (Bourges, 1922), Pierre Bouvier published many insights which won widespread acceptance. But he also maintained (pages 77-79), like A. Ponlevoy some sixty years earlier, that Ignatius based the Foundation solely on natural reason, not faith; and consequently, that he did not presuppose our elevation to the supernatural order. This opinion drew a steady flow of disagreements. The Spanish scriptural expert José Bover, for example, argued against it in "El Principio y Fundamento: por razón o por fe?" (*Manresa,* 1 [1925]: 321-326), in which he also praised the rest of Bouvier's monograph. Similar refutation came from Walter Sierp, *Hochschule der Gottesliebe* (1935), pages 119-122. In "La méditation fondamentale à la lumière de S. Paul," Jean Levie maintained that the Foundation supposes the supernatural economy of salvation and the beatific vision; it gets its full value and complete meaning in the light of the ascetical and mystical teaching of St. Paul.[3] In 1965 Iparraguirre wrote that the opinion of Ponlevoy and Bouvier limiting the Foundation to reason alone was virtually abandoned.[4] Interpretation in the light of revelation is supported also by other authors.[5]

---

1. On this see note 15 in *IgnCLWS*, p. 372; also "Jesus Christ, God and our Lord" in *Cons,* 758; also Aldama, *An Introductory Commentary on the Constitutions*, p. 272; J. Solano, "Cristología de las Constituciones," in *Ejercicios-Constituciones: unidad vital* (Bilbao, 1975), pp. 207-208.

2. Solano, in *Miscelanea Comillas* 26 (1956): 173.

3. *Nouvelle Revue Théologique* 75 (1953): 815-827; see esp. 815, 816.

4. L. González and I. Iparraguirre, *Ejercicios Espirituales: Comentario pastoral* (Madrid, 1965), p. 135.

5. Noteworthily here, by M. A. Fiorito, "Cristocentrismo del . . .

Cusson (1968 and subsequently) has presented the Foundation from the viewpoint of biblical theology.[6]

Highlights in the History of the Foundation

In treating the history of the Foundation we should distinguish its literary expression (which first appears in Paris in 1535) from its substance (which in some rudimentary form seems to date from Manresa in 1522).

Our earliest written expression of the Foundation with its present structure is found in the notes written by the English humanist John Helyar after he made the Exercises, probably under Favre in 1535.[7] There it was still among the introductory explanations (*anotaciónes*) used to prepare the dispositions of exercitants, and it had a form only a little simpler than the definitive Spanish text which is in the Autograph, *A*, a copy made most probably in 1544. A literal translation of this definitive text into Latin is found in the First Latin version, P^1, used in Paris from about 1529 to 1535. But our manuscript of this version dates only from 1541.

However, the chief principles contained in the Foundation functioned so prominently in Ignatius' thought from Manresa in 1522 onward that many experts have thought that its substance must have existed in some sketchy form already at Manresa.[8] Pertinent features are the descent of all creatures from God, their return to God through praise and service from free persons, and the principles which Ignatius used in guiding people through elections. The Foundation seems to have been influenced by Ignatius' mystical experiences at Manresa. There "the manner in which God had created the world was presented

---

Fundamento," (*Ciencia y Fe* 17 [1961]: 3-42); Cusson, (*La pédagogie d'expérience spirituelle personelle* [1968], pp. 67-89; *BibThSpEx*, pp. 47-67); Coathalem, *Ignatian Insights* (1971), pp. 63-68; S. Lyonnet, "A Scriptural Presentation of the Principle and Foundation," *Ignis* 6 [1973]: 24-32; J. Losada, "Presencia de Cristo in el Principio y Fundamento," *Manresa* 54 [1982]: 45-57; Granero (*Manresa* 40 [1968]: 327-336; see esp. 334. For further references see *Obras-compl*, p. 214.

6. *BibThSpEx*, pp. 47-67; see also 68-80, 98, 135, 138-139.

7. *SpExMHSJ69*, pp. 31-32, 425, 429.

8. See, e.g., Leturia, *Estudios*, 2:21; Iparraguirre, *Obrascompl*, p. 190; Dalmases with Calveras, *SpExMHSJ69*, pp. 31-32; *DalmIgn*, p. 67; Coathalem, p. 61.

to his understanding with great spiritual joy" (*Autobiog*, 29). Moreover, his exhilarating illumination beside the Cardoner gave him a synthesized vision of his previous thoughts, especially those from Ludolph's *Life of Christ*.

A little later other probable influences on the Foundation appear. In Barcelona (1524-1526) and Alcalá (1526-1527) Ignatius made his first attempts at giving the Exercises, sometimes in the hope of winning companions for his apostolic life.[9] Such work was likely to make him aware of the necessity of indifference for making sound decisions. There too he probably read[10] some of Erasmus' *Handbook of the Christian Soldier* (*Enchiridion militis Christiani*). In it Erasmus urged:[11]

> Take this as your Fourth Rule: Set before you Christ as the only goal of your whole life, and direct all your efforts, all your activities, all of your business in his direction. . . .
>
> For one who is pressing straight forward toward the goal of the supreme good, whatever things turn up along the way should be rejected or accepted to the extent that (*eatenus . . . quatenus*) they further or obstruct one's progress. Of such things there are three categories.
>
> Some of them are so base that they can never be upright. . . . Other things . . . are so good that they can never be base. . . .
>
> Still others are midway between these two: for example, health, good looks, strength, eloquence, learning, and the like. In this category of things nothing should be sought for itself alone, and such things should not be used in greater or less measure except to the extent that (*eatenus . . . quatenus*) they are conducive to the final goal.

The striking similarity here to Ignatius' treatment of indifference in the Foundation makes influence on it from Erasmus probable. Although Ignatius was later cool toward Erasmus in general,[12] he may well have found this passage useful and

9. See *DalmIgn*, pp. 88-89; *Obrascompl*, p. 42.

10. Ribadeneira in *FN*, 4:172-174; *DalmIgn*, pp. 91-92.

11. The Latin text is in *SpExMHSJ69*, p. 57.

12. Some of Erasmus' books were harshly satirical of ecclesiastical authorities and practices and later he was among the authors who were suspect to Ignatius (*Cons*, 465). But the *Enchiridion militis Christiani* is not thus satirical. This has cast doubt on some of Ribadeneira's statements in *FN*,

taken notes on it which went into his principle of indifference, far more tersely expressed in the Foundation (23:4,5,6) than in Erasmus' ample page. If so, Erasmus' *eatenus . . . quatenus* became Ignatius' *tanto . . . cuanto*: We ought to use or reject these things "to the extent that" they help or hinder us. But if Ignatius borrowed from Erasmus, he also added an original emphasis characteristically his own, his norm for making decisions: We ought to choose "only that which is *more* conducive to the end for which we are created" (23:7).

We turn our attention again to the statement from Peter Lombard's *Sentences* quoted above on page 206:

> The rational creature . . . [was created] to praise God, to serve him, and to enjoy him. . . . And just as human beings were made for God, that they might serve God, so the world was made for humanbeings.

As was mentioned above, this statement of Peter may have been the origin of Ignatius' phraseology in "to praise, reverence, and serve God" (23:1,2), and of his statement that all other things are created to help human beings toward salvation (23:3). But why, it is often asked, did Ignatius write "to praise" and "to serve," and omit "to love"? A possible reason is that he was writing notes on this sentence of Peter Lombard (or some similar source which did not contain the word love); and hence Ignatius too omitted the word "love" just as his source did. Other commentators have devised more elaborate theories.[13] In the Foundation he was aiming principally to inculcate the premises which conclude to the need of indifference and wise choice. Affective love might distract attention from that need, and hence he omitted it. It would suffice to bring it in later, especially in the concluding Contemplation to Attain Love. Since he himself has not told us why he omitted the word "love," in these discussions we are confined to conjectural theories. It should be noticed, however, that reverential praise of God clearly implies love of him; and Ignatius nowhere forbade the consideration of love during the ruminations on the Foundation.

After the Foundation reached its definitive form in Helyar's notes and the Autograph text of 1544, another long history

---

4:172-174 about him and Erasmus in Barcelona in or near 1525.

   13. See, e.g., J. Calveras in *Manresa*, 7 (1931): 107-115.

began: that of continual discoveries of new wonders contained within it. Ignatius himself and many of his contemporaries used the Foundation especially to teach the principle of indifference, the hinge on which the election depends. In his Directory dictated to Vitoria Ignatius advised keeping some exercitants "on the consideration of the Foundation and on the particular and general examens for three or four days or even more."[14] As its fundamental importance became more and more recognized it was divided into points (e.g., the end of human beings, the means to it, the necessity and difficulty of indifference) and placed within the First Week.[15] Different directors such as Polanco, Canisius, and other early Jesuits used variant manners and emphases in presenting the *Exercises*, or in writing Directories on them. Miró, for example, used a viewpoint of idealistic but rigid theory, while Polanco saw them from a viewpoint of what went on in a retreatant's heart.[16]

In the minds and hearts of retreatants, too, the Foundation functioned in other ways which slowly came to light. It contained the outlook of Christian faith, that vision of the whole which was an inspiring introduction to Ignatius' own worldview on God, the created universe, and the role which the exercitant as a free human being can play in shaping the evolution of this divine salvific plan.[17] An example in point is the case of Ignatius' contemporary, Martín de Olave, a doctor of Scripture. After he made the Exercises before entering the Society, he stated that he learned more from his meditation on the Foundation than from all his previous study of theology.[18]

To what extent Ignatius was aware of the growing insights and unanticipated spiritual fruits the Foundation was producing we do not know. But we do know that he did not wish to bind others to the details of his own knowledge or practice. His pedagogical method was, as he states (*SpEx*, 2), to stimulate exercitants to think things out for themselves and make their own new discoveries. He also wanted directors to adapt the Exercises for the benefit of their exercitants (18). For centuries retreat directors, following these directives, have devised new

---

14. *SpEx*MHSJ19, p. 791; *DirSpEx*, p. 100.
15. *BibThSpEx*, p. 49; also pp. 47-50 on the history of the Foundation.
16. Iparraguirre, in *Historia de los Ejercicios*, 2:430.
17. Cusson expounds this worldview well in *BibThSpEx*, pp. 44-67.
18. Iparraguirre, *História de los Ejercicios* 1 (1532-1556): 179, 189.

ways of presenting the Foundation. Many exercitants too have, after their retreat experience, preserved and deepened its fruits by studying the *Exercises*, including the Foundation in which they found ever-growing significance. Further still, scholars and writers have been studying the Foundation; and the more they explored the more have they made explicit the new inspirational truths they found latent within it. Examples in point are the statement of La Palma in 1626 quoted above, and in our day Cusson's presentation of the Foundation in the full light of biblical theology.[19] Through procedures such as this we today know many aspects of the Foundation which were unnoticed by Ignatius—just as scholars of Scripture today know more aspects of its truths than any sixteenth-century expert.

While the directors and writers were adjusting themselves to the prevailing ideas of their respective eras they naturally varied their ways of presenting the Foundation. Some have stressed our creation by God, our dependence on him, and the obligations we owe him. Others have found it more inspirational to stress the attractive and inspirational goal in which Ignatius' first statement in the Foundation comes to its climax. This goal, salvation in the beatific vision, inspires retreatants and motivates them to accept the work or sacrifices necessary to attain it. In our era when spirituality is becoming more and more biblical, many directors have devised presentations increasingly scriptural. All these approaches are legitimate, and can be adapted to elicit "experiences filled with reverence and awe, like Iñigo's Cardoner experience."[20] Such experiences have often elicited great inspiration and desire and thus done much to make the *Exercises* effective. Probably each director can succeed best with the experiences of the Foundation found most inspirational in his or her own life. To the retreatant the Foundation can bring orientation, inspiration, and desire of spiritual growth.

---

19. *BibThSpEx*, pp. 44-67.

20. See J. A. Tetlow, "The Fundamentum: Creation in the Principle and Foundation," *Studies in the Spirituality of Jesuits* 21/4 (Sept. 1989): esp. 37, 49-50.

SELECTED BIBLIOGRAPHY

of all the works referred to in the present book,
and a few others.
It focuses especially on works in English.

I. BIBLIOGRAPHIES

Begheyn, Paul, and Kenneth C. Bogart. "A Bibliography on St. Ignatius' *Spiritual Exercises.*" *Studies in the Spirituality of Jesuits* 22/3 (May, 1991).

Iparraguirre, Ignacio. *Orientaciones bibliográficas sobre San Ignacio de Loyola.* Subsidia ad historiam Societatis Iesu, no. 1. 2nd ed. rev. Rome, 1965. Pages 75-99 are on the *Exercises.*

Polgár, Lázló. *Bibliographie sur l'histoire de la Compagnie de Jésus. 1901-1980. Vol. I. Toute la Compagnie.* Rome, 1980. Pages 265-373 are on the *Exercises.*

Ruiz Jurado, Manuel. *Orientaciones bibliográficas sobre San Ignacio de Loyola. Vol. II. (1965-1976). Vol. III (1977-1989).* Subsidia ad historiam Societatis Iesu, nos. 8 and 9. Rome, 1977 and 1990.

II. THE CHIEF PRIMARY SOURCES

MHSJ—MONUMENTA HISTORICA SOCIETATIS JESU, the Historical Records or Sources of the Society of Jesus in critically edited texts, most of them from the Society's archives in Rome. This scholarly series of 131 volumes was begun in Madrid in 1894 and transferred to Rome in 1929, where it is being continued by the Jesuit Historical Institute.

MI—Monumenta Ignatiana. The writings of St. Ignatius of Loyola.

Series I

EppIgn—S. Ignatii . . . Epistolae et Instructiones. 12 vols. Madrid, 1903-1911. The letters and instructions of St. Ignatius.

Series II

SpExMHSJ19—*Exercitia Spiritualia S. Ignatii ... et eorum Directoria.* Ed. A. Codina. Madrid, 1919. The *Spiritual Exercises* and Directories.

SpExMHSJ69—Vol. I. *S. Ignatii de Loyola Exercitia spiritualia: Textuum antiquissimorum nova editio.* Ed. C. de Dalmases. Rome, 1969. (A revision of *SpExMHSJ19*).

DirSpEx—Vol. II. *Directoria Exercitiorum Spiritualium (1540-1599).* Ed. I. Iparraguirre. 1955. (Also a revision of *SpEx-MHSJ19*.)

Series IV

FN—*Fontes narrativi de S. Ignatio de Loyola et de Societatis Iesu initiis.* Ed. D. Fernández Zapico, C. de Dalmases, P. de Leturia. 4 vols., 1943-1960. Vol. 1. 1523-1556; 2. 1557-1574; 3. 1574-1599; 4. Ribadeneira's *Vita Ignatii Loyolae* (1572). 1965.

MonNad—*Epistolae P. Hieronymi Nadal.* 6 vols. Vols. I-IV. Ed. F. Cervós. 1898-1905. Vol. 5. *Commentarii de Instituto S. I.,* 1962, and 6. *Orationis observationes,* 1964. Ed. M. Nicolau. Letters and instructions of Ignatius' companion Jerónimo Nadal.

DalmMan—Dalmases, Cándido de. *Ignacio de Loyola. Ejercicios Espirituales: Introducción, texto, notas y vocabulario* por Cándido de Dalmases, S.J. Santander: Sal Terrae, 1987.

III. OTHER BOOKS

Arzubialde, Santiago. *Ejercicios Espirituales de San Ignacio: Historia y análisis.* Bilbao-Santander, 1991.

Blaise, A. *Dictionnaire Latin-Français des auteurs chrétiens.* Strasbourg, 1954.

Brou, Alexandre. *Ignatian Methods of Prayer.* Trans. W. J. Young. Milwaukee, 1949.

Calveras, José. *Ejercicios espirituales, Directorio, y Documentos de S. Ignacio de Loyola: Glosa y vocabulario de los Ejercicios.* 2nd ed. Barcelona, 1958.

Cisneros, García de. *Book of Exercises for the Spiritual Life: Written in the Year 1500.* Trans. E. Allison Peers. Monastery of Montserrat, 1929.

Clancy, Thomas H. *An Introduction to Jesuit Life.* St. Louis, 1976.

Coathalem, Hervé. *Ignatian Insights: A Guide to the Complete Spiritual Exercises.* Taichung (Taiwan), 1971.

Covarrubias, Sebastián de. *Tesoro de la lengua Castellana o Española, segun la impresión de 1611.* Ed. Martín de Riquer. Barcelona, 1943.

Cusson, Gilles. *Biblical Theology and the Spiritual Exercises.* St. Louis, 1988.

————. *The Spiritual Exercises Made in Everyday Life: A Method and a Biblical Interpretation.* St. Louis, 1989.

Dalmases, Cándido de. *Ignatius of Loyola, Founder of the Jesuits: His Life and Work.* St. Louis, 1985.

Directory of the Spiritual Exercises of Our Holy Father Ignatius: Authorized Translation. London, 1925.

Divarkar, Parmananda R., trans. *Ablaze with God: A Reading of The Memoirs of Ignatius of Loyola.* Anand, India, 1990.

Egan, Harvey D. *The Spiritual Exercises and the Ignatian Mystical Horizon.* St. Louis, 1976.

English, John. *Choosing Life.* New York, 1978.

————. *Spiritual Freedom: From an Experience of the Ignatian Exercises to the Art of Spiritual Direction.* Guelph, Ontario, 1975.

Fleming, David L. *The Spiritual Exercises: A Literal Translation and a Contemporary Reading.* St. Louis, 1972.

See also *Notes on the Spiritual Exercises,* below.

Frank, Francine W., and Paula A. Treichler. *Language, Gender, and Professional Writing.* New York: The Modern Language Association of America, 1989.

Ganss, George E. *Ignatius of Loyola: The* Spiritual Exercises *and Selected Works.* The Classics of Western Spirituality, no. 72. Mahwah, N.J., 1991.

Giuliani, Maurice, et al. *Ignace de Loyola: Ecrits, traduits et présentés sous la direction de Maurice Giuliani, S.J.* (Paris, 1991).

Gueydan, Edouard, et al. *Ignace de Loyola: Exercices Spirituels: Traduction du texte Autographe.* Collection Christus, no. 61. Paris, 1985.

Guibert, Joseph de. *The Jesuits: Their Spiritual Doctrine and Practice.* Trans. W. J. Young. Chicago, 1964. 3rd ed. St. Louis, 1986.

————. *The Theology of the Spiritual Life.* Trans. Paul Barrett. New York, 1953.

Hausherr, Irénée. *The Name of Jesus.* Kalamazoo, 1979

Hernández Gordils, Emmanuele. *Que su santísima voluntad sintamos y enteramente la cumplamos.* Rome, 1966. Excerpts from a dissertation, Gregorian University.

Ignatius of Loyola, St. *Letters of St. Ignatius of Loyola.* Trans. W. J. Young. Chicago, 1959.

Ignatius, His Personality and Spiritual Heritage. Ed. F. Wulf. St. Louis, 1977.

Iparraguirre, Ignacio, and Cándido de Dalmases, ed. *Obras completas de San Ignacio.* 4th ed. Madrid: Biblioteca de Autores Cristianos, 1982.

————. *Vocabulario de Ejercicios Espirituales: Ensayo de hermenéutica Ignatiana.* Rome, 1972.

Knauer, Peter. *Ignatius von Loyola: Geistliche Übungen und erläuternde Texte.* Übersetzt und erklärt von Peter Knauer. Leipzig, 1978.

Léon-Dufour, Xavier. *Dictionary of Biblical Theology.* New York, 1973.

Leturia, Pedro de. *Estudios Ignacianos.* Ed. I. Iparraguirre. 2 vols. Rome, 1957.

————. *Iñigo de Loyola.* Trans. A. J. Owen. 2nd ed. Chicago, 1965.

Longridge, W. H. *The Spiritual Exercises of Saint Ignatius of Loyola. Translated from the Spanish with a Commentary and a Translation of the* Directorium in Exercitia. London, 1919.

McKenzie, John L. *Dictionary of the Bible.* Milwaukee, 1965.

Morris, John. *The Text of the Spiritual Exercises of St. Ignatius, Translated from the Original Spanish.* 4th ed. Westminster, Md., 1943.

Mullan, Elder. *The Spiritual Exercises of St. Ignatius of Loyola, Translated from the Autograph.* New York, 1914.

National Conference of Catholic Bishops. *Criteria for the Evaluation of Inclusive Language Translations of Scriptural Texts Proposed for Liturgical Use.* Publication No. 421-X. Washington: United States Catholic Conference, 1990.

The New Dictionary of Theology. Ed. Joseph A. Komonchak et al. Wilmington, 1987.

The New Jerome Biblical Commentary. Ed. R. E, Brown, J. A. Fitzmyer, R. E. Murphy. Englewood Cliffs, N.J., 1988.

Nicolás, Antonio T. de. *Powers of Imagining: Ignatius de Loyola. A Philosophical Hermeneutic of Imagining through the Collected Works of Ignatius de Loyola with a Translation of These Works.* Albany, 1986.

Notes on the Spiritual Exercises: The Best of the Review. Ed. David L. Fleming. St. Louis, 1983. A collection of articles from *The Review for Religious.*

Obras completas de San Ignacio. 4th ed., 1982. See Iparraguirre, above.

Ong, Walter J. *The Barbarian Within.* New York, 1962.

Oxford Dictionary of the Christian Church. Ed. F. L. Cross. 2nd ed. New York, 1974.

Palma, Luis de la. *Camino espiritual . . . de los Ejercicios.* Alcalá, 1626.

Petri Lombardi Sententiarum libri quattuor. Ed. Migne. Paris, 1853.

Puhl, Louis J. *The Spiritual Exercises of St. Ignatius: A New Translation. Based on Studies in the Language of the Autograph.* Westminster, Md., 1951, and Chicago, 1968.

Rahner, Hugo. *Ignatius the Theologian.* Trans. Michael Barry. New York, 1968.

————. *St Ignatius Loyola: Letters to Women.* Trans. K. Pond and S. A. H. Weetman. New York, 1960.

————. *The Spirituality of St. Ignatius Loyola: An Account of Its Historical Development.* Trans. F. J. Smith. Chicago, 1968.

RB 1980: The Rule of St. Benedict in Latin and English with Notes. Ed. Timothy Fry. Collegeville, 1981.

Richards, Innocentia. *See* Vandenbroucke below.

Sheldrake, Philip. *See* The Way of Ignatius Loyola, below.

Stanley, David. *A Modern Scriptural Approach to the Spiritual Exercises.* Chicago and St. Louis, 1967 and 1986.

————. *"I Encountered God!" The Spiritual Exercises with the Gospel of St. John.* St. Louis, 1986.

Tetlow, Elisabeth Meier. *The Spiritual Exercises of St. Ignatius Loyola: A New Translation.* Lanham, Md., 1987.

Tetlow, Joseph A. *Choosing Christ in the World: Directing the Spiritual Exercises according to Annotations Eighteen and Nineteen: A Handbook.* St. Louis, 1989.

Toner, Jules. *A Commentary on St. Ignatius' Rules for the Discernment of Spirits.* St. Louis, 1982.

————. *Discerning God's Will: Ignatius of Loyola's Teaching on Christian Decision Making.* St. Louis, 1991.

Vandenbroucke, François, and Joseph Pegon. *Discernment of Spirits.* Trans. Innocentia Richards, from *Dictionnaire de Spiritualité,* 3: cols. 1222-1291. Collegeville, 1970.

The Way of Ignatius Loyola: Contemporary Approaches to the Spiritual Exercises. Ed. Philip Sheldrake. London and St. Louis,

1991. A collection of articles from *The Way*.
The Westminster Dictionary of Christian Spirituality. Ed. Gordon S. Wakefield. Philadelphia, 1983.

IV. ARTICLES

Aschenbrenner, George A. "Consciousness Examen." *Review for Religious* 31 (1972): 13-21.

Buckley, Michael J. "Rules for the Discernment of Spirits." *The Way*, Supplement 20 (Autumn 1973): 19-37.

Donnelly, Philip J. "St. Thomas and the Ultimate Purpose of Creation." *Theological Studies* 2 (1941): 53-83.

————. "The Doctrine of the Vatican Council on the End of Creation." *Theological Studies* 4 (1943): 3-33.

Fiorito, M. A. "Cristocentrismo del 'Principio y Fundamento' de San Ignacio." *Ciencia y Fe* 17 (1961): 3-42.

Ganss, George E. "Prudence and Vocations." *Review for Religious* 22 (1962): 434-442.

————. "'Active Life' or 'Contemplative Life'?" *Review for Religious* 22 (1963): 53-56.

————. "Thinking with the Church: The Spirit of St. Ignatius' Rules." *The Way*, Supplement 20 (1973): 72-82.

Kinerk, E. Edward. "Eliciting Great Desires: Their Place in the Spirituality of the Society of Jesus." *Studies in the Spirituality of Jesuits* 16 (November 1984).

Leturia, Pedro de. "Génesis de los Ejercicios de san Ignacio y su influjo en la fundación de la Compañía de Jesús." *Estudios Ignacianos* 2:3-55. Rome, 1957.

————. "Sentido verdadero en la Iglesia militante." *Estudios Ignacianos* 2:149-174.

Ong, Walter J. "'A.M.D.G.': Dedication or Directive?" *Review for Religious* 11 (1952): 257-264.

Quay, Paul. "Angels and Demons: The Teaching of IV Lateran." *Theological Studies* 42 (March 1981): 20-45.

Solano, Jesús. "Cristología de las Constituciones." In *Ejercicios-Constituciones: unidad vital*, pp. 207-208. Bilbao, 1975.

Tetlow, Joseph A. "The Fundamentum: Creation in the Principle and Foundation." *Studies in the Spirituality of Jesuits* 21/4 (Sept. 1989).

EDITORIAL NOTE ON THE TERM
"SPIRITUAL EXERCISES"

To solve the editorial problems arising from the term "Spiritual Exercises," we use *Spiritual Exercises* (in italic type) when the term refers chiefly to Ignatius' book, and Spiritual Exercises (in roman type) when the term refers chiefly to the activities of an exercitant within a retreat. At times the two meanings overlap and require an arbitrary decision as to which is predominant. This term "Spiritual Exercises" gives rise to many editorial problems. The procedures by which they are handled are shown by example in the following paragraphs.

Long before Ignatius various spiritual exercises, such as attendance at Mass or recitation of the Office, were common. He gradually composed directives for a sequence of such exercises. Before 1535 his companions Xavier and Favre made his Spiritual Exercises for a period of thirty days. Ignatius assembled his notes in his book *Spiritual Exercises*, which was (or were) published at Rome in 1548. To make references easier, in an edition published at Turin in 1928, Arturo Codina divided the *Exercises* into 370 sections, with each section designated by a number in square brackets to indicate that it was an addition to Ignatius' manuscript. For example, the purpose of the Exercises is stated in *Spiritual Exercises*, [21] or, to use our abbreviation, *SpEx*, [21]. In some editions since then the numbers were placed in the margins, sometimes with and sometimes without the brackets.

By 1991 evolving stylistic customs have brought modifications to some former practices. For example, some editors have ceased to use the brackets [ ] in references to the sections of the *Exercises*. However, the brackets [ ] are still used to indicate cross references run into Ignatius' own text; for example, in *SpEx*, 189: "an Election as explained above [175-188]." Ordinary references run into our own texts are indicated by parentheses. Other examples of our usages follow. The Introductory Explanations (*Anotaciones*) are in *SpEx*, 1-20. Important exercises in his book are the Principle and Foundation (23) and the Call of the King (91-98), which is an introduction to the Second Week or division of the *Exercises*. Since 1548 the *Spiritual Exercises* have been read or made by many persons. The making of the Exercises is often a deep spiritual experience.

Recently further additions have been devised because of the computerization of Ignatius' texts to facilitate studies of his vocabulary and texts. The section numbers introduced in 1928 have been retained; but each section has been subdivided into thought units or numbered verses for the sake of precisely detailed locations; for instance, *SpEx* 23:2, 95:4,5, 189:6-9. The term "mortal sin" (*pecado mortal*) means a sin punished by damnation in 33:3 and 48:4; but it means one of the capital sins in 18:5,7, 382:2, 242:3, 245.

INDEX

The numbers in **bold face** refer to **sections** of the *Exercises;*
and those in light face, to pages of this book.

Abstinence, **210-213, 229, 359;**
181

Adam, sin of, **51;** 156

Adaptations of the Exercises,
18-20; 4, 145

Additional Directives (*adiciones*), **6, 73-90, 130, 131,
206, 207, 229;** 158

Adrianssens, A., letter to, 182

Affections for each Week, **3, 74,
130, 206, 229, 342**
See also attachments

Aim of this book, vii, 10-12
its relation to *Ignatius* published by Paulist Press, xi

Aldama, Antonio, 209

Alms, distribution of, **337-344;**
196

Amending one's own life, **189;**
177

Angels, sin of, **50;** 154-156
existence of, 191

Annotations. *See* Introductory
Explanations

Aschenbrenner, G., 154

Application of senses. *See* Senses

Attachments, affections, or inclinations:
disordered **1, 16, 21, 149-
157, 172, 179;** 143, 147-
148, 161, 169, 171, 172
well ordered, 148, 161, 169,
171-172

Augustine, St., **344, 363;** 167

Benedict, St., Rule of, 174, 187,
201

Benefice, **16, 169, 171, 178, 181;**
145

Bernard, St, **351;** 174, 196

Bible in Spanish, 188

Binario, meaning of, 170-171

Bonaventure, St., **363;** 164

Bouvier, P., 151, 209

Buckley, M. J., 190

Busa, R., ix

Calveras, J., 10, 180, 186, 193,
210, 212

Carthage, Third Council of, **344**

Christ, his standard, **137; 143-
147** 167-169
imitation of in use of the
senses, **214, 248**
interior knowledge about,
104; 163
model to be imitated, **143,
344;** 181
present in Week I, **23, 53;**
150, 157, 206-208
apparition of to Mary, **219,
299;** 182

Christology of the Foundation,
23; 150, 157, 208-210

Church, proper attitude toward, **352-370;** 197-200
Ignatius' concept of, **353;** 199

historical background, 197-198

sentido, attitude, 199

fundamental principle, **353**; 199

on practices, **354-361**; 199

on superiors, **362-364**; 199-200

on doctrines, **365-370**; 200

Classes, Three, **148-157**; 169-172

Coathalem, Hervé, 148, 158, 163, 164, 177, 179, 186, 190, 191, 193, 194, 210

Colloquy, how made, **53, 54, 199**; 156, 157

to Christ on cross, **53**

triple, **62-63, 147, 156, 159, 168**

Commandments, praying about the, **239-243**; 186

the state of the, **135**; 166

of the Church, **361**

Communion, at end of Week I, **44**

Comparing saints with persons still alive, **364**

Composition of place, **47, 55, 65, 91, 103, 112, 151, 192, 220, 232**; 155

Confession, general, **44**; 153

frequent, **44, 354**

Conscience, and good or evil spirits, **313-326, 347, 350**; 189-195

See also Examination.

Consideration, **170**; 176

Consolation, spiritual, **6, 7, 13, 316**; 192, 193

sign of God's will, **175, 176**

sign of the good spirit, **318**

without preceding cause, **336**; 194-195

Constitutions S.J., 150, 200

Contemplation, a major method: of persons, words, deeds **106-108, 114-116**; 162-163

acquired. *See* Prayer, mental

See also Application of senses,

Contemplative in action, **233**; 184

Counterattack (*agere contra*), **13, 97, 325, 350, 351**; 161

Creation, gifts of, **234**.

Cusson, Gilles, or *BibThSpEx*, 2, 14, 145, 147, 157, 179, 182, 183, 189, 210, 213, 214

Dalmases, C., or *DalmIgn*, or *DalmMan*, 3, 9, 10, 145, 149, 150, 153, 155, 157, 159, 167, 170, 172, 178, 188, 190, 192, 196, 197, 199, 200, 210, 213

Damascus, **51**; 156

Death, judgment, etc. **71**; 158

thought of in election, **186**

in distributing alms, **340**

Deceits of devil, **139, 326, 334**

Deeds, examination of, **42**; 183

manifesting love, **230**; 183-185

Defects, Particular Examen against, **24-31**; 153

revealing those of another, **41**

Deliberación, decision, **182**, 178

Desire, **48**; 156

Desolation, spiritual, **6, 7, 13, 176, 317-336**; 189-195

causes of, **322**

how to act in, **318-321**

Devil. *See* Satan.

Director, giver of the Exercises, **1, 2, 6, 7, 9, 10, 15, 17**; 4, 143-145

Directories, vii, 12-13

Discernment of spirits, **6, 8**
  meaning of the term, 190
  rules for Week I, **313-327**; 189-193
  outline of, 192
  suitable for which Week? **9, 10**; 192-194
  origin of the rules, 190
  consolation and desolation, **316-324**; 192-193
  rules for Week II, on deceits of the devil, **328-336**; 194-195
  outline of, 194

Discernment of the will of God, **169-189**; 176-179, 195

Discretion and generosity, 152

Disordered affections. *See* attachments

Disposition, **18; 166**; 145, 175

Divinity of Christ, in Passion and risen life, **196, 223**

Doctors, positive and scholastic, **363**; 199-200

Drink, **211**

Editorial procedures, viii, x, 219-220

Egan, Harvey D., 194, 195

Election, **18, 135-189**; 166-179
  the term, **169**; 176
  text deals directly with electing a state of life, **23, 135, 170-188**; 7, 146, 147, 162, 176-177
  but applies also to other matters, **170, 174, 178, 181, 189**; 135, 147, 162, 176-177
  periods in treatment of. *See* Time periods
  introduction on the states of life, **135**; 166
  life of Christ as preparation, **135, 158**; 173
  mulling ways of humility and, **164**; 173
  when should a director explain the election? **163**; 173
  introduction to making an election, **169**; 176
  about what, **170, 174**; 147, 176-177
  changeable and unchangeable elections, **171-174, 189**
  correcting one, **172, 174**
  interacting contemplations and reflections, **158**; 173
  three suitable times for making, **175-178**; 177
  first method of making, **178-183**; 177-178
  second method **184-188**; 177

End, of human beings, **23, 177, 179, 180, 189, 140**; 148-151, 208-210. *See also* Glory; Plan of God
  of the *Exercises*, **21**; 3, 146-147, 208-210

Erasmus, 197, 200, 209, 211-212

Examination, of conscience, **18, 19**; 5, 153-154
  particular, **24-31, 90, 160, 207**; 153-154
  general, **32-43**; 153
  of success in prayer, **77**

Exercises, the Spiritual:
  explanation of the term, **1, 2, 4, 18**; 221-222
  their purpose, **21**; 146-147
  duration of, **4, 12, 13**
  at what hours, **72, 128, 159**; 173
  light or easy, **18, 238-260**; 185-187
  order and number in Week II, **128, 159**; in Week III, **204**; in Week IV, **226, 227**
  number each day, **129, 133**
  in everyday life, **19**; 145-146
  retreats preached to groups, 4, 6
Exercises, i.e., the book:
  an application of the divine redemptive plan to daily living, vii, 212
  its gradual composition, 2
  its structure, 5-8
  its influence, 8, 208
  manuscript texts of, 8
  varying interpretations, 13-14
  study of it is often prayerful, vii, 180, 213-214
  enriching its text through modern knowledge or study, vii, 14, 180, 183, 188-189, 206, 211, 213-214
Exercitant, one receiving the Exercises, **3, 5, 11-13, 16, 20**; 4, 7, 144

Faculties. See Powers
Faith, during consolation and desolation, **316, 317**; 192-193
  caution in speech on, **366, 368**

Fasts, **229, 359**
Faults, **43, 65, 90, 241, 322**
Fear, **9, 65, 370**
Finding or seeking God in all things, **39, 233-236, 351**; 172, 184-185
Fiorito, M. A., 209
Fischer, P. C., xi
Fitzmyer, J. A., 2, 156
Fleming, D. L., 190, 196
Following of Christ, **100**
Food, rules for taking, **210-217**; 181-182
Forma, contrast of matter, **105, 119**
  procedure, **186, 204**; 178, 186
Foundation, Principle and, **23, 169**; 3, 5, 146, 148-151, 176, 208-214
  reason or faith? 150, 208-210
  history of, 210-214
  finding new wonders in it, 213
Friends, alms to, **338-342**

Ganss, G.E., or *IgnCLWS*, xi, 2, 158, 162, 164, 166, 167, 175, 176, 188, 189, 198, 200, 209
Gender-inclusive language, 11, 12, 144
Generosity in retreatant, **5**.
Glory or praise of God, **16, 23, 152, 167, 179, 180, 185, 189, 264, 339, 351**; 2, 5, 149, 169, 171, 172, 175, 179, 185, 194, 195, 202, 203
  greater glory, Ignatius' norm for decision making, **23, 152**; 5, 149, 152, 171
  equal glory from options, **166**; 175
  of Christ, **221, 276, 303**

God, compared to myself, **58, 59**

  moving the will, **155**; 172

  present in all things, **39, 233-236, 351**; 172, 184-185

"God our Lord," **23**; 150, 209

Good, temptation under appearance of, **10, 332-334**

Grace, actual, **21, 155, 366, 369**; vii, 172, 195

  sanctifying (justification), **50, 51**; 195

Gueydan, Edouard, ix, 171, 172, 178, 184, 186

Guibert, J. de, or *DeGuiJes*, 3, 4, 5, 13, 14, 144, 147, 153, 156, 162, 164, 165, 176, 177, 178, 180

Hell, meditation on, **65-71**

History, the, **2, 102, 150**; 143, 163, 188

  of sin, a global view, 6, 7, 154, 157

Honor, step toward vices, **142**

Hope, in consolation and desolation, **316, 317**

Human beings, end of, **23, 135, 167, 177, 179, 180, 181, 189, 240**; 148-150, 208-210

  composed of body and soul, **47**; 150, 155

  See also Foundation

Humble, three ways of being, **164-166**; 7, 173-176

  maneras, many translations, 173, 174

  and the *Spiritual Diary*, 175

  summit of humility as love, 174-175

  love and suffering, 175-176

  prepares for election, **167**

  petitioning for third way, **168**

Humility, opposite of pride, **146**; 169

Ignatius, St.

  mystical illuminations and life of, 3, 165, 175

  his worldview or outlook, 1, 2, 248, 201, 206, 211

  which he expressed through the *Exercises*, 2, 8, 211-212

Illuminative way. *See* Way.

Illuminism, **22**; 148

Incarnation, Meditation on, **101-109, 262**; 161-163

Indifference, **16, 23, 155, 179**; 6, 151-152, 163, 172, 177-178, 208-211

  the Three Classes and, **149-157**; 169-172

  second Way of Being Humble and, **166**; 175

  See also Humble; Three Classes

Injuries, bearing of, **146-167**; 174-176

Intellect, in meditation, **4, 50**

Intention, basic meaning, 155

  pure, and election, **169**

Interior knowledge, **104**; 163

Introductory explanations (*anotaciones*), **1-20**; 143

Iparraguirre, I., or *Obrascomp*, ix, 8, 10, 12, 143, 164, 168, 170, 173, 184, 193, 196, 209-211, 213

John of the Cross, St., 165, 195

Johnson, Elizabeth A., xi

Judgment, Last, **71, 107, 341**; 158

Kinerk, E. E., 156
Kingdom of Christ, meditation
   on, **91-99**; 159-161
   the term or title, **91**; 159
   the parable, **92-94**; 160
   Christ's mission, achieved
      through the Church, **95**;
      160
Krumpelman, Frances, xi

Lectio divina (prayerful reading), 187, 201
   second method of praying is
      like it, **249-257**; 187, 201,
      206
Léon-Dufour, X., 168
Leturia, P. de, 3, 199, 210
Light, use of, **79, 130, 229**
Longridge, W. H., 11, 158, 162
Love, carnal, **97**. See Counterattack
Love of God
   and avoiding hell, **65, 184**
   what true love is, **230-231**
   manifested by deeds, 183
   affective and effective love,
      230; 183, 184, 212
   arises from gratitude, **231**;
      184
   love and suffering, the
      Cross, **167**; 175, 176
   Contemplation for, **230-237**;
      183-185
   and almsgiving, **338**
   love and fear, **65, 370**
   and 3rd way of humility,
      174-175
Ludolph of Saxony, 2, 156, 182,
   188, 196, 206, 210, 211

Majesty, His Divine, an Igna-
   tian expression of rever-
ence, **5**
our translation of the
   phrase, 144
Man. See Human beings
Manresa, 3, 8, 182, 188, 196, 207
Mary, Blessed Virgin, colloquy
   to, **63, 147**
   in various mysteries, **102,
      108, 208, 218, 262, 273,
      276, 297, 299**
   apparition of Christ to, **219,
      299**; 182
   imitation of, **248**
Mass, **20, 355**
Matrimony and celibacy, **356**
McCarthy, J. L., xi
McKenzie, J. L., 156, 160, 182
Medida, norm, **186**; 178
Meditation. See Prayer, mental
Memory, use in meditation, **50-
   52**.
Mercy, **18, 61, 71**.
Midnight, **88, 129**
Motions, **6, 21, 176, 313, 316,
      327, 329, 330**; 144, 147,
      177, 189-195
   racional and sensual, **182**; 178
   from ourselves, or good or
      bad spirits, **32**; 154
Mullan, Elder, 11
Mysteries, events of Christ's
   life, **262-312**; 187-189
   for use after retreat, **162**; 188
   same sequence as Ludolph's,
      188
Mystery of Christ. See Plan of
   God

Nativity, contemplation on,
   110, 264; 162-163
"Negative" factors in Ignatian
   spirituality (= purifica-

tions), **21, 189**; 146, 179

Nicolás, A. T. de, 149

Norm for decisions or election, **23, 152, 155**; 5, 149, 152, 171, 212
   See also Glory of God, the greater

Oaths, **38-39**

O'Flaherty, V. J, xi

Ong, W., 156

Ordering one's life, **2, 21, 97**; 5, 147, 161

Ortiz, Pedro, 174

Overcoming oneself, **21**; 146

Padberg, J. W., xi

Palm Sunday, **4, 161, 287**

Palmer, M. E., xi

Paschal Mystery, 179

Passion, how to contemplate it, **4, 190-207, 289-298**;179-180

Patience in desolation, **321**

Paul, St., **175, 311**

Penance, kinds and fruits of, **82-89, 130, 229, 319, 359**

Pentecost, exercise on, 189

Perfection, counselling it, **14, 15**
   the state of, **135**; 166
   seeking it in whatsoever state, **135, 173, 185, 189, 339**; 166
   means toward it, **189**

Persevering in prayer, **12, 13**

Peter Lombard, **363**; 210

Peter, St., **201, 275, 280, 284, 289-291, 302, 306**

Petition in preludes
   in Week I, **48, 55, 65**
   in Week II, **91, 104, 139, 152**
   in Week III, **193, 194, 203**
   in Week IV, **221, 233**

Pilgrimages, **358**

Plan of God, the salvific, unfolding in the history of salvation, **23, 45, 50, 51, 101, 190-209, 218-225**; also the sequence of mysteries from **45-229**; 1, 2, 5, 7, 146, 153, 162, 168, 179, 180, 183, 185, 201-207, 208, 213
   Scripture texts showing God's redemptive plan, 1, 201-205

Points, the **2, 228, 261-312**

Polanco, Juan de, 12, 13, 164, 177, 183, 189, 198, 213

Positive theology, **363, 369**; 199-200

Posture in prayer, **76, 239, 252**

Poverty, **14, 357**
   in Scripture, 168
   indifference about, **23, 166**
   as emptiness of self, 168
   offering oneself for it, **98**
   spiritual and actual, **98, 146-147, 157**; 161, 167-169
   of religious life, 168

Powers or faculties of the soul, **45, 51, 246**; 154, 155, 158, 187

Prayer, mental
   discursive, "meditation," **45-52, 136-148, 157**; 154, 186
   affective, "contemplation," **101-126**; 162-165
   acquired contemplation, **2, 49, 121-126, 254**; 154, 158, 164-165, 186
   infused contemplation, 145, 164-165, 193

relation to the three ways, 144. *See also* Ways

Prayer, the preparatory, **46, 49, 105, 240, 244, 246, 248, 251**

Prayers, vocal, **54, 61, 63, 147, 241, 248, 253-255**

Praying, three methods of, **238-260**; 185-187

prayerful reading (*lectio divina*) and 2nd method, **249-257**; 187, 201

rhythmic measure, **258-260**; 187

Predestination, **366, 367**

Preludes, the, **47, 48, 49, 104, 105, 111, 112**

Presence of God, in prayer, **75, 239**

in all things **39, 233-236, 351**; 172, 184-185

Presupposition, **22**; 148

Pride, in fall of angels, **50**

in Satan's strategy, **142**; 167

brings desolation, **322**

Principle, **23**; 148-152. *See also* Foundation

Progress, **17, 189**; 178-179

Purgative way. *See* Ways

Quay, P., 191

Rahner, Hugo, 164, 193

Rahner, Karl, 194-195

Reading during retreat, **100**; vii, 189

not about future topics, **10, 127**

Redemptive Plan. *See* Plan of God

Reformation of one's life, **189**; 178, 179

Rejadell, Teresa, 158, 164, 211

Religious life, **14, 15, 135, 356, 357**

Repetitions, how made, **62, 118, 119**; 157

Retreatants, their aim, vii

Reverence, **3, 23, 38, 39, 75**; 212

Riches, **23**

snare of Satan, **142**

and indifference to, **157**

and ways of humility, **166, 167**

Rules, meaning of term, **210, 344, 352**; 181, 199

for an election, **169-189**; 176-179

for taking food, **210-217**; 181-182

for discerning spirits, **313-336**; 189-195

for discerning the will of God, **169-189**; 176-179, 195

for distributing alms, **337-344**; 196

for proper attitude toward the Church, **353-370**; 197-200

Saints, lives of, **100, 215, 358**

Salvation, the term. For Ignatius it usually connotes also one's growing perfection, **23, 135**; 149, 150

Satan, his sin, **50**

leader of the enemy, **140**; 167

standard of, **140-142**; 167

Satisfaction in prayer, full, **76, 254**; 158, 163-165

Scruples, notes on, **345-351**; 196

Seclusion for the Exercises, **20**

Secret, keeping temptations so, **326**

Senses, prayer on, **18, 247-248**
in meditation on hell, **69-70**
application of the, **65-70, 121-126, 129, 132-134, 204, 208, 209, 226, 227**; 158, 163-165

Sensuality, meaning of, **97**; 159, 161

Sin, venial and mortal **35, 36**
exercises on sin, **45-64**; 154-157
in salvation history, 6, 7, 154, 157
capital sins, **18, 238, 242, 244, 245**; 145, 187
the opposite virtues, 187
sorrow for sin, **55-61**

Sleep, **73, 74, 84**

Solano, J., 209

Soul, often means the self or person, **23, 313**; 150, 192
"parts of the soul," **87**; 158

Soul of Christ, **63**; 20, 157

Solitude for Exercises, **20**

Spirits, good (God or angels) or bad (devils) **4, 6, 32, 176**; 143, 154, 189-195
existence of, 191.
See also Discernment of spirits

Standards, the Two, **136-148, 156, 169**; 167-169

Stanley, D. M., 180, 187, 189

States of life, **135**. *See* Election

Suffering, and love, 175-176

Superiors, **362**; 199

"Take, Lord, and receive," **234**

Tears, **55, 87, 195**

Temperance, **83, 84, 229**

Temptations, **9, 345**
under appearance of good, **10, 332, 351**
to shorten an exercise, **12, 13**
to covet riches, etc., **142**

Teresa of Avila, St., 144, 165, 194

Tetlow, Joseph A., xi, 146, 214

Texts of the *Exercises*, 8-10

Theology, scholastic and positive, **363**; 199, 200

Thomas Aquinas, St., **363**; 174, 201, 205

Thoughts, and a director, **17, 326**
from self, or good, or bad spirit, **17, 32, 317, 332-334, 351**; 154
examining them, **32-37**
cherishing helpful thoughts, **74, 78, 130, 206, 229**
in desolation and consolation, **320, 323, 324**
examining a train of, **333, 334**

Time Periods in Week II, 162
1: days 1-3, **101-134**; 162-165
2: day 4, **135-157**; 166-172
3: days 5-8, **158-189**; 173-179

Times suitable for an election, **175-177**; 177
exemplified in Ignatius' *Spiritual Diary*, 177

Toner, J. J., 161, 190-195

Touch, the sense of, **70, 125**.

Translations of *Exercises*, 9-12

Vainglory, **322, 351**

Verse numbers for computers, viii

Virginity, **15, 356**
Vocation and God's initiative, **15, 155**; 172
  one from God is pure, **172**
Vows, **14, 15, 357**

Ways or stages of spiritual pro-
    gress, the three, **10**; 5,
    144, 154, 159, 164, 183
Week, meaning of term, **4**; 5
  lengthening or shortening
    Weeks, **4, 162, 209**
  views on Week III, **190**; 179
  on Week IV, **221**; 183
Will of God, seeking it, **1, 5, 15,
    21, 234**
  discerning it, **169-189**; 195
Will, the human,
  use of in the Exercises, **50-52**
  thoughts arising from, **32**

God moves our will, **155** 172
  total surrender to God's will,
    5, 175, 189, 234
  free will and grace, **369**
Women, as directors, 144
Words, examination of con-
    science on, **38-41**
  reflecting on the persons,
    words, and deeds, **106-
    108**; 162
  and deeds, in love, **230**.
Works, good, **14, 278**
  not to be omitted from fear,
    351
  and predestination, **367-369**
World, knowledge of, **63**; 157
  its vain honor, **142**.
  worldly love, **97**
Worldview of Ignatius, 1, 2,
    248, 201, 206, 211